YAQUI DEER SON
MASO BWIKAM

Volume 14

SUN TRACKS

An American Indian Literary Series

YAQUI DEER SONGS
MASO BWIKAM

A Native American Poetry

LARRY EVERS and FELIPE S. MOLINA

Sun Tracks and The University of Arizona Press

Tucson & London

ABOUT THE AUTHORS

FELIPE S. MOLINA grew up in the Yaqui settlement near Marana, Arizona, which is now called Yoem Pueblo. He credits his grandmother, Anselma Angwis Tonopuamea, and his grandfather, Rosario Bacaneri Castillo, who was a famous *pahkola*, with educating him in the Yaqui language and ways. He has served as governor of Yoem Pueblo, as a member of the Pascua Yaqui Tribal Council, and is at this writing a member of the Pascua Yaqui Language Policy Commission. He is godfather to many Yaqui children and an active deer singer.

LARRY EVERS has lived in Tucson, Arizona, since 1974, the year he met Felipe Molina. He is a professor of English at the University of Arizona. He edited *The South Corner of Time* (1980) and produced *Words and Place: Native Literature of the American Southwest* (1979), a series of videotapes of performances by American Indian singers, tellers, and authors.

All authors' royalties from this book will be donated in the memory of Jesús Yoilo'i to projects within Yaqui communities that foster the verbal arts and the visual arts.

Third printing 1993

THE UNIVERSITY OF ARIZONA PRESS

Copyright © 1987
The Arizona Board of Regents
All Rights Reserved

This book was set in Linotron Pilgrim and Baker Signet types.
∞ This book is printed on acid-free, archival-quality paper.
Manufactured in the U.S.A.

Library of Congress Cataloging-in-Publication Data
Yaqui deer songs, Maso Bwikam.
(Sun tracks : an American Indian literary series : v. 14)
English and Yaqui.
Bibliography: p.
Includes index.
1. Yaqui poetry. 2. Yaqui Indians—Rites and ceremonies. 3. Indians of North America—Arizona—Rites and ceremonies. 4. Yaqui poetry—Translations into English. 5. American poetry—Translations from Yaqui. 6. Indians of Mexico—Rites and ceremonies. I. Evers, Larry. II. Molina, Felipe S.
III. Series: Sun tracks ; v. 14.

PS501.S85   vol. 14   810'.8s   87-19313
[PM4526.Z77]   [897'.4]
ISBN 0-8165-0991-3 (alk. paper)
ISBN 0-8165-0995-6 (pbk. : alk. paper)

This book is dedicated to
Don Jesús Yoilo'i

CONTENTS

YAQUI DEER SONGS
MASO BWIKAM

PROLOGUE

✤ On the table there is a pair of antlers I brought in from a walk in the desert. For the area where we found them they are not especially large, a little longer than my forearm and hand, but they are very graceful, mirror reflections of the same sinuous arch. They have weathered to the white-bellied gray of storm clouds in the dusk.

I have come on other things in the desert: tortoise shells, the skull of a javelina, scattered bones of various kinds, and, many times, single antlers. I am told that deer shed their antlers one at a time. When I walk I watch for them.

Often I have found them on the soft benches just above washes. These lay together in the open, high on a desert ridge. Up there they made me think of a nest. When I rock them here among the papers, the tines flicker like tongues of a flame.

A pair of antlers and pages of song words, we sit and talk about these objects on the table: the coincidence of their discovery, the elegance of their symmetries, the new growth they represent. If they are also vestiges, they promise more.

I

Aa yeweli hiweka
   tolo pakuni
      tolo pakun hikawi
Yeweli hiweka
   tolo pakuni
      tolo pakun hikawi

Aa wainavo su
  itou weyekai
Wainavo su
  itou vuitema
Yeweli hiweka
   tolo pakuni
      tolo pakun hikawi

Aa look out,
   to the light blue outside,
      up to the light blue outside.
Look out,
   to the light blue outside
      up to the light blue outside.

Aa from that side,
   to us, as he is walking,
From that side,
   to us, as he is running,
Look out,
   to the light blue outside,
      up to the light blue outside.

Miki Maaso
Vicam Pueblo
May 29, 1983

3. Deer dancer
Luis Cinfuego ..

1

YOPO NOOKI
ENCHANTED TALK

IT IS HARD to go far in the borderlands country of Arizona and Sonora without en-
countering an image of the Yaqui Indian deer dancer. Fixed in bronze and larger than
life, the deer dancer stands as a public monument at the edge of Ciudad Obregón.
Travel posters, postcards, promotional brochures, hotel directories, mescal and salsa
labels, even the official seal of the State of Sonora, all feature his image.[1] These are
public images, and they are fixed, immobile, and silent. What speaks are the political
and economic motives that cluster around them. They serve as an aboriginal connec-
tion for the politicians, a romantic lure for the admen, the borderlands equivalent, in
many ways, to the warbonneted Plains Indian horsemen of the Wild West.

Yaqui Indian people call themselves the *Yoemem*, People.[2] They know the deer
dancer as *saila maso*, little brother deer. And when their little brother comes walking,
comes running to dance for the *Yoemem*, he has a voice. The voice speaks to all
through the songs to which the deer dancer moves. The songs are the voice of *saila
maso*. "All that he should talk about, that is what we sing," one deer singer told us.
"He does not talk, but he talks in an enchanted way."

Maso bwikam, deer songs, are a traditional kind of Yaqui song usually sung by three
men to accompany the performance of the deer dancer. Yaquis regard deer songs as
the most ancient of their verbal art forms. Highly conventionalized in their structure,
their diction, their themes, and their mode of performance, deer songs describe a dou-
ble world, both "here" and "over there," a world in which all the actions of the deer
dancer have a parallel in that mythic, primeval place called by Yaquis *sea ania*, flower
world. Deer songs describe equivalencies between these two real parts of the Yaqui
universe. They are verbal equations, developed richly with phonological, syntactic,
and rhetorical parallelisms and repetitions. They participate in "an aesthetics of
regularity" as they describe vivid single images.[3] Readers with a vantage from the
Yaquis' ecological homeland will recognize common things from the natural world of
the Sonoran desert imaged in the songs: insects and plants, birds and animals; and
those rarer ones, more powerful in combination: rain, flowers, the deer.

The poet Kenneth Rexroth admired deer songs as "pure poems of sensibility."[4] But heard with Yaqui ears, deer songs are not so much "pure poems of sensibility" as they are narrative poems. Image by image, from the point of view of *saila maso* and the other living things with whom he shares the *sea ania*, Yaqui deer songs tell a continuing story of life and death in the wilderness world of the Sonoran desert.

This is a collection of writing about the enchanted talk of Yaqui deer songs. In it we offer our translations of the words of deer songs which continue to be sung in Yaqui communities in both Sonora and Arizona. These are translations from a living tradition which stretches back past the time the Spanish slave trader Diego de Guzmán first encountered Yaquis in 1533 into time immemorial. The songs are still sung, and those who are interested will not have a hard time finding a place to stand and listen. Those who do will know that deer songs are more than words. Yaquis relish the preparations in smoke and silence, the sermons and speechmaking, gossip, the smell of mesquite fires and stew, as well as the rasp and rattle and rush of the dance. Before the deer singers ever utter a word, the *ramá* is already full of meaning. So along with our representations of the words in transcription and translation, we describe some of the contexts in which they continue to exist, and, because we have each lived around deer songs in different ways, we give our individual appreciations of them, too.

In all, we work for two goals: for the continuation of deer songs as a vital part of life in Yaqui communities and for their appreciation in all communities beyond. Most of the time these goals coincide.

Nau Tekipanoawame: Working Together

You know from the title page that there are two of us responsible for this book. You may have guessed from our names that one is Yaqui and one is not, and, if you have read other collections of this kind, you may have some expectations about the way our collaboration worked.

The two of us decided to work together on this project in 1979. Since then we have spent time together, when we could, listening to deer songs and talking about what we hear. Felipe Molina is a native speaker of Yaqui. He continues to live in Yoem Pueblo, a Yaqui community in Marana, Arizona, the community in which he was raised. He has studied at the University of Arizona, and during much of the time we worked on this project, he taught Yaqui language and culture at the Richey Elementary School in Tucson. Larry Evers is a native speaker of English. He has studied Yaqui language with Molina but does not speak it. He has lived in Tucson since 1974 when he moved here to work in the English Department and the American Indian Studies Program at the University.

Neighbors in an urbanizing Sonoran desert world, we both have ongoing interests in the oral traditions of this place. We traveled together throughout southern Arizona and into the Río Yaqui area in Sonora, Mexico, to visit deer singers and to record their songs and talk about songs. When we returned, Molina transcribed the tapes into written Yaqui, and the two of us sat down together to work out English translations. Then we talked about them, sometimes with the transcriptions and translations in hand at one of our houses or offices, sometimes far from papers on walking trips into the desert northwest of Tucson.

As we began to convert our talk into writing, we found we had some things to say together and some things to say as individuals. We decided to try to keep those voices separate when we wrote. The "we" voice you are reading comes out of discussions of what we have read and recorded together. We talked through an outline; Evers wrote a draft; Molina revised. Evers wrote the bibliographic end notes. We each wrote in an "I" voice as well. We think of these voices as our own, of course, but we proofread, commented, and made suggestions on each other's writing as we went along. The two of us worked together in constructing the sequence of voices which make this publication.

The historically exploitative aspects of the relationships between Euroamericans and native Americans, teachers and students, investigators and informants, employers and employees, all cast long shadows around our effort to make this a fully collaborative project. It would be arrogant for us to suggest that we have avoided them completely. By presenting our collaboration in this way, however, we want to remind you that we have tried. At the same time we want to echo a method of the deer songs themselves in which, as we understand it, there are also many voices in one.[5]

We hope that our collaboration provides perspectives on some central Yaqui expressions which until now have been out of reach of most readers. But more than that we hope that our working together will prompt others to undertake similar collaborations. Kenneth Hale's contention that "significant advances in the study of American Indian languages can be made...only when a significant portion of the field is in the hands of native speakers of the languages concerned" should be extended to include the study of American Indian literatures as well. Unless efforts to engage native speakers actively in the study of their verbal arts succeed, it is unlikely that the study of American Indian oral literatures will advance significantly.[6]

✠ I began working with Larry in September 1978. I worked as a consultant in the Yaqui language, mainly as a translator. The material I translated concerned deer songs and ceremonial speech. The material consisted of many long hours of song and dance which Larry recorded working with my godfather and some others in 1976. I enjoyed this work because I learned many new things that I didn't know before. This is also the time when I started to use my Yaqui language writing system more. The writing in Yaqui started when I was in junior high in Marana, and I continued it in high school. During that time, I wrote to my girlfriend in Yaqui, and she sometimes also answered in Yaqui.

The deer songs on the video tapes finally turned into a program called *Seyewailo.*[7] I was the narrator, and I helped Larry and the others to edit it. Then the project turned into another project which we called the Deer Song Project. Working on the video tape *Seyewailo*, I came to appreciate the deer songs more. I learned a lot, as I mentioned before. During that time I became a deer singer and a deer song teacher myself. I had an interest in deer songs before the projects with Larry, but it intensified while I worked. My grandfather was a *pahkola* dancer, so I witnessed many *pahkom* and much dancing. When we started the second project, I thought that I would go ahead and learn as many songs as possible so that I could teach the younger generation about the ways of the *Yoemem* because I think it is very important for us *Yoemem* to continue our ways.

❋ Felipe was a student in a freshman composition class I taught in the fall of 1974, the first year I worked at the University of Arizona. I remember only that the class was too large, that Felipe said little, and that his weekly essays were meticulously proofread and full of mention of the grandfather with whom he was living in the Yaqui village at Marana, Arizona.

Three years later Felipe turned up again in an upper-division course I was teaching. Outside class, I was at the time trying hard to complete a series of films and videotapes of American Indian singers, storytellers, and writers for the public television affiliate in Tucson. One of the eight programs in the series focused on Yaqui deer songs. At the suggestion of Professor Edward Spicer, I had planned that program with Yaqui consultants Fern Cupis and Anselmo Valencia. The two of them orchestrated a recording session in October of 1976 during which we recorded parts of a Yaqui *pahko* on videotape. Anselmo Valencia promised translation of the more than five and one-half hours of song and talk in the Yaqui language, but for over a year after the recording his many civic and religious duties repeatedly took precedence. One day, after I had shown some of the unedited video to my class, Felipe came forward to offer his help. He spoke fluent Yaqui and had developed a system for writing it. Anselmo Valencia was his godfather. I arranged to hire him immediately to translate and to help edit the videotape. We worked together weekly until we completed *Seyewailo/The Flower World: Yaqui Deer Songs* in the fall of 1979.

By that time, I knew I needed to know much more about deer songs if I were going to appreciate them as a part of what we had called the native literature of the American Southwest on the videotape. I suggested to Felipe that we continue to work together at learning more about deer songs and at finding ways of making their poetry more available to both Yaqui and non-Yaqui audiences. He agreed immediately, and we began what we called the Yaqui Deer Song Project in which we set out to review together what had already been recorded and to see what continued to be sung in contemporary Yaqui communities.

The longer I live here in the Sonoran desert, the more I wonder about how it has been imagined by the others who have lived here before. There are those who refuse to accept even the possibility that there might have been imaginative life here and elsewhere in the West before English speakers arrived. Editors of a collection of poetry of the American West recently argued that "the first

stump of verse in what would become the literature of the American West" was Captain William Clark's utterance in 1803 over what Clark took to be the Pacific but which turned out after a closer look to be a spot along the Columbia River days away from the ocean: "Ocian in view! O! the joy."[8]

To see the beginnings of western American poetry in that ejaculation is to repeat its error. American Indian peoples knew the shorelines, the waterways, the mountain ranges, the basins, and the valleys of this continent intimately centuries before Lewis and Clark stumbled through, and by all reports almost every native American community maintained rich traditions of story and song about the place they knew. It is a rare mountain in this part of the continent which has not been the subject of story and song in a native community. Never mind springs, rivers, and oceans. When I pointed this out to one of the editors, he replied, "Oh that was all just in the air."

"Oral literature" is a contradiction in terms. Traditionally, Yaqui deer songs—like the *Illiad*, the *Odyssey*, *Beowulf*, and the *Chanson de Roland*—were not written down. They were "just in the air." "Yet we live in a time," as Harry Levin writes, "when literacy itself has become so diluted that it can scarcely be invoked as an esthetic criterion."[9] Deer songs have rhythm, are organized into lines and stanzas, employ metaphor, parallelism, and other features we think of as poetic. The way in which they are performed sets them apart from other uses of the Yaqui language, and, most importantly, they are regarded by Yaqui people themselves as containing some of the most aesthetically pleasing Yaqui language spoken or sung. Yaqui deer singers have survived "cycles of conquest."[10] They continue to work with themes and forms which are easily centuries old. The artistic continuity which they represent in their songs is something those of us who wish to talk about a literature of the American West cannot ignore.

The Yaqui Deer Song Project has had several results. In December 1982, we compiled selections from previously collected sources on deer songs, both published and archival, into a Xeroxed anthology format. We distributed copies of this compilation to ten Yaqui communities in Arizona and Sonora. In June 1983 we duplicated sets of audio cassette tapes from original recordings we had made with deer singers both in Arizona and Sonora for distribution in Yaqui communities. This publication is our attempt to translate and discuss the portions of the tapes which Felipe Molina felt could be appropriately presented to non-Yaqui audiences.[11]

U Masobwikame: The Deer Singer

The songs and the talk about songs that we translate here were given to us for this purpose by several singers, among them Guadalupe Molina, Marcos Savivae, Tani Masobwikame, Hopom, Miguel Cinfuego, Porfirio Yokiwa, and Miguel Matus Hu'upamea. But our primary source for this publication was Don Jesús Yoilo'i, who was also known by his Mexican name Jesús Alvarez Vasquez. Born in Potam, Sonora, around the turn of the century, Don Jesús grew up during the turbulent times surrounding the Mexican Revolution of 1910.[12] While still a boy, he served the *Yoem Vatayonnimmake*, the Yaqui Battalion, as a soldier and was wounded. When the fighting stopped, he came north across the border to work on the railroad along borderlands tracks from Yuma into Texas. For a time he lived in one of the Yaqui camps near Scottsdale, Arizona, and worked in the cotton fields there. Very early in his life, Don Jesús lived with hardship, suffering, war and death. These early experiences left him with a tragic sense throughout his life. "That is how man is," he told us on several occasions. "He is born to die."

After these travels, Don Jesús returned to Potam in 1918 or 1919 and "went to work for the elders." Antonio Potakovanao, one of the most remembered deer singers in the Río Yaqui area, became his teacher, and Don Jesús learned all of the arts of the *pahko* from him. He played the water drum, he danced the *pahkola* dances, he learned the flute and drum songs of the *tampaleo*, and he was a deer dancer to Antonio Potakovanao's singing. When Don Antonio died, Don Jesús "sat down to these raspers and stayed with them." Later in his life, Don Jesús himself became a teacher of the deer songs and of the other arts of the *pahko*, directing sessions that became so formalized he called them *ehkwelam*, schools.

By the time we came to Don Jesús early in 1980, he had retired from deer singing and was living with his sons in his house on the edge of the plaza at Potam. It was one of Don Jesús' students who urged us to approach Don Jesús if we wanted to know about deer songs. When we did, it turned out that Don Jesús was an old friend of

Felipe's grandfather. Probably because of this connection, Don Jesús was from the beginning enthusiastic about our proposal to record some of his songs. Later we were told he was was not always so open to such proposals and that he had on several occasions gone away from his house into the desert to avoid teaching songs to some other Yaqui singers who sought him out. When we asked him about this, he said that his songs were for everyone but that he must feel right in *hiapsi*, heart, before he could sing for someone.

Over two years and more than a dozen trips to Potam, we sat down to work with Don Jesús. Most were weekend trips, sandwiched between long night drives back and forth to our jobs in Tucson. In May of 1981, we brought Don Jesús across the border to stay in Tucson. During that time we talked with him and his son Aleho intensively for a week. It was during that week that we recorded most of the songs that we translate here.

Bright, witty, and quick to smile, Don Jesús was partially deaf all during the time we knew him and racked by tuberculosis and other respiratory problems from at least the mid-1960s on. When last we visited him in the morning of April 13, 1982, he was very weak, but he talked about all the songs which he would like to sing and record. By that evening, Don Jesús had fallen into a coma. He died four days later.

For at least the last century it has been common for collections like this one to begin with a lament, mourning the passing of a last tradition-bearer and his stories and songs, and a prediction, describing the day soon to come when those stories and songs will be found only in the printed pages of the collection itself. That is not the way we see this work. We have mourned Don Jesús and we miss him now, but his songs did not die with him. They continue. The most vital way in which they continue is in the repertories of the many singers he taught in Sonora. But they continue, too, on the audio tapes we made with him and in the translations we offer here. We hope that other singers will take the songs up and work with them. This is the reason that Don Jesús gave them to us.

To some extent this is already happening. The young deer singers Felipe works with at Yoem Pueblo were learning and singing Don Jesús' songs even as we sat transcribing them into print. And these young singers now use the songs when they perform for ceremonies in their own community and elsewhere.

There is a view that print spells the end of oral traditions, that stories and songs are fast-vanishing relics performed only for anthropologists and folklorists, that in order for them to survive they must be captured between the covers of books. Our experience suggests that Yaqui deer songs and the traditions which surround them are very much alive and that more than sixty years of recording and printing versions of them has complemented and reinforced more traditional oral modes of continuance, rather than contributing to their disappearance.

✠ I saw Don Jesús for the first time in June 1978 during the Santísima Trinidad *pahko* in Potam. But before then I knew about him. My grandfather always talked about Don Jesús because my grandfather danced with him when Don Jesús came up from Potam to dance in *pahkom* in the Arizona Yaqui villages. My grandfather told me that Don Jesús could do everything. He was a *tampaleo, pahkola, maaso,* and a *maso bwikame.* He seemed to be a very bright person. I was aware of my grandfather's desire to see Don Jesús again, because everywhere he went in Potam he asked for Don Jesús. Finally on the blue side, my grandfather asked this middle-aged man if he knew Don Jesús. The man told us that Don Jesús was on the red side. My grandfather thanked the man and we went over to the red side of the plaza to ask for Don Jesús.[13]

Juan Cruz from Vicam Pueblo was the deer dancer there. Juan Cruz recognized my grandfather right away, and he came over to greet my grandfather where we stood on the side of the ramada. Juan Cruz went to find Don Jesús.

When Don Jesús came to greet my grandfather, he was very happy and surprised to see my grandfather once again. All the *pahkolam* came to greet my grandfather even though they didn't know him. All the people at the *pahko* were fascinated by the two old men. Later the *pahkolam* were making jokes about how the old men found each other. People were smiling and happy. Since that day I had always wanted to talk with Don Jesús about his past and about deer songs.

I met with Don Jesús again in February 1980 on the first Friday of Lent on the outskirts of Tahimaroa. Tahimaroa is a small village which is part of *Ko'oko'im* Pueblo. I knew Don Jesús lived in Potam and asked for him there. But his sons told me that that day he was visiting his nephews in Tahimaroa.

When my cousin Josephine and I arrived in Tahimaroa that Friday, we asked for Don Jesús at one house and a man there knew him. He said that Don Jesús was staying at his nephews' house on a small hill about a mile away.

When we got to the house, a man and his wife came out and greeted us. We told them we wanted to see Don Jesús. We explained we wanted to talk with him about deer songs. The man's name was Chico, and he invited us into the ramada. We sat down on some chairs and coffee was brought to us.

Chico was out looking for Don Jesús. He was out in the back working on a drum rim. Chico came walking back with Don Jesús at his side. Don Jesús had the drum rim in his hand. He came up to us and greeted us, *"Dios em chaniavu, kechem allea."*

We answered, *"Dios enchiokoe, kette allea."*

After some conversation about the weather and Yaqui people in Arizona, I told Don Jesús that I wanted him to talk about deer songs. He told me there was a lot to talk about, but he didn't have time to talk now. He was going to the *Konti,* Procession, in *Ko'oko'im* because it was the first Friday of Lent.

I told him I understood, but still I wanted to talk a little at least. He said okay. He didn't know me until I told him I was Rosario Castillo's grandson. When I said that, right away he asked for my grandfather. I told him my grand-father had died a year and a month before. Don Jesús was unhappy, but he said: "That is the way we people are; we are made to die."

Then he began to talk about the begin-nings of the deer songs. He talked about the first real Yaquis who were called *Surem.* After this, he began to talk about his days as a railroad worker in Arizona. Finally he sang some songs. He sang the beginning songs for a *pahko* and the songs for the Gloria on Holy Saturday. He also sang one badger song and a buzzard song. I was very happy that he sang the songs. I thanked him for taking the time to talk with me, and I gave him some money. He was very happy.

Then Don Jesús wanted to know if we could give them a ride to *Ko'oko'im* Pueblo. It was about three miles away. I told him I would be glad to, and all of them got in. Chico's wife got in the truck, too, and also the man who brought us to Don Jesús.

5. Juan Tampaleo's drum ...

✤ All morning we have been over at Don Jesús' house listening to him talk about rain songs—and sing a few. Now we are sitting in the drum maker's yard on the edge of Potam drinking coffee. Felipe and the drum maker are negotiating. Felipe wants to take a drum back to Arizona and hopes the drum maker will take his dark green Stetson in trade. It is a handsome hat, and the drum maker has admired it before. Felipe keeps it wrapped in a plastic bag behind the seat of the pickup away from the dust.

The drum maker is a short stout man. As he talks, he sits on his burlap cot in the mottled shade beside the house languidly shelling white corn. His left leg is tucked up on the cot, and the right one dangles over the edge, rocking to the rhythm of his talk. Behind him, on a wire stretched from the corner post of the house to a lacy castor-bean tree along the side of the yard, three drum frames hang. There is a completed drum there too, but it is spoken for. The frames are made from narrow circles of *guasima* wood. The three empty ones are like round picture frames enclosing details along the horizon to the north. It is late afternoon and across the huge open fields the Vacateteve Mountains are beginning to pick up a light salmon glow. The talk circles around the fields.

The drum maker begins to tell a story about water. Sometimes there are problems with irrigating. There was a man whose fields are out a way toward Rahum who was in a hurry. He wanted to irrigate before it was his turn. So when the water came down the ditch, he cut it

into his fields. Two who should have had the water before him came to him. They asked him to wait. Why was he in a hurry? There is plenty of water for everyone. But the man would not listen. So they told him again to stop the water and wait for his turn, but he just continued to work the water through his fields. Finally, the two who were before him threatened. If you don't stop, maybe this will be the last time you are able to irrigate. Later on that night when he got home, that man became sick. He was all stopped up. Whatever he ate and drank did not come out. And by the next day he was dead. The family of the dead man accused the two of cursing him because he took their place in the irrigating. But who can say? The man shouldn't have been in such a hurry.

The drum maker's wife brings us more coffee. And as the sugar goes around, he takes the completed drum down from the line and begins to play some rhythms on it. Behind him, in the middle distance, along the irrigation ditch, a boy is bringing his animals in from the fields: a small herd of goats, three long-horned cows and a couple of calves, and two yearling horses. The drum is passed around to us. We inspect it. Felipe goes to the truck for the Stetson. He takes some time getting it out of the plastic bag.

Finally, the drum maker tries it on.

It doesn't fit! Too bad, the drum is spoken for anyway. We give the drum maker fifty pesos to buy a goat skin and promise to come back for a drum during Santísima Trinidad.

Yoemtuwame: Being Yaqui

Yaqui traditions tell of the deer dance and deer singing as a part of a ritual performed before the hunting of deer. That connection seems only a memory now. Some Yaquis, especially in the Sonoran communities, continue to hunt deer regularly. And deer songs and the deer dance are still performed regularly on a variety of occasions in every Yaqui community we know. There seems now, however, to be no direct connection made between the two activities. Perhaps it was for this reason that some observers in the middle of this century felt that the deer dance was "going out of vogue" or that it was tending "steadily toward obsolescence in Yaqui culture."[14]

Over the several years that we have been paying close attention, just the opposite seems to be occurring. The deer dance and deer singing seem to be increasing in popularity. The reasons for this resurgence are complex, but some stand out.

Deer singing has always been an important entertainment for Yaqui communities. People gather to see the dancing of the deer, to watch the antics of the ritual clowns, the *pahkolam*, who dance with the deer, and to hear the poetry of the songs themselves. Even when there is no *pahko*, people gather around the homes of deer singers when they practice just for the pleasure of hearing the songs. But the continuance of deer singing in Yaqui communities into the last quarter of the twentieth century is far more than a matter of entertainment.

Yaquis have always believed that a close communication exists among *all* the inhabitants of the Sonoran desert world in which they live: plants, animals, birds, fishes, even rocks and springs. All of these come together as a part of one living community which Yaquis call the *huya ania*, the wilderness world. Like their neighbors the Papagos, whom Yaquis call *hua yoemem*, wilderness people, Yaquis regard song as a special language of this community, a kind of "lingua franca of the intelligent universe."[15] It is through song that experience with other living things in the wilderness world is made intelligible and accessible to the human community. In fact, deer songs often take the form of dialogues in which *saila maso* and others in the wilderness world speak with one another or with the deer singers themselves. It is in this way, according to deer singer Miki Maaso, that "the wilderness world listens to itself even today." Deer songs continue in Yaqui communities as a very real vehicle for communication with the larger natural community in which Yaquis live.

Yaquis do not, however, regard deer songs as some sort of "natural" language, at once wholly inspired, spontaneous, and mystical. Deer songs are made and sung in the Yaqui language, a language with systems of sound, syntax, semantics, and a web of relations with other languages every bit as complex and human as German, Japanese, or American English. The Yaqui language is part of a large family of native languages which stretches north to include Shoshoni, Paiute, and Hopi in the western United States and south into central Mexico to include Aztec.[16] Within this Uto-Aztecan family, Yaqui is most closely related to the language spoken by the Mayos, their neighbors immediately to the south, but it has close affinities with most of the languages spoken by the native peoples who occupied the lands around the Yaqui homeland along the northwest coast of Mexico: the Tarahumara, Guarijio, Opata, Tepehuan, Papago, and Pima. We have included a guide to reading Yaqui words in the References section. Almost all Yaquis living in Sonora speak Spanish as well as their native language. Among Yaquis living in southern Arizona, it is not unusual for individuals to be able to converse easily in English, as well as Spanish and Yaqui. Yaqui and Spanish have been spoken together in Yaqui communities for some 450 years now, and the language of many Yaqui speakers shows considerable Spanish influence. The impact of Spanish on the language of deer songs, however, seems limited. Most Yaquis believe that deer songs perpetuate the oldest form of their language. In that sense deer songs are regarded as one of the most essential expressions of what it is to remain Yaqui after four and one-half centuries of attempts to destroy their communities and to dissolve them as a people. The continuance of Yaqui deer songs is thus directly related to Yaqui memories of their history and survival as a people.

There are probably about 30,000 people who think of themselves as Yaquis today. Most live in communities along the Río Yaqui in southern Sonora on a part of their aboriginal lands which President Lázaro Cárdenas established as Mexico's first "Indigenous Community" in 1939. Other Yaquis maintain communities in the Sonoran cities of Empalme, Guaymas, and Hermosillo. Of the 5 – 6,000 Yaquis in the United States, most live in the communities of Old Pascua, 39th Street, and Pascua Pueblo in Tucson and in the community of Guadalupe near Phoenix. A map of these Yaqui communities is included in the References section.

Yaquis have lived in permanent communities in southern Arizona since well before Arizona was declared a state in 1912. But until very recently Yaquis were not recognized as American Indians. In the 1970s a group of Arizona Yaquis set out to change that and, with the sponsorship of Representative Morris Udall, they succeeded. In 1978, President Carter signed into law S. 1633 which provided trust status for the Pascua Yaqui Indians of Arizona. What is of special interest to us here is how Yaquis went about proving that they were "real" Indians. At a hearing on this matter before the U.S. Senate Select Committee on Indian Affairs, September 27, 1977, Yaqui leader Anselmo Valencia introduced a series of arguments: Yaquis had lived within the area we call the United States long before there were international boundaries to divide the continent; most of the members of the Pascua Yaqui community were born in the United States; many Yaqui Indians have served in various branches of the Armed

Forces of the United States. But the heart of Mr. Valencia's successful argument was this:

> *The Yaquis are Indians in every sense of the word. We have our own language, our own culture, such as the Pascola dancing, the deer dancing, and the coyote dancing. These dances are Indian in origin. In the deer dance, we sing to honor the great mountains, the springs, the lakes. We sing of our father the Sun, and of creatures living and dead. We sing of trees and leaves and twigs. We sing of the birds in the sky and of the fish in the ocean. Our drummers play their music in their drums and flutes. All the songs sung and played are to the olden times—ancient Yaqui Indian stories....The Catholic faith and the various governments under which the Yaquis have had to suffer have tried for centuries to undermine our "Yaquiness," but after 400 years they have not succeeded. We have retained our language, our culture, and our Indianness.[17]*

The continuance of the deer dance and deer singing through four centuries of attempted conquest is, in Mr. Valencia's judgment, one of the primary evidences that Yaquis remain Yaqui. In this way, the deer dance and the enchanted talk of deer songs which it accompanies have emerged as perhaps *the* symbol of Yaqui identity in the last quarter of the twentieth century.[18]

Yoememmet Hiohte: Writing About Yaquis

Europeans and Euroamericans have been writing about Yaquis since at least the middle of the seventeenth century when the Spanish Jesuit Andrés Pérez de Ribas published an account of the six years he spent in the Yaqui River valley as *Historia de los Triunfos de nuestra Santa Fé entre Gentes las mas Bárbaras y Fieras del Nuevo Orbe* (1645).[19] So far as we can tell, however, it was nearly three hundred years later that Yaqui deer songs were first recorded and published for audiences outside Yaqui communities. The Europeans who had contact with Yaquis during those centuries, whether they were sympathetic or hostile to native cultures, viewed Yaquis as anything but poetic. De Guzmán grudgingly complimented them for being the fiercest fighters he had encountered in the new world he was trying to conquer. But to him and to those who followed, Yaquis were enemies and heathens, who, of course, had no writing system anyway. Ruth Finnegan has observed that, wherever European visitors have found no print, they are quick to assume an "intellectual and artistic barrenness" as well. Because most native peoples in the Americas, including Yaquis, were without letters when Europeans first encountered them, they were widely assumed to be artless and unreflective.

There are prominent exceptions. Such men as Bernardino de Sahagún, Jerónimo de Alcalá, and Cristóbal de Molina saw the value of native verbal arts and very early worked vigorously to translate them into Spanish.[20] Shortly after his arrival in Mexico in 1529, for example, the Franciscan Sahagún actually set up a college for native translators of Náhuatl in Tlatelolco. There Náhuatl texts were written down, translated, and discussed by the native peoples Sahagún was training. Náhuatl is a language related to Yaqui, and these early recordings show some provocative parallels with contemporary Yaqui texts. Unfortunately, however, no efforts like Sahagún's took place in northwestern Mexico. Yaqui tradition holds that Yaquis began to write down their language and traditions for their own use as early as the seventeenth century. But Yaqui verbal arts went largely unappreciated outside their own communities until early in the twentieth century.

The English-speaking Americans who worked their way southwest toward the Yaquis during the nineteenth century were no more receptive to native American verbal arts than the Spanish speakers surging northwest. Dr. Jonathan Letherman, for example, came southwest as far as the Navajo Indians in northern Arizona and New Mexico on behalf of the Smithsonian Institution in the 1850s. He was charged, among other duties, with assessing the cultural achievement of the Navajos. Letherman's estimates appeared in the First Smithsonian Report (1856). "Of their religion little or nothing is known," he wrote of the Navajos, "as, indeed, all inquiries tend to show that they have none. The lack of tradition is a source of surprise.... Their singing is but a succession of grunts and is anything but agreeable."[21] Within a generation of this report, however, the archives of several American institutions were filling up with recordings of the great song cycles of the Navajo chantways. These remain today some of the true masterworks of American literature.

The assessment of the Yaqui verbal arts offered by the Mexicans who went among the Yaquis during the nineteenth century would probably have been even harsher. Mexicans seem to have been well aware of deer singing and the other traditional arts throughout the nineteenth century, for, as Edward Spicer notes, nearly every Mexican writer on Yaquis referred to them. However, it was only after the Revolution of 1910 that there was any sentiment for considering traditional Yaqui art forms as anything other than marks of savagery and barbarism.[22]

It was at about that time, during the decades on either side of the turn of the twentieth century, that a transformation in attitude toward native American verbal arts was taking place. Stories and songs from native communities went from being regarded as disagreeable "grunts" to being considered "remains" valuable to science and on to being hailed as our first American literature.

In 1883 Daniel Brinton published a wide-ranging survey of the American Indian verbal art known at his time, including selections intended to "engage in their presentation and publication the interest of scholarly men, of learned societies, of enlightened governments, of liberal institutions and individuals, not only in [this] country but throughout the world."[23] By 1888 an American Folk-Lore Society was founded to promote "the collection of the fast-vanishing remains of Folk-Lore in America." Among these "remains" the verbal arts of American Indian people were regarded as "the most promising and important part of the work to be accomplished." What followed these calls, chronologically if not causally, was an intense period of recording native American traditions. During the last decades of the nineteenth century and the first of the twentieth, enormous numbers of narratives and songs were recorded from tribal peoples all over this continent.

It was as a part of this move to record the verbal arts native to this continent that Frances Densmore began the work which brought her eventually to the Yaqui village of Guadalupe, Arizona, in the spring of 1922.[24] Working there with singer Juan Ariwares on the Monday after Easter, Densmore recorded some thirteen deer songs on phonographic cylinders. These she published along with some Yuman deer songs ten years later in *Yuman and Yaqui Music*. For each of the deer songs she published, Densmore gives a musical notation, a brief analysis of musical features, and a "free translation." The free translations appear to be paraphrases of the words of the deer songs provided by translator Loretto Luna.

In 1933, Francisco Domínguez, "musician, composer, and collector of folk music of the Ministry of Education," visited the Yaqui village at Potam, Sonora. Domínguez first reported on this visit in several articles in a short-lived journal called *Mexican Folkways*. In "Música Yaqui" he describes the melodies of two deer songs sung for him by Santana Valenzuela and gives texts and translations for them. It appears likely that these are Mayo rather than Yaqui deer songs. A more complete report of the 1933 Domínguez trip to Río Yaqui was finally published in 1962 as a part of a collection of reports on field projects sponsored by the Mexican office of public education between 1931 and 1937. That collection, titled *Investigación Folklórica en México*, also includes a separate report on Yaqui deer song texts recorded in 1931 when some Yaqui singers visited Mexico City.[25] The five songs in 1931 are probably the first deer song texts recorded and translated accurately in print. Unfortunately, it was not these but the Yaqui/Mayo song texts recorded by Domínguez in 1933 that got reprinted for wider public appreciation—first as a part of Alfonso Fabila's extensive discussion of the Yaqui arts in *Las Tribus Yaquis de Sonora* (1940) and then again in Frances Toor's *A Treasury of Mexican Folkways* (1947), along with the most bizarre "deer song" we have seen reported. "The deer dance of the wilder Yaquis of the Bacatete Sierra," Toor writes, "is danced around a bonfire and over its flames, while the singers sing:

Vamonos, vamonos a bailar   Come on, let us dance
A la hoguera de Satanas;   At Satan's bonfire,
A ver que fin tenemos,   To see what happens,

A ver si no nos quemamos.	To see if we get burned.
Y antes que no vayamon,	But before going,
Vamos a persignarnos,	Let us cross ourselves
En nombre de Dios.	In the name of God.
Que fin hemos de tener?	What can happen to us then?

Toor does not give a source for this song.[26] We have never encountered any deer songs, in Arizona or Sonora, even remotely like it.

This "deer song" points to a tendency of some writers to publish depictions of Yaquis that are so dominated by their own fantasies as to be suspect as anything but outright fiction. The notion that Yaquis retire to the Vakateteve Mountains in order to pursue secret ceremonies and worship the Devil is a fantasy as old as Pérez de Ribas and his Jesuit brothers. In 1645, he wrote "with some trepidation" on the subject of witchcraft among the Yaquis: "A Yaqui woman of those who had been engulfed in such darkness, after becoming enlightened pointed out to a Padre a great range of mountain peaks and ridges whose skyline could be seen across the Yaqui River, explaining that all these were places of superstition to the Yaquis, which they reverenced and, at the same time, held in dread and fear. She asserted further to this Padre that the devil often appeared in these places."[27] More recently, popular folklorist J. Frank Dobie salutes "the fiercest defenders of their wild liberty and the most tenacious clingers to their wild land that the continent of North America has spawned—the Yaquis," only to launch into a telling of "the secret Easter dance of the Yaquis in the Vaca Tete Mountains" which revolves around defiling a dead body. See *Apache Gold and Yaqui Silver* (1939) for the sensationalized story, perhaps prompted by the same Sonoran Mexican folklore which inspired Toor's "deer song."[28]

This may be the tradition to which Carlos Castaneda's *The Teachings of Don Juan: A Yaqui Way of Knowledge* (1968) and its sequels most closely relate.[29] Felipe Molina notes that there are some Yaquis who have some of the abilities described by Castaneda. *Yenanasonteme*, those who damage (from *nasonte*, to damage or ruin), for example, are said to be able to transform themselves. At the same time, Molina feels that Castaneda's books "make Yaquis into something they are not." A full review of the Casteneda books from a Yaqui point of view might be of interest to many non-Yaqui readers; however, we have yet to come across a Yaqui who admits even to reading all the books, much less to trying to review them. And, as poet Wendy Rose observes, "the last thing a 'Don Juan' cultist wants is to meet a genuine Yaqui holy person."[30] Richard de Mille, a non-Yaqui, devoted at least six years to detailed researches into the question of what is fact and fiction in Castaneda's writings. De Mille concludes that Casteneda is a con artist in the tradition of such native American tricksters as Coyote, a trickster who "abuses people's trust while teaching them valuable lessons." "One thing Trickster could teach us," de Mille writes, "is not to go on forever being fooled."[31] G. C. Edmondson writes a more recognizable science fiction about Yaquis in *Chapayeka* (1971), a tale of an alienated anthropologist who journeys to a remote Yaqui village in the Vakateteve Mountains in search of exotic data for his next paper. There he finds a retarded alien from another solar system, whose forbearers provided Yaquis with a model for chapayeka masks on a previous visit to planet earth sometime before the beginning of the archaeological record![32]

We do not wish to equate the responsible work of such early recorders as Frances Densmore or Francisco Domínguez with these fantasies about Yaquis. Still, even these early recorders of deer songs on both sides of the border had only a casual acquaintance with the Yaqui language and culture and little inclination to spend time to acquire more. Neither Densmore nor Domínguez appears to have spent much more than a week in Yaqui communities before they were off to other researches. And it is clear that neither involved Yaqui collaborators in any significant way in their work.

In 1936 Edward H. Spicer began a lifetime of study of Yaqui history and culture. Working with his wife Rosamond, Spicer maintained an active interest in the Yaqui arts throughout his long career, and that interest is reflected in the attention he gave to the Yaqui arts in most of his major publications. Although he recorded few deer songs himself, Spicer urged many students to explore deer songs and deer singing, and he was instrumental in arranging a number of sound recording sessions.[33] Spicer and his student Carleton S. Wilder arranged to make phonographic recordings of deer songs sung by deer singers from Pascua village in January 1940. During one morning recording session at a studio on the University of Arizona campus, lead singer Juan Silvas (José Angel Alvarez), working with Luis Robles, Frank Acuña, and Juan Maaso (Juan Alvarez), recorded twenty deer songs. These songs became a major part of a thesis which Wilder prepared under Spicer's direction titled "The Yaqui Deer Dance: A Study in Cultural Change" (1940). In that study Wilder included a transcription and word-for-word translation along with explanatory notes for each song. He also gave two additional translations for each song: one "a modern native translation" written by Yaqui translator Joe D. Romero, the other a free translation of Wilder's own "incorporating all or most of the ideas specifically mentioned in the song, something which is not always included in the native translation." This set of translations is the most satisfactory presently available. Comparing them to the original recordings, we find both the transcriptions and translations accurate.[34] Wilder's goal for the study, however, was not to focus on deer-song texts themselves but rather upon the deer dance in "an attempt to describe the form of the deer dance in Pascua in 1940...and to inquire into the function of the deer dance in Yaqui culture."

Ten years later, Amos Taub, a student of Spicer and novelist Frances Gillmor, wrote a thesis in which the primary focus was on deer-song texts. In "Traditional Poetry of the Yaqui Indians" (1950), Taub gives interlinear translations of some thirty deer and coyote songs, analyzes them as "song-poems," and offers his own literary translations of each of the songs. We will take up some of Taub's observations about deer songs later, but his was the first attempt to translate the words of deer songs for appreciation by a wider American audience as a part of what he called "folk poetry."

Bwika Nokita Hiohte: Writing Song Talk

We too are offering the translated words of Yaqui deer songs as a native American poetry. In so doing we take a part in a movement growing from many quarters to recognize the aesthetic achievement of native American verbal arts. This is a movement, as we have noted, which was already building around the turn of this century in response to the publications of the likes of Frances Densmore. Especially over the last ten years, it has flowered as a part of what has been called a Native American Renaissance.[35] One thrust has come from linguists, ethnologists, and folklorists; another from poets and writers; and a third has come from within native communities themselves, especially in recent years, as a part of bilingual education programs. The first group has tended to publish translations distinguished by their documentary and analytical merits; the second by their aesthetics; and the third has looked to translations of story and song for help with language maintenance and strengthening tribal identity. From our perspective, the *sine qua non* of all three is an accurate transcription of a native language text along with an English translation faithful to it. Unfortunately, there are many who fail to meet even these fundamental criteria. Several have "translated" or "retranslated" Yaqui deer songs.

In his influential book *Assays* (1961), poet Kenneth Rexroth praises the translations of Frances Densmore. Noting that all the texts of Densmore's translations are extremely "simple," Rexroth writes that "most of them are pure poems of sensibility resembling nothing so much as classical Japanese poetry or Mallarme and certain other modern French and American poets, notably some of the Imagists at their best." At the conclusion of the discussion, Rexroth gives some Yaqui examples from Densmore's work:

The bush   The deer
Is sitting   Looks at a flower.
Under a tree
And singing.

Re-lined from Densmore, the two are striking epigrams, and they may even be "pure poems of sensibility" to the tastes of some readers. But even as they are presented in

Densmore's monograph, it is evident that they have other much more important aesthetic dimensions for Yaqui audiences. Rexroth says nothing about these: nothing about the deer dance which accompanies the songs, nothing about the songs' relation to the larger world of Yaqui belief, nothing about hints that the songs are as much narrative as lyric. As readers we are left to respond to the song not as a Yaqui song in any sense, but as words on the page that look very much like printed poems from both Oriental and Occidental literary tradition. The problem with this, as Karl Kroeber notes in writing of a similar sequence of recent "retranslations" of an Ojibwa deer song also recorded by the ubiquitous Densmore, is that "because we receive the song 'beyond' its originating culture, any comparison such as the one to Imagism is sure to be falsifying—and to that degree diminishing of the original's power to let us perceive our own art from a new perspective." The Ojibwa song text is more like a libretto score for a dance drama, Kroeber continues, "a transactional event, a process by which dream power is realized as cultural potency."[36]

But there is an even more fundamental problem with our Yaqui example: the accuracy of the translation Rexroth worked from. Densmore recorded Juan Ariwares's songs on phonographic cylinders which are still preserved at the Smithsonian Institution, so we are able to evaluate her original "free translations." Although the singer's voice is unintelligible in many of the songs on those cylinders, Felipe Molina was able to transcribe one as follows:

Sikili...
    kaita va vemu weamakasu
        hakun kukupopoti hiusakai
Sikili...
    kaita va vemu weamakasu
        hakun kukupopoti hiusakai

Iyiminsu seyewailo
    huya nainasukuni
        kaita va vemu weamakasu
            hakun kukupopoti hiusaka
Sikili...
    kaita va vemu weamakasu
        hakun kukupopoti hiusakai

This is the song Densmore translates as:

The quail in the bush is making his sound (whirring).[37]

Although the word for quail is not intelligible in the first line of the recording, the singer is probably saying *sikili suva'i*, little red quail. A new translation of the song indicates some of what is lost in the original "free translation":

> Little red [quail],
>> walking afar where there is no water,
>>> where do they make the kukupopoti sound?
>> Little red [quail],
>>> walking afar where there is no water,
>>>> where do they make the kukupopoti sound?

> Over here, in the center
>> of the flower-covered wilderness,
>>> walking afar where there is no water,
>>>> where do they make the kukupopoti sound?
>> Little red [quail],
>>> walking afar where there is no water,
>>>> where do they make the kukupopoti sound?

The song's line and stanza structure, its rhetorical structure, the action it describes, its onomatopoeic representation of the sound of the quail, and other features which must contribute in some way to its aesthetic effect in Yaqui are completely absent in the "free translation," and, of course, in Rexroth's re-lined version. Appreciations of verbal art provoked by such translations, then, must be suspect. They are grounded, as Dell Hymes notes, "solely on the reader's sense of the English and ethnological appropriateness of the translation, and respect for the linguistic ethnographer."[38]

"The problem in studying Indian music," Densmore herself recognized later in her career, "is not simply to describe it accurately but to acquire the native standpoint."[39] We include Yaqui language transcriptions for all the deer song texts which we translate. This gives Yaqui readers a ready gauge of their accuracy. Audio recordings are available to those who would listen. Acquiring "the native standpoint" is, we agree, a more difficult matter. Felipe Molina's collaboration ensures that *a* native standpoint is represented here. Moreover, we have asked all the deer singers with whom we worked to comment on their songs. The Pawnee singer Tahirussawichi explained to Alice C. Fletcher that "the words of the song do not tell all that the song means; the meaning has been handed down from our fathers and taught to the [singers], who may teach it to anyone who is serious-minded and sincerely desires to learn."[40] We have found this to be true of Yaqui deer songs as well. Because he did not have access to such explanations of the Yaqui deer songs he wanted to appreciate as a "traditional poetry," Amos Taub felt that deer song words would never be clarified, that "the long passage of time and the gradual change in the nature of the culture have obliterated too many references, allusions and contexts."[41] Although we agree that many meanings of deer-song words seem too far removed to bring back into the present, we found that the commentaries of deer singers on their songs keeps much alive into the 1980s. Don Jesús was particularly helpful in his explanations and commentaries, and we have used quotations from them to accompany our translations of his song sets.

Like other languages, Yaqui may be used in many special ways. Expressed in some of its own terms, for example, the Yaqui language may be used *nooka*, to talk; *lionoka*, to pray (from *Dios* + *noka*, God talk); *hinabaka*, to give a sermon; *etehoi*, to tell, especially in the sense of an *etehoim*, story; and, of course, *bwiika*, to sing. There are likewise many special ways to sing in Yaqui tradition. *Suru bwikam*/messenger songs, *vachi vino bwikam*/corn wine songs, *nahi bwikam*/fly songs, *wo'i bwikam*/coyote songs, and the *maso bwikam*/deer songs that we discuss here are some of the kinds of traditional Yaqui songs that continue to be sung. Each one has its own subject matter, its own style of performance, and its own performance settings. All Yaqui songs are not the same. One who wishes to sing a deer song cannot come out with just any words, rhythm, or melody. He, almost always the singer is a he, must express himself in Yaqui within the conventions which Yaqui audiences have come to expect of *maso bwikam*/deer songs. In preparing the translations that follow we have tried to take account of these conventions. Some of them we can represent in print, some we cannot.[42]

During our talks about deer songs, Don Jesús distinguished between *bwika hiawa*, song sound, which we understood to refer to the song's rhythm and melody, and *bwika noki*, song talk, which we understood to be the verbal part of the song. In this book we attempt to translate only the song talk, the verbal part of deer songs. Since neither of us is trained in music, we leave attempts at translating the song sound to others.[43] As readers you may get some better sense of the way the song words, which we translate, work with the song sounds, which we do not, by listening to the audio recording which accompanies this book.

In translating the words of Yaqui deer songs, we note as a first thing that they *are* words. Many native American song traditions have kinds of songs which are made in part, sometimes entirely, from vocables, syllables without meaning. Yaqui deer singers use vocables only rarely in their deer songs. Some singers use /mmmm/or /aaaa/ to find their pitch at the beginning of each of their songs, as Felipe does on the accompanying audio tape. Others regularly use an /aa/ to carry them into repetitions of the first part of the song. But the deer singers we have heard and recorded for this book rarely use vocables within the songs.

One of the comments we have heard frequently in Yaqui communities about deer songs is that the words in them sound different from regular Yaqui. Some suggest that deer singers use a special language, a song language which is all but incomprehensible to anyone but the singers. We do not find this to be the case. There are a number of key words in deer songs that are not often used in ordinary Yaqui conversation. "Old words," Don Jesús called them. Two from this archaic lexicon that we discuss at some length later are *seyewailo* and *yevuku yoleme*. More commonly, however, the song words sound different from ordinary words because of changes the singer makes in individual sounds. Don Jesús said that he made such changes in his song words so that they would "sound better." To illustrate, we compare the verbal part of one of the rain songs we recorded from him with equivalent contemporary conversational Yaqui supplied by Felipe Molina:

ORDINARY LANGUAGE	SONG LANGUAGE
Uva uvaka	Yuvali yuvalika
toloko bwiapo	tolo bwiapo
yewe	yeyewe
Uva uvaka	Yuvali yuvalika
toloko bwiapo	tolo bwiapo
yewe	yeyewe
Hunaman ne seyewailo	Ayaman ne seyewailo
huya nasukuni	huyatanaisukuni
kiane yo tevuhria namuei	kaine yo tevulia namulia
vahewa sililiti komisu yumao	vaiwa sililiti komisu yuyumao
Uva uvaka	Yuvali yuvalika
toloko bwiapo	tolo bwiapo
yewe	yeyewe
Uva uvaka	Yuvali yuvalika
toloko bwiapo	tolo bwiapo
yewe	yeyewe

This step from song language to ordinary language amounts to the first "translation" of the song in some native American song traditions, as Donald Bahr has shown for Pima/Papago and Leanne Hinton for Havasupai.[44] Our illustration gives evidence that the amount of such "translation" required to turn the language of deer songs into conversational Yaqui is modest. Many of the kinds of changes that happen in this song occur regularly in the other songs we have recorded. Looking just at Don Jesús' set of four rain songs, for example, we find the following differences between song words and contemporary conversational words:

ORDINARY WORDS	SONG WORDS		
vasevo'imtea	*vaesevolimtea*	/a/	/ae/
		/'/	/l/
yeusu	*yeulu*	/s/	/l/
aniachi	*aniwachi*	/ia/	/iwa/
namutakane	*namutakaine*	/a/	/ai/
vahurina	*vaulina*	/ahu/	/au/
		/r/	/l/
machia	*machiwa*	/ia/	/iwa/
yoeme	*yoleme*		/l/
yova'ata	*yoyovata*	/yo/	/yoyo/
		/va'a/	/va/
uva	*yuvali*	/y/	
		/li/	
toloko	*tolo*	/ko/	
yewe	*yeyewe*	/ye/	/yeye/
hunaman	*ayaman*	/hun/	/ay/
nasukuni	*naisukuni*	/a/	/ai/
tevuhria	*tevulia*	/hr/	/l/
namuei	*namulia*	/ei/	/lia/
vahewa	*vaiwa*	/ahe/	/ai/
yumao	*yuyumao*	/yu/	/yuyu/

We note that two of the most common kinds of sound change listed here *do* occur as well in some conversational Yaqui. This blurs further any case that a special "song language," requiring a special translation, exists. The addition of /l/ to a word, as in *yoeme*/*yoleme* or *vai*/*vali*, or the substitution of /l/ for another phoneme, as in *vasevo'imtea*/*vaesevolimtea* or *tevuhria*/*tevulia*, both occur in conversational Yaqui. There, as in the songs, Felipe believes that the /l/ indicates special affection. A second case is reduplication, which Felipe believes occurs "mostly in action verbs not only in the songs but also in our elders' talk." *Yewe:* play/*yeyewe*, *weche:* fall/*weweche*, *vuite:* run/*vuivuite*, *tekipanoa:* work/*tekipapanoa*, and *bwikola:* edge of/*bwibwikola* are examples of reduplication in words used in songs which Felipe has also heard used in speech of elder Yaquis in southern Arizona. Thus, the language we encountered in the deer songs we worked with seemed remarkably close to contemporary conversational Yaqui and, therefore, posed few of the barriers to translation that some have described in their work with other native verbal art traditions. We experienced difficulties, of course. Some of these we report later. Although we were able to recognize and translate the meaning of the words in deer songs, our experiments with trying to find equivalents for the *sounds* in our English translations were unsuccessful.[45] For the most part the sound texture of the songs, one of their most "poetic" features to Yaqui listeners, remains untranslated here.

The line and stanza structure of deer songs is accessible in translation. Don Jesús talked about two parts of deer song: *u vat weeme*, the first part, and *u tonua*, the concluding part. These parts are the two large units out of which all deer songs are made. They are equivalent to what we call "stanzas" in English and American poetry. When a deer song is sung, the first part may be repeated a number of times, from one to eighteen are the extremes in our collection, three or four the norm; then the concluding part is sung once to complete one full repetition of the song. Don Jesús cautioned us to "remember that the first part is sung many times and then the concluding part will fall down there." Throughout this book we repeat the first part the same number of times as did the singer we recorded, even if this means an exact repetition of the same line ten or twelve times.

There can be considerable variation in the way the first part is organized, but most often in the songs we recorded it consists of a single line which is repeated once. Or a single line may be repeated with slight variation, for example, the deletion or addition of single words:

Ala ini kun maiso yoleme
  hunu kun maiso yoleme
    ini kun tua maiso yoleme

So now this is the deer person,
  so he is the deer person,
    so he is the real deer person.

Frequently singers make an antithesis of the repetition, as Felipe does in *Sewa Huya*:

Sewa huya
  yeu ne wevalika
    sewa huya
Sewa yo huya aniwapo
  yeu ne sika
    sewa huya

Flower wilderness,
  as I want to go out,
    flower wilderness.
In the enchanted flower wilderness world,
  I went out,
    flower wilderness.

But the most common is a single line repeated once in perfect parallelism.

Don Jesús described the *tonua*, the concluding stanza (fr. Sp. *tonada*, tune, song?), as having two parts. It begins with a long line which describes a place in the flower world and, then, the action(s) in it. This opening line commonly begins with the locative *ayaman*, over there. The concluding line of the *tonua* is usually a repetition of the first line of the first part. This pattern is made more complex in a number of ways which we take up later.

Translating song words requires attention to more than the matters of semantics, sound, and structure that we touch on here. "When the totality is considered," writes Acoma poet Simon J. Ortiz of translating song, "it doesn't break down so easily and conveniently. And there is no need to break it down and define its parts. Language as expression and perception—that is at the core of what a song is."[46] We take a step toward consideration of "the totality" in the next section, as we discuss what might be called originative contexts of deer songs: their sources in Yaqui myth and history, their sources in the lives of individual singers, perception and expression, cultural and individual.

Aa hita sea kutataka
   wana yo vampo
     voka noka
Hita sea kutataka
   wana yo vampo
     voka noka

Ayaman ne seyewailo
   mayachiala vevetana
     weyeka
       im ne
         yo toloko bwiapo
          yeu ne yolemtaka
Hita sea kutataka
   wana yo vampo
     voka noka

Aa what flower stick,
   there in the enchanted water,
     is lying, talking?
What flower stick,
   there in the enchanted water,
     is lying, talking?

Over there, I, from
   the flower-covered dawn,
    I am walking,
      here, I,
        out on the enchanted light blue earth,
      I am a person.
What flower stick,
   there in the enchanted water
     is lying, talking?

Miki Maaso
Potam Pueblo
May 28, 1983

6. Taking a break from deer singing …

2

YEU A WEEPO
WHERE IT COMES OUT

WHERE DO Yaqui deer songs come from? What are their sources in Yaqui myth and history? And what are their sources in Yaqui lives? How do they come to individual singers? To offer answers to these questions we gather stories from many tellers around talks we had with Don Jesús. In this way we begin to translate some words and concepts that inform our translations of the deer songs themselves.

U Kuta Nokame: The Talking Stick

There is a Yaqui story about *u kuta nokame,* the talking stick. It is often told, and there are many versions set down in print. Some speak of the story as an account of the Yaqui creation. We came to ask Don Jesús about that talking stick one day when the palo verde trees were in bloom and a dry Sonoran wind pushed pale yellow blossoms in eddies along the packed earth of his patio. It was not yet mid-morning, but the spring sun was intense. In the shade of his kitchen *ramá,* Don Jesús sipped the soda we brought along and spoke about a time "when the earth was becoming new here." His voice was low and even, and as he spoke his left hand caressed the worn mesquite walking stick he had placed on the table beside him.

Sometime in the past the tree talked.
All the elders do not know of it,
But, yes, some wise ones spoke of it.
When the world was becoming new here,
There was one who could hear the sounds of the tree.
The one who could hear it,
That one told about it.
They were old things from long ago,
But only one could hear it.
That talking stick was a long time ago,

When the earth was becoming new here,
When the Surem lived here,
When they lived here, that is when the stick talked.
When it talked, it was just like a song.

Leaning forward on his wooden bench, Don Jesús began to hum in the rhythm of a deer song, here and there bringing words into the single line he repeated over and over.

There is one in deer singing about that.
It goes like this:

> Ala senu kuta kun noyoka noyokai   So one stick may be talking, talking.
> Ala senu kuta kun noyoka noyokai   So one stick may be talking, talking.

That one is an alavansa, *a song.*
That stick wants to talk in a deer song.

> Ala senu kuta weyeka noyoka noyokai   So one stick is standing, talking, talking.
> Ala senu kuta weyeka noyoka noyokai   So one stick is standing, talking, talking.

That one is just an alavansa.
Some deer singers sing that one.
When we do, we are singing about the talking stick in the deer song.
The talking stick.[1]

With characteristic repetition and gentle antithesis, Don Jesús' deer song preserves a recognition of sound as language that is central in Yaqui tradition. In a significant way, all beginnings in Yaqui oral history involve such recognitions. The sounds that need to be understood may come from fishes, caves, or invading Spaniards. They may be a part of what we call myth, history, vision, or dream, but time and again in Yaqui stories the people must understand sound from beyond the limits of the everyday language of their communities in order to continue. In this sense there are no creators in Yaqui tradition, only translators. All beginnings are translations.

The talking stick which Don Jesús refers to is imagined in various ways by Yaqui people. Some talk of it as just the thick bare trunk of an unidentified tree which vibrates. Others describe fully branched trees of particular varieties from the Sonoran desert, such as palo verde or mesquite, which sing with some unnatural sounds. Don Jesús' comments make a link not between the talking stick and some particular kind of tree but between the talking stick of ancient Yaqui narrative and the instruments which he used all his life to practice the art of deer singing. For the deer singer's raspers, which are named *hirukiam*, are often also referred to as a *kuta*, stick. We have heard them called *sewa kuta*, flower stick; *yo kuta*, enchanted stick; *maso kuta*, deer stick; and other things.[2]

The many versions of the story of the talking stick or talking tree which have been printed all tell of a time before the coming of Europeans to the Yaqui world when a translator needed to be found to understand the future in a language of the past.[3] Always the translator is a young woman. She is variously named, and sometimes she is a twin. One version calls her *Seahamut*, Flower Girl. In another telling she is *Yueta*, an appropriate name for it connects her with what she does in the story. In Yaqui language, *yueta* is a sound carried in the wilderness air, especially a sound which is unusual and out of the ordinary. Often the young girl or her parent is named for another sound, perhaps also metaphorical of sound she translates: *Yomumuli*, Enchanted Bee. Yaqui poet Refugio Savala compares the sound the young girl translates to "the chords of a harp" in a literary version of the story published in his *Autobiography of a Yaqui Poet*. In the 1940s, the Sonoran Yaqui poet Ambrosio Castro said that when the tree "spoke it made a noise like a telephone apparatus."

The focus of the story is not so much on what the talking stick sounded like as it is on what the young woman is able to hear. In the vibrations of the talking stick the young woman hears a message that marks a boundary between an ancient Yaqui way of living and a way of living that takes account of the new world created by the European presence, a boundary between myth and history, immortality and death, a boundary between the language of the wilderness and the language of the town. It marks, then, not so much a creation as a re-creation, a time "when the earth was becoming new here."

Felipe Molina wrote down this version of the story of the talking tree after hearing Luciano Velasquez tell it at Kompwertam, Sonora, in August 1982.

In the time before the Spanish conquest the Surem *lived in the area that is now west of Ciudad Obregón. Their river was called* Yo Vatwe, Enchanted River. *In this region the* Surem *had their homes, and they lived on both banks. Their houses were called* hukim. *They were built of sticks and mud and were about four or five feet high. They hunted, fished, and farmed to stay alive.*

Well, anyway, during those early times a tree was heard talking on a small hill called Tosai Bwia, White Earth. *Some say it was heard at* Omteme Kawi, *but we say it was at* Tosai Bwia. *This tree was an old dead mesquite tree, and it made strange humming sounds. Nobody could understand the sounds. That bothered the* Surem. *All the intelligent men in the* Surem *land were notified and told to visit the tree. None of those intelligent men could figure it out. They all had to admit failure. They could not decide what the meaning of the tree was.*

These wise men knew of one other wise man who lived near a little mountain called Asum Kawi, Grandmothers' Mountain. This man's name was Yomomoli, and he had twin daughters. The wise men visited him and requested that his two daughters interpret the talking tree. Yomomoli told them that the girls didn't have a good vocabulary, so they would be incapable of doing such a task. The men insisted. Finally they convinced Yomomoli to take the girls to the talking tree. But Yomomoli did one thing first. He took his twin daughters to the ocean. There they talked to a fish, so that they might better understand the talking tree.

At Tosai Bwia the girls stood on either side of the tree, and they began to interpret. The tree predicted Christianity and baptism, wars, famine, floods, drought, new inventions, even drug problems, and so on. After the tree had given all the information it stopped making the sounds.

The Surem were happy, but they didn't really like some of the things they heard, so they planned a big meeting. The meeting was held near a water hole called Yo Va'am, Enchanted Waters. This is in the region between Vicam and the modern town of Colonia Militar. There the Surem held both a meeting and a dance of enchantment. At this meeting some of the Surem decided to leave the Yaqui region, while others decided to stay and to see these new things. At this dance of enchantment, they say a real live deer came to dance for the Surem. After the dance the Surem who were leaving cut up a portion of the Yo Vatwe, wrapped it up in a bamboo mat, and took it north to a land of many islands. Other Surem stayed around and went into the ocean and underground into the mountains. There in those places the Surem now exist as an enchanted people. Those who stayed behind are now the modern Yaquis, and they are called the Baptized Ones.

The separation described in this story is definitive. From the time of the talking tree there have been two kinds of Yaquis. On the one side are the *Vato'im*, Baptized Ones, those who accepted the seventeenth-century Spanish Catholicism offered them by Jesuit missionaries and absorbed it into their lives. On the other side are those who refused baptism, the *Surem*, the enchanted people, those who went away to preserve the Yaquis' aboriginal relation to the world. The relation between these two parts of the Yaqui world is complex and reciprocal, and it bears directly on our understanding of deer songs.

❋ Coming along a back road out of Vicam that snakes in and out of fields and mesquite bosques until it opens up along one of the irrigation canals, we stop to look at all the turtles climbing up out of the water onto the concrete apron of the canal. They have a good spot to watch the sun go down, so we join them. From where we sit we look out across the canal and the open fields toward the west, and the only thing that stops us from seeing all the way to the Gulf of California is a low, black volcanic mountain with a huge microwave tower on its flat top. Felipe says that must be the Talking Stick. Timothy and the other Yaqui boys who are traveling with us laugh. I need to ask to find out that the mountain is called *Omteme Kawi*, Angry Mountain, and that it is one of the places where it is said that the talking stick was found.

Vato'im: Baptized Ones

Yaquis are a religious people. Today the most visible parts of their religion are practiced within the villages and centered on their churches. It was by Yaqui invitation that the Spanish Jesuit missionary Andrés Pérez de Ribas became the first European to live on Yaqui lands in 1617. Over the next 125 years, he and his successors engaged in a peaceful collaboration that transformed the economic and religious lives of Yaquis. It is clear that from the beginning Yaquis took a very active role in the exchange with the Jesuits, and the result was "a vigorous vitalization of Yaqui culture—in contrast with the stultifying dominance which the Spaniards assumed over the Aztecs and other peoples to the south of the Yaquis."[4] One effect of the long tenure of the Jesuits, which lasted until their expulsion from the New World in 1767, was an insulation of Yaqui lands from Spanish colonial settlement and redistribution policies. Another was the concentration of the Yaqui population into eight villages that were organized around churches. Long after the expulsion of the Jesuits, the Baptized Ones maintained these churches, and they remain today the center of Yaqui community life. Other churches modeled on them are found in Yaqui communities in both Sonora and Arizona.

Under the direction of lay priests called *maehtom*, the Baptized People are organized into a number of societies. Membership in these societies is usually open to anyone who is willing to make a *manda*, a binding vow to carry out the religious obligations of the society. In this way the Baptized Ones work for their salvation through a rich liturgy on such occasions as weddings and baptisms, funerals and death anniversaries, as well as such major calendrical feasts as Holy Trinity Day, San Juan Day, All Souls Day, Christmas, and so on. The formal religious year comes to a climax each spring in Yaqui communities during Holy Week, when a dramatization of the passion and death of Christ enhances the Yaqui observance of the regular Christian lenten liturgy. In all of this ceremonialism, "Yaquis to a large extent have maintained in their religious lives the kind of unity which existed in Europe between religious and aesthetic expression four hundred years ago."[5]

Over the four and one-half centuries since the Conquest, the Baptized Ones have developed a substantial verbal art. It includes not only the formal latinate prayers, litanies, and sermons of the *maehto* and his assistants but a large body of apochryphal Biblical narratives as well.[6] In these stories the pantheon of the Jesuits walk the Río Yaqui country. The stories demonstrate dramatically how Yaquis have made the Catholicism given them into something distinctly their own. Stories tell how *Dios*, God the Father, created the cow, the horse, and tobacco; how *Eva*, Eve, organized the first *pahko;* how *Jesucristo*, Jesus Christ, himself, roamed through Yaqui lands creating mountains and pointing out medicinal herbs to the Yaqui people. One narrative locates Christ's passion, death, and resurrection in the Yaqui country and even attributes the creation of the deer songs to the inspiration of the moment of the Resurrection. This story may help explain the support the deer singers and other dancers and singers give the Baptized Ones throughout the Christian year. But we should regard it carefully. The deer singers and the deer dancer cooperate with the *maehto* and the other church people in many ways throughout the year, but always they remain significantly apart.

Yaqui translator and poet Refugio Savala gives a balanced view of the relationship between the words of the *maehto* and the words of the deer singers in his *Autobiography of a Yaqui Poet*. There he writes: "Singing the deer songs is like praying because there are no bad words used. It is like a prayer because the songs are inspired."[7] In this way Savala suggests that praying and deer singing are complimentary ways of speaking the sacred, but he is careful to note that the kind of inspiration manifested in the deer songs has a source very different from the Resurrection. The deer songs, he continues, "come from the wilds—just like when you dream, you go to a place in nature. Nature is the source of inspiration and prayer. Therefore the songs are like prayers." The deep connections Savala points to here between deer songs and the worlds of wilderness and dream take us back to the talking stick and those the Baptized People left behind there.

✠ My grandfather and many other Yaqui elders did not really know what kind of dance our ancestors danced during the time just before the arrival of the Spaniards, before the people separated into two groups. My grandfather knew the name of a dance that the *Surem* danced though. He called it *yo yiwak*, dance of enchantment.

He understood it this way. After hearing the statements of *Yomumuli*, the young *Surem* girl who translated the prophecies of the talking tree on *Omteme Kawi* near Vicam Pueblo, the *Surem* decided to have a great dance. The dance was held near *Akitavampokatekapo*. That means "where the organ pipe cactus is in the water." It is a place near the present village of Pitahaya. Grandfather said that the place where the dance took place is all flattened out and that there is no vegetation growing on it. My grandfather thought that this dance was like a farewell dance where all the *Surem* gathered and danced for a great departure. The way the ground is flattened out there, he felt that there must have been much footwork from many dancers and that it must have lasted for days.

According to my grandfather, after the dance many *Surem* went underground into big mountain caves and beneath the sea and there became an enchanted people. The other *Surem* became the modern *Yoemem* of today. Many Yaquis say that the *Surem* turned into ants and dolphins but, according to my grandfather, the *Surem* retained their human image but were very magical. Traditional Yaquis perceive the *Surem* on earth as an enchanted nation. Once in a while a *Yoeme* will run into a little *Surem* in the wilderness world. Grandfather believed that, if a *Yoeme* encountered a *Surem*, the *Yoeme* might be shocked greatly or even die from the encounter. For that reason my grandfather and especially my grandmother disapproved of me going into the desert alone.

7. *Reyno Romero's tenevoim ...*

Ume Tua Vat Hiakim: The First Real Yaquis

When we asked Don Jesús about the story of deer songs being created at the time of the Resurrection, he laughed. He told us that, while today the deer songs are performed "for God," they originated long before the time of the talking stick:

The ones who started this were the first Yaquis,
The first real Yaquis.
They didn't wear pants like us. Some had loincloths,
Some had white pants. They didn't dress like us.
Some had long hair like you see in the villages again now.
They were the real Yaquis.
They didn't understand the Spanish language.
They spoke nothing but their own language.
They didn't hold pahkom for God like us.
They were the ones who started it,
There in the wilderness world,
The first real Yaquis.

Before we talk about the relation deer songs have with this wilderness world, we want to reflect for a moment on the term Don Jesús chooses to use for the ancestors— *ume tua vat hiakim*, the first real Yaquis.

As we have seen, Yaqui tradition remembers the first named ancestors as the *Surem*, a race of people of small stature, "little people," who inhabited what are now Yaqui lands in the days before European contact. The *Surem*, it is widely understood, were people of great knowledge, attuned to all the ways of the Sonoran desert and the living things in it. After the great division of the people, the *Surem* stayed on to inhabit the wilderness world of the desert in magical and enchanted ways. Those who split from the *Surem* to inhabit villages are known to Yaqui oral history as the *Yoemem*. And that is what they remember calling themselves when they encountered the first Spaniards in Diego de Guzmán's party in 1533. They were the *Yoemem*, People; the Spaniards were the *Yorim*, other, non-people.

The story of the talking tree tells how some of the *Yoemem* came to be known as the Baptized Ones. Just how they came to be the *Hiakim* is not so clear, but the naming is almost certainly the result of the garbled communication and partial understandings characteristic of the early contacts between Europeans and native people all through the Americas.

During the same era, Spanish missionaries, hearing the close resemblances between the Yaqui language and those of neighboring tribes in northwest Mexico, chose the native word *cahita* to describe the common language. Linguists and others continue to use that word today as the name for the language group which includes Yaqui and Mayo. And some persist in calling Yaquis "Cahitans." *Cahita* is the Yaqui word for "nothing," making Yaquis literally "Nothings" to these scholars.[8] *Hiakim* probably derives from a similar, if less poignant, misunderstanding.

Some early Spanish historians claimed that "Hiaki" was what the people called the major river which runs through their lands and so named the people for the river. In an account of his time among the Yaquis published in 1645, Pérez de Ribas writes that people said to him: "*no ves que soy hiaqui*/Don't you see that I am a Yaqui?" He explains: "*y decíanlo porque esa palabra y nombre significa el que habla a gritos*/and they said this because this word and this name signified the one who speaks in shouts."[9] Yaqui tellers have other stories. Felipe notes that *hihiame*, from *hia*, would be "one who makes a sound," while *chatchaime*, from *chai*, is "one who shouts." Thus, one line of speculation among contemporary Yaqui tellers centers on the verb *hia*, to say or to sound, especially the third person form in the past tense *hihiak*, it sounded. Yaqui poet Ambrosio Castro worked his own etymological theories into a dramatic narrative.

He speculates that the name *Hiakim* originated when the Spaniards, after subduing the Yaquis' neighbors—the Mayos, the Opatas, the Papagos, and others—came once again to try to overcome the Yaquis. When again they failed, the Spaniards decided it was time to be friends. In this way they were at last able to enter Yaqui country. And so it could happen that one day a Yaqui was walking in the desert near Torim, eating fruit from the organ pipe cactus, when suddenly he came upon a Spaniard. The Spaniard began to ask the Yaqui questions: "What is your name? Who are you?" The Yaqui could not understand the Spaniard, but thinking that the Spaniard might be asking: "What are you doing?" the Yaqui replied: "*aakim.*" *Aki* is the Yaqui name for the organ pipe cactus and for its fruit; *akim* the plural form. Castro concludes the scenario triumphantly: "Then the Spaniard took out a pencil and piece of paper saying: 'Ah ha, you are called Yaqui!' and he wrote down these letters: y-a-q-u-i."[10]

In any case, Yaqui is now the principal name the *Yoemem* apply to themselves. And they commonly now refer to the whole of their lands as *hiakimpo*, literally translated "in Yaquis," or more truly as "in the homeland." When Don Jesús talks of the beginning of the deer songs, he extends the term even further. The *Surem*, the original people, he tells us, are *ume tua vat hiakim*, the first real Yaquis.

Huya Ania: Wilderness World

Guadalupe Molina, a deer singer from Vicam Switch, learned to sing from Don Jesús. Once when we asked Don Lupe to tell us more about the *huya ania*, the place where the first real Yaquis lived, he gestured to the desert out toward the Vakateteve Mountains. "That is the *huya ania*," he said; then he sang this deer song:

Empo sewa yo huya aniwa
  empo yo huya aniwa
    vaewa sola voyoka
Empo yo huya aniwa
  vaewa sola voyoka
    huya aniwa

You are an enchanted flower wilderness world,
  you are an enchanted wilderness world,
    you lie with see-through freshness.
You are an enchanted wilderness world,
  you lie with see-through freshness,
    wilderness world.

Ayamansu seyewailo
  huyata naisukunisu
    yo huya aniwapo
      usyol machi hekamake
        usyolisi vaewa sola voyoka
      huya aniwa
Empo yo huya aniwa
  vaewa sola voyoka
    huya aniwa

Over there, in the center
  of the flower-covered wilderness,
    in the enchanted wilderness world,
      beautiful with the dawn wind,
        beautifully you lie with see-through freshness,
      wilderness world.
You are an enchanted wilderness world,
  you lie with see-through freshness,
    wilderness world.

We translate *huya ania, huya aniwa* in the language of the song, as "wilderness world." That translation requires some comment.

Huya encompasses a range of meanings in conversational Yaqui. It may signify an individual plant or bush or tree growing in the Sonoran desert, or it may refer to just a part of one of them, say, a branch. In other contexts, *huya* may signify a whole group of trees, bushes, or plants, taken in the collective sense of "brush." But the most common use of the word is to refer to the whole of the desert around the Yaqui towns and villages, all that enclosed by the sweep of Don Lupe's hand. This sense of the word is often translated by the Spanish *monte*. We translate *huya* as "wilderness" not only because it suggests a region of uncultivated land but also for the appropriateness of its etymology. Wilderness derives from the Old English *wilde*, wild + *doer*, deer. At the same time we want to be quick to say that such associations of the word as "barren," "empty," "pathless," and "uninhabited by human beings" as we find in Webster's *Third New International Dictionary* are not appropriate to the Yaqui sense of the word. For, as Don Lupe's song suggests, the *huya ania* encompasses a rich poetic and spiritual and human dimension of the area surrounding the Yaqui villages as well.

Before the coming of the Spaniards, "the *huya ania* was the source of all things—the food and tools of everyday reality, as well as the special powers of dance and song."[11] The special powers which can be found in the *huya ania* are today thought to exist in certain specialized areas. These too are called *aniam*, worlds, in the sense of a realm or domain. Yaquis speak of a *tuka ania*, night world; a *tenku ania*, dream world; a *yo ania*, enchanted world; a *sea ania*, flower world; and others.[12] The special character of each of these areas, and the relations of the worlds, one to another, are not understood in the same way by the Yaquis we have talked with. Some feel that it is not appropriate to discuss some aspects of them with outsiders at all. It is safe to say, though, that all of these realms are associated with the *Surem* and that they name the spaces in which the *Surem's* religion, what has been called the religion of the woods, continues.[13]

All these worlds are considered to be supernatural and dangerous if not approached correctly. They are visible only in the private eye of dream and vision, and they are made public only when they are put into words in stories individuals tell of their own experiences and those of others. The actions of the *pahkolam* and the deer dancer during a *pahko* may be thought of as reflections of experience performers have had in one of the other worlds. Of greatest importance to understanding deer songs are the *sea ania* and the *yo ania*.

✠ A *yoeme* by the name of Francisco Onamea once told me that he went out to hunt for deer one morning with his friend José Sanava. He said they both took old, powerful rifles for the hunt. While they were walking in the desert toward the *Vakateteve* Mountains, they spotted a small deer standing at a distance watching them curiously. José told Francisco to take a shot at the deer. So Francisco aimed his rifle at the small deer. It was a *soutela*, a small species of deer in the Yaqui country.

Francisco carefully focused his eyes on the small deer and pulled the trigger and shot. The *soutela* was hit and fell to the ground. While both of the men watched, the deer made his last agonizing movements in the dirt. But then to their amazement the *soutela* staggered on his front legs and lifted himself up and shook his body to remove the dirt. Then he stood there and watched the men curiously again.

Once more José told Francisco to shoot at the deer, so Francisco took aim right away and fired. Again the deer fell to the ground, made his agonizing movements, and made a cloud of dust. When the dust settled, the deer again stood at the spot watching the two men curiously.

For the third time José ordered Francisco to shoot at the deer and to kill it. So Francisco took aim and fired at the deer. The deer fell and made so much dust they could hardly see. José and Francisco waited for the dust to settle. When the dust settled, the *soutela* stood on the same spot watching the men. Francisco and José were dumfounded. As they stood there amazed, the deer finally ran away.

Francisco realized later that the *soutela* was from the *yo ania,* and that it wanted to offer them some powers. Unknowingly, they had refused.

8. *Totoitakusepo, Where the Rooster Crows ...*

Sea Ania: Flower World

Located in the east, in a place "beneath the dawn," the *sea ania*, flower world, is described as a perfected mirror image of all the beauty of the natural world of the Sonoran desert. It is filled with flowers, water, and natural abundance of all kinds. And it is home to the prototypical insects, birds, and animals of the Sonoran desert as well. Chief among these is the deer known to Yaquis as *malichi* or *saila maso.* There may be many deer in the *sea ania*, but only one is named in the stories and in the deer songs. During a *pahko*, the deer dancer takes on the spirit of that deer, giving him physical form even as the deer singers describe him with words and bring his voice from the *sea ania* through the deer songs.

Maso refers to a mature deer, and *malit* to a fawn. *Malichi*, *malit*/fawn + -*chi*, an affectionate, is thus "little fawn," a name which focuses on the age of the deer. *Malichi* may also be called *ilimaso*, *ili*/little + *maso*, deer. The two epithets may also refer to the physical size of the deer. Don Jesús was very explicit that *malichi* was a *tua maso*, a real deer, the Yaqui term for the small Coues whitetail deer (*Adocoileus virginianus couesi*), as opposed to a *sevis maso*, the burro deer (*Odocoileus hemionus eremicus*), which is the large variety of mule deer common west of Hermosillo in the Seri Indian country. Felipe describes the *soutela* as "like the little whitetail deer, but smaller with straight antlers like an antelope."

Saila maso focuses on a kin relation. *Saila* is the Yaqui kinship term for younger brother. *Saila maso*, little brother deer, as a term emphasizes the kin relation Yaquis believe exists between themselves and the deer. It may have added the force of traditional kin obligations to the hunt for deer. *Malichi* is referred to by several other names and epithets. Sometimes he is characterized with regard to his antlers, as *vaetatakalim awakame*, the one with the three pointed antlers. A more common epithet for him in the deer songs, as we have seen, is *sewa yoleme*, flower person.

Deer songs were first used to placate *malichi* and to ask his permission for hunting and killing him. To accomplish this, the songs describe and celebrate the *sea ania* and the living things in it. In older times, it is said that Yaqui stalked the deer by wearing masks and a deer skin disguise. The hunters held a stick in one hand and bow in the other to simulate the forelegs of the deer as they imitated his movements. The hunters were able to come quite close to the deer and to overhear their speech. In this way the hunters learned the secrets of the deer and their language; and that deer language came to be translated into the deer songs of the hunters. During the hunt the hunter should not let his mind wander but should concentrate. He would be successful, though, only if he didn't "think," thereby leaving his mind open to communication with the deer. One Yaqui told anthropologist Ralph Beals of an encounter between a hunter and *malichi*, in which the deer challenged the hunter saying, "I'm going to kill you." The hunter's riddle-like reply—"Until my fingers are the same length, you can't kill me"—saved him, for *malichi* cannot respond. By winning this verbal contest in the language of the deer the hunter was given the power to find and kill deer by *malichi*. Those who survived encounters of this sort in the wilderness world "might be classed as shamans, and their aid in the hunt sought. They did not marry, frequently slept alone in the woods, and are said modernly to have been sent a deer 'wife' by the chief of the deer."[14]

There is a prototypical deer hunter in the *sea ania* as well. He is known as *Yevuku Yoeme*. Many consider him the first deer hunter. As we have seen, *yoeme* may be translated as a Yaqui person, as distinguished from a *yori*, a non-Yaqui. A *yoeme, person, may also be distinguished from a yoawa*, an animal or *yoeria*, an insect. An adequate translation for *yevuku* eludes us. The particle *-ku* may be translated "in the wild." And a *vuki* in contemporary Yaqui usage may be either a slave or one who keeps animals. The field notes of the dedicated student of Yaqui life Murial Thayer Painter indicate that Yaquis she worked with translated *yevuku yoeme* as "trainer or tamer person." Amos Taub, translator of Yaqui deer songs in the 1950s, chose "Big Animal Tamer" as a translation for *yevuku yoeme*.[15] One Yaqui man we talked with suggested that *yevuku yoeme* was anyone who lived entirely in the wilderness world. "You can still be a *yevuku yoeme*, if you are willing to go out and live that way," he told us.

There is a story about *Yevuku Yoeme* which is set in the wilderness world. The version we will give in part here was told to Ambrosio Castro in the early 1940s by Juan Maria Santime'a, "a very old man, leader of the most conservative faction in the pueblo of Potam."

This is the story of the first Yaqui deer hunter. In Yaqui, he is called Yevuku Yoeme. *Because he was very young, this man lived alone with his mother. They lived in a place called* Poobetame'aka'apo.

Well, this Yevuku Yoeme *was a very good hunter. He had great power over the deer. He dominated them so that they became as tame as burros. The deer were very wild and dangerous like broncos, but* Yevuku Yoeme *could catch up with them and kill them. Sometimes he would tie two deer together and drive them like a team of horses.*

Throughout all his youth, Yevuku Yoeme *didn't know a single man or another woman except his mother. All he knew were the animals and the desert. He did nothing but bring his mother water from the large lagoon which was near their house. Then he would go off into the desert.*

Well, it happened that one day after running after a big deer to kill it, Yevuku Yoeme *lay down under a tree and fell into a deep sleep. He was lost in his dreams when a rabbit and a female deer approached. They came very close to him. The rabbit said to the deer, "Look, it's* very important that you, and all the deer, know the odor of this creature. If you don't learn to know his smell, he will finish all of you. If you can recognize his odor, then you will notice it from a long distance, and you will be able to flee and save yourself. So come over here close." The rabbit lifted a corner of the skin which served as Yevuku Yoeme's clothing. Then the rabbit wiped sweat from Yevuku Yoeme's body with a piece of the skin and held it to the deer's nose. "Smell it," he said.

"Ah, yes," said the deer. She was very appreciative for what the rabbit had done. And from that time on, the deer run and try to hide when they smell anything associated with man.[16]

In the deer songs *Yevuku Yoeme* appears in the singular role of hunter. In that role Don Jesús explains that he stands for all of us. "He is a hunter," Don Jesús told us, "*Yevuku Yoeme* is all of us. We are all *Yevuku Yoeme*, and he is all of us." We have chosen to leave *Yevuku Yoeme*'s name untranslated throughout.

So far as we know, Yaqui tradition does not associate this *Yevuku Yoeme* with the creation of deer songs or with the creation of the deer dance. That distinction falls to one named *Wok Vake'o*. "Only a brave man," Yaquis told Ralph Beals in the 1920s, "will spend a night in the woods, and he must have special powers." As cowboys do so often, Beals notes that in the Río Yaqui area they "have become associated with the magical quality of the forest."[17] Knowing that makes it less surprising that the first deer singer was a cowboy without a horse. *Wok Vake'o* means walking cowboy.

The first man to sing deer songs among the Yaqui people lived in a section of Ko'oko'im *called* Bwawisim Kayehon, Barn Owls' Alley. *He was called* Wok Vake'o, *but the man didn't have any cattle. He had many goats and sheep though, and because he herded them on foot, they called him* Wok Vake'o.

Wok Vake'o *noticed that all of the hunters had beautiful clothes made of skins of many colors from different animals. He too wanted to be a hunter, so he left his animals with a relative of his by the name of* Hunama Wo'i, Big Coyote. Wok Vake'o *prepared his bow and many arrows. Then he began to enter the wilderness to search for deer and other animals. He wanted to have many kinds of hides to make clothes for himself.*

One of the times he went into the wilderness he crossed the river and headed for a low range of hills called Roma Kawi, Rome Mountain, *which is on the edge of the Río Yaqui and very close to the village that is now called Corral.* Wok Vake'o *climbed to the top of* Roma Kawi *very early in the morning. From there he scanned the little bench that lay between him and the river. He was sitting on a dry tree trunk, when he saw two large deer with long antlers. A little way from them was a small deer. The two big deer were standing, facing one another, their heads tilted down and their antlers entwined. They were moving their heads and scratching each other's antlers. The young deer lowered his head toward the ground, then he lifted it, and he looked from side to side. He began to leap high in the air, and he ran* to where the two big deer were. The two pulled their antlers apart. Then they stood looking at the young one for a long time. Finally they began to rasp their antlers again. The little deer began to circle them and to jump around happily.

Wok Vake'o *watched all of this. He believed that the big deer were singing and that their antlers served them as musical instruments to accompany the song. He thought that the little deer was dancing to the music. In this way, the three deer sang and danced for a long time. Then they disappeared. Wok Vake'o had had no desire to kill any of them.*

Wok Vake'o *walked away from Roma Kawi with many thoughts in his head. He had a desire to sing to the deer. So he did. He began to be inspired. Early the following morning he went to the foot of a hill called* Otam Kawi, Bones Mountain. *There he found a fawn. The mother deer ran off and left her little baby deer. Wok Vake'o picked up the baby. It had been born among the flowers that were blooming there. Wok Vake'o composed a song and dedicated it to the little fawn he found among the flowers. The words of the song went something like this:*

> Little one, born in the night,
> Caressed by the fresh wind.
> Little one, born in the night,
> Caressed by the fresh wind.
> Where are you going then,
> Flower fawn among the flowers?
> Dressed in flowers, I am going.

Wok Vake'o *took the little fawn with him. When he arrived in* Ko'oko'im, *he talked with his friends, both old and young. He told them that he wanted to make songs to the deer and that he wanted someone to dance to the music. Then he prepared two sticks, one large and one small. Both sticks were slender, and the larger one had notches on its surface. Then* Wok Vake'o *prepared a young Yaqui boy for the dancing. He gave the boy instructions, teaching him to make motions like those he saw the young deer make at Roma Kawi.*

In this way they danced and sang, perfecting the songs and the dance more and more until today.[18]

Refugio Savala tells much the same story. "The dance," he writes, "started when a man who lived in the country—one who probably made his living by hunting and was much in the wilds—saw the deer, mostly young ones, having a fiesta of their own.... The man studied their dancing and was able to interpret it and do it himself."[19]

"Look out to the east early in the morning," Don Lupe told us, "and the ground will be covered with flowers. That's *seyewailo*." We had asked him for help in under-ing a word that appears in almost all the deer songs we have recorded. Usually the word appears in the opening line of the concluding stanza of a deer song as an adjective that describes a quality of the *huya*: as in the line, *ayaman ne seyewailo huyatanaisukuni*, over there, I, in the center of the *seyewailo* wilderness. Especially in its shortened form *sewailo, seyewailo* may be used in other places in deer songs as well. *Seye* is a word for flower. The translation for *wailo* is less clear. The /l/ adds a sugges-tion of affection and the diminutive, as it often does elsewhere in Yaqui. *Wai* is a word for younger brother or sister. Assuming the *wai* was somehow related to the meaning of the word, Felipe's grandfather used to say of *seyewailo*: "there is a big one and a little one." A little flower place for little brother deer? Over the years, other Ya-quis have consistently suggested that *-wailo* could be translated "covered with," so that *seyewailo* becomes for them a place name indicating "the earth covered with flowers." In the song translations that follow we have settled for "flower-covered" as a translation for *seyewailo*, but not without some regret at our inability to do better.[20] What Don Lupe's comment adds to this translation is a very specific denotation of time and direction. *Seyewailo* names, we think, that convergence of time, place, direc-tion, and quality of being that is for Yaquis the essence of what they call the *sea ania*, the flower world, the convergence at which *Wok Vake'o* found the little fawn and the inspiration for the first deer song.

From this first deer song of *Wok Vake'o*, all Yaqui deer songs describe the flower world. After *seyewailo*, the most common words in the deer song lexicon are the Yaqui words for flower: *sewa, sea, seya,* and *seye*. In the songs they may refer to specific flowers, such as *choi seya*, palo verde flower, or *masa'asai sewa*, queen's wreath flower. Or, more commonly, they may be used adjectivally. Thus the songs speak of *sea tevatchiapo*, flower patio; *sewa heeka*, flower wind; *sewa huli*, flower badger; *sea hilukiam*, flower raspers; and so on. The sense of the use of *sea, sewa, seya,* and *seye* in this way is sometimes stated by Yaquis as "all that is good and beautiful." But we should note that the adjectival sense of those words is more "all that is good and beautiful from the flower world," for there are more general Yaqui words for good and beautiful: *tutuli, tu'ulisi,* and *uhyoi*.

On some occasions songs use *sewa* in a metaphoric way, as in Don Lupe's song *Sewa*

Yotume, Growing Flower, where the "growing flower" is a figure for the rising sun. Almost every piece of regalia and every instrument used in deer dancing and deer singing may be called a *sewa* or *sea* as well.

When the singers settle in with their raspers and other instruments to begin the *pahko,* they may sing "*vesate sewau hotekate,* already let's sit down to the flower." And the metaphoric use of the words for flower reaches far beyond deer songs and deer singing to permeate virtually the whole of Yaqui ceremonialism and everyday Yaqui life.[21]

9. Luis Maaso's gourd rattles ...

✠ We Yaquis believe that there is this special power we call *seatakaa*, or flower body. This power is received during the birth of a child. Some children have it and some don't. Usually the power will increase with age if you have it. Many Yaquis have *seatakaa* but do not know that they have it. The elders tell stories about *seatakaa*, and some tell about dreams that involve the *seatakaa*. This is the way that those people who have it and do not know of it will become aware of what their power is. I think *seatakaa* is a protective energy of the *hiapsi*, the heart or spirit of a person.

As a person grows up and gets older, he or she might become mean or evil. This will make their *seatakaa* diminish greatly. If a person continues to be evil and mean and so on, he will eventually lose that special power and never gain it back. People with the *seatakaa* must always be with a good heart and never think about harming another person.

I will give some examples of *seatakaa* as I know of it. When you dream of a big, mean mountain lion chasing you, and all of a sudden you are on a tall cottonwood tree looking down at the mountain lion running past you, that might mean you have *seatakaa*. The ability to escape to safety in the nick of time shows that a person has *seatakaa*. Things go right for people who have *seatakaa* without them trying. Also if you dream of flying, that might show that you have it. Or people might see you at a certain place and tell you about it, but you tell them that you were at home or work and never at that place they describe. This also shows that the *seatakaa* is at work. The image of the physical body that contains the *seatakaa* travels around while the main physical body remains at home or work or wherever. For many Yaquis it is very hard to understand the workings of *seatakaa*. Some people who know that they possess the *seatakaa* are afraid of it.

Possessing *seatakaa* can be good or bad. *Seatakaa* can protect a person from *erim*, evil thoughts, and other dangers, if the person has taken care of his *seatakaa*. The bad thing about *seatakaa* is that it is playful and can get you into trouble for no reason. A husband might see the *seatakaa* of his wife some place she is not supposed to be, or maybe she might see his some place it is not supposed to be, while in fact the wife or the husband is really out working somewhere. So the *seatakaa* can play these harmless tricks on people.[22]

In Yaqui usage, within and without deer songs, *sewa, sea, seya*, and *seye* evoke images not only of the *sea ania* but also of *teweka*, heaven. One of the most cherished stories of the Baptized Ones tells of the flowers which poured from the side of Christ when it was lanced on the cross on Calvary. Hence flowers have become, too, a symbol of divine grace. Working in the Río Yaqui area in the 1940s, Ruth Giddings asked one Yaqui if the use of flowers for Christian purposes was the same as the use of flowers in the deer songs. The man replied that "the flowers with which the Virgin is worshipped are sacred flowers and quite different from the wild flowers with which the *maaso* is associated."[23] The contemporary Yaquis we have talked with both in Sonora and in Arizona do *not* maintain or recognize this distinction. Rather the single concept *sewa* provides a place for the notions of the good and the beautiful from both sides of the Talking Tree to come together, a place where the *sea ania* and *teweka* can meet.

Thus, in some deer songs the classic description of place in the flower world, which almost always begins the concluding stanza, gives way to a direct Christian displacement. *Ayamansu seyewailo naiyoli yo aniwapo*, over there in the flower-covered cherished enchanted world, may become *ayamansu seyewailo santo teweka*, over there in the flower-covered holy heaven. In other songs, the concluding stanza spirals through even more specific Christian images:

Ayaman seyewailo machilo aniwaita	Over there in the flower-covered dawn world,
kalasoiti hikauwi chatuko	when it lifts up brightly,
im ne vae kusimne habwekapone	here, where the three crosses
tolobololoti...	are standing...

In still other songs, a whole layer of Christian meaning is added. One deer song asks:

Sewailo bwiapo weyekai	As you are going on the flower-covered earth,
Sewa yoemta ka tata'a	Do you not know the flower person?

As we have seen, *sewa yoemta*, flower person, is a common epithet for *saila maaso*, little brother deer. Here, in a song that is sung on Holy Saturday evening, it is clear that the singers intend to allude to both *saila maaso* and the risen Christ. The only songs in which any of these Christian references occur are songs which are used on Holy Saturday morning or during the processions which open and close the *pahkom* during which any of these Christian references occur are songs which are used on Holy Saturday morning or during the processions which open and close the *pahkom* during in emphasis on the symbol within which the Christian and the original Yaqui worlds can come together.

Looria Bwikam: Gloria Songs

When we asked Don Jesús how the *sea ania* and *teweka* were related, his response was to sing the three deer songs which he used during *Looria Tenniwa*, Running the Gloria, the climactic event of the Yaqui lenten drama. He called these songs *looria bwikam*, gloria songs. He sang them for us May 14, 1981.

On Holy Saturday morning, near the conclusion of Holy Week and six weeks of intense lenten observances by the Yaqui community, the deer singers and the deer dancer, along with the *pahkolam* and their musicians, align themselves with those Baptized Ones who are defending the Yaqui church against the final ritual attempts of the "evil ones" to storm the village church and capture an image of Jesus Christ. In Yaqui, the evil ones are known as *Fariseos*, Pharisees. The role of the *Fariseos* is a dramatic one taken on by some Baptized Ones out of a deep sense of religious obligation. Some of the *Fariseos* are known as *chapayekam*, literally "those with long noses." They wear masks some of which evoke images of the sun and moon and stars. Another style of *chapayekam* masks caricatures various non-Yaqui types: pink-skinned white men with vacant stares, Mexican soldiers, hobos, cowboys, war-bonneted Plains Indians, even such contemporary movie characters as Darth Vader.

All during Holy Saturday morning, while the *maehto* and other devout Yaquis work through the liturgy for the day, the *Fariseos* march menacingly in front of the church. And when at last the *maehto* chants the Gloria, the culminating prayer of the service, the church bell begins to ring as the *Fariseos* make a wild running charge upon the church. They are repelled by the Baptized Ones who protect the church. They throw "flowers," that is, shouts, confetti, cottonwood leaves, and flower petals as ammunition at the charging *Fariseos*. The charge is made three times, until finally the *Fariseos* are routed, their masks burned, and they are brought back into the church.

Positioned in front of the church, to one side but on the front line of defense, the deer singers are in the thick of the ritual battle. Their contribution is to sing a different deer song over and over throughout each of the three charges. Don Jesús sang these three. *San Malekos*, Saint Mark, is also mentioned in a *looria* song sung by Don Lupe. Felipe understands *San Malekos* as "a messenger, one who is sent to check things out and then report back."

Ala aman tewekapo
  tua yosi machi
    in achali
Ala aman tewekapo
  tua yosi machi
    in achali

Ala aman tewekapo
  tua yosi machi
    in achali
Ala aman tewekapo
  tua yosi machi
    in achali

Ala aman tewekapo
  tua yosi machi
    in achali
Ala aman tewekapo
  tua yosi machi
    in achali

Ayamansu seyewailo santo teweka
  loriau vichakai
    tua yosi machi
      in achali
Ala aman tewekapo
  tua yosi machi
    in achali

But there in heaven
  truly it is as if enchanted,
    my father.
But there is heaven
  truly it is as if enchanted,
    my father.

But there in heaven
  truly it is as if enchanted,
    my father.
But there in heaven
  truly it is as if enchanted,
    my father.

But there in heaven
  truly it is as if enchanted,
    my father.
But there in heaven
  truly it is as if enchanted,
    my father.

Over there in the flower-covered holy heaven,
  to see the glory,
    truly it is as if enchanted,
      my father.
But there in heaven
  truly it is as if enchanted,
    my father.

Vanseka weyema
  Señor Santo San Malekos
Vanseka
  yo telika
    sea telika
Weye
  Señor Santo San Malekos

Vanseka weyema
  Señor Santo San Malekos
Vanseka
  yo telika
    sea telika
Weye
  Señor Santo San Malekos

Vanseka weyema
  Señor Santo San Malekos
Vanseka
  yo telika
    sea telika
Weye
  Señor Santo San Malekos

Ime woh mamni ama woi
  apostolosimmake
    Ime woh mamni ama woi
    serafinimmake
      Aman santo teweka
      Ioriau vichaka
Weye
  Señor Santo San Malekos

Go ahead and walk,
  Holy Lord Saint Mark.
Go ahead,
  with enchantment as they say,
  with flower as they say,
Walk,
  Holy Lord Saint Mark.

Go ahead and walk,
  Holy Lord Saint Mark.
Go ahead,
  with enchantment as they say,
  with flower as they say,
Walk,
  Holy Lord Saint Mark.

Go ahead and walk,
  Holy Lord Saint Mark.
Go ahead,
  with enchantment as they say,
  with flower as they say,
Walk,
  Holy Lord Saint Mark.

With these twelve
  apostles,
    With these twelve
    seraphims,
      There in holy heaven,
      toward the glory,
Walk,
  Holy Lord Saint Mark.

Huya aniwai
    sea lihlihti heka
        huya aniwai
Huya aniwai
    sea lihlihti heka
        huya aniwai

Huya aniwai
    sea lihlihti heka
        huya aniwai
Huya aniwai
    sea lihlihti heka
        huya aniwai

Huya aniwai
    sea lihlihti heka
        huya aniwai
Huya aniwai
    sea lihlihti heka
        huya aniwai

Ayaman ne
    seyewailo yo yevuku yolemta
        sea tevachiaposu
            sea rihrihti heka
                huya aniwai
Huya aniwai
    sea lihlihti heka
        huya aniwai

Wilderness world,
    flower freely, is blowing,
        wilderness world.
Wilderness world,
    flower freely, is blowing,
        wilderness world.

Wilderness world,
    flower freely, is blowing,
        wilderness world.
Wilderness world,
    flower freely, is blowing,
        wilderness world.

Wilderness world,
    flower freely, is blowing,
        wilderness world.
Wilderness world,
    flower freely, is blowing,
        wilderness world.

Over there, I, in Yevuku Yoleme's
    flower-covered, enchanted,
        flower patio,
            flower freely, is blowing,
                wilderness world.
Wilderness world,
    flower freely, is blowing,
        wilderness world.

At the Enchanted Fall of the Yaqui Deer Dancer: A Mural

Danny Leon spent almost a year working out his own visual interpretation of the Flower World in a mural which he completed in August of 1980. The mural is painted on a wall along the south edge of the community plaza in the village of Old Pascua in Tucson. Born December 19, 1953, Danny has lived in Old Pascua all his life, save a six-month period when he went with his father to the Yaqui village of Guadalupe near Phoenix to look for work. Danny took art courses as he worked his way through the Tucson Public School system, but he feels he really began to develop as an artist when Arturo Montoyo took him on as an apprentice when Danny was eleven years old. It was Arturo Montoya who took Danny to Sabino Canyon, just north of Tucson. There among the boulders and water tumbling down the Santa Catalina Mountains he was inspired and resolved to paint the mural.

When we began to talk about how we might describe and discuss the Flower World, we decided that we should go talk with Danny and ask his help. When we asked Danny to talk with us about his understandings of the elements in his mural, he said he'd be happy to talk with us but that he wanted to talk with his teacher Arturo Montoya first. What follows here is a statement that the two of them prepared for us.

AT THE ENCHANTED FALL OF THE YAQUI DEER DANCER ©

The Yaqui people have always believed in other worlds. One of these worlds is called the sea ania, the Flower World. The mural depicts that world. The waterfall is in this enchanted world. The waterfall gives life to the flower world, its forest, and its creatures. I used glitter to try to show how the light glitters and shines through the water. The flowers represent the flower world. Flowers are very sacred to Yaqui people because we believe that when Christ was crucified his blood turned to flowers when it touched the ground. The regalia of all the Yaqui ceremonial society groups is called sewa. That means flower. On Easter Saturday morning the attacking forces of evil (which are represented by the Chapayeka Society) are defeated by the forces of good (the Matachinis, the Angelitos, the Deer Dancer, the Pahkolam, and other church groups) by the use of flowers as weapons. The flowers are thrown at them.

The flower world is the legendary home of our little brother who is called saila maso. We Yaquis believe that we are brothers to nature and especially to the deer. The fawn in the mural represents saila maso and his rebirth into human form to give us the deer dancer. The little animals and birds that surround the saila maso in the mural are in the songs that are sung by the deer singers. The pahkola mask, belt, and rattles symbolize that the enchanted

world is believed to select certain people to be pahkolam *and that it supplies them spiritually with the desire and the skills that they will need to carry out their work. The selection is made mainly through dreams.*

The Mayo Indians also have a deer dancer. I put the Yaqui flag into the mural to identify the scene as Yaqui and not Mayo. The eagle grasping the flag symbolizes the Yaqui spirit of courage and tenacity, a unified struggle for survival. The eagle, an endangered species, survives as the Yaqui people survive. That is why I chose the eagle.

Sometimes I used to participate in the ceremonies as a matachini to please my grandfather who was the governor of the matachinis. When my aged grandfather became crippled and confined to the wheelchair, he could no longer attend ceremonies. It was then that I drifted away from participating. It was not the same without him. If I could dedicate my murals to someone, I would dedicate them to my grandfather, Don Felipe Garcia, and to all the Yaqui elders who have passed away, and also to those elders who are still living. I feel that they are true Yaquis. They fought hard for their beloved homeland and for the ceremonial life they have preserved for us. They were very strong people. These murals are my contribution to the support and preservation of the Yaqui culture they have given to me.

Yo Ania: Enchanted World

Don Jesús was never much interested in talking with us about the *sea ania*. We suppose the songs were his way of doing that. Likewise he showed little interest in talking about the stories of *Yevuku Yoeme* and *Wok Vake'o*. Rather, when we raised the question of the source of deer songs, he spoke of another space within the *huya ania* which he called the *yo ania*, enchanted world.

Yo is another Yaqui word that is not easily translated. The verb *yo'otu* means "to grow old" and the verb *yo'ore* "to respect or venerate." In Yaqui communities an old and respected elder is called *yo'owe*, and, in these contexts, *yo* may itself be translated as "old." But especially when it is used with *ania*, *yo* suggests not just "old" but the oldest old, the ancient, the primordial.[24] The *yo ania* is an ancient world, a mythic place outside historic time and space, yet it can be present in the most immediate way. *Yo* refers to the essential and originative quality of being in that time and place. Both Felipe's grandfather, Rosario Castillo, and Don Lupe translated *yo* as "*encanto*"; we translate *yo* as "enchanted."

The relations between the *sea ania* and the *yo ania* as specialized areas within the *huya ania* are not clear to us. From most accounts they seem to be regarded as distinct and complimentary realms. Refugio Savala suggests that before the time of the talking tree "it (was) true that the *yo ania* was all the Indians could live by." Since the time of the talking tree, Savala writes that the *sea ania* has evolved as a source for good powers and the *yo ania* as a source for bad, even demonic, ones.[25] In the way that the *sea ania* has become aligned with Christ and Heaven, the *yo ania* has become associated with the Devil and Hell to some Yaquis. Others strongly resist this suggestion that the *yo ania* is somehow an "evil" realm. Don Jesús was one of these. In fact, in one of his deer songs, he describes *saila maso* himself as coming out from an "enchanted house" which he explained was in the *yo ania*. Spicer understood the *yo ania* as the spiritual dimension of the whole of the *huya ania* and as the "domain of respected powers."

In any case the experience of the *yo ania* seems always to be a solitary one, and what we know of it is from the stories individuals tell when they return, stories that may be retold until they become legendary themselves. Individuals tell of entering the *yo ania* through dream or vision or simply a visit at the right time and place in the wilderness world. Once entered, the *yo ania* may provide the power to perform the whole range of Yaqui occupations. Accounts of encounters with the enchanted world tell of entrances into caves and meetings with enormous snakes and monsters.

Don Jesús called these beings *chupiarim*, literally "completed ones," and he called the places where they live *yo hoaram*, enchanted homes. The enchanted homes, he suggested, were the source of Yaqui deer songs. The first real Yaquis, the *Surem*, got the songs there.

The first real Yaquis,
They didn't live like us, but they still held pahkom.
Those real Yaquis—the tampaleos, the deer singers—
They didn't hold pahkom for God.
Somewhere they entered enchanted homes.
They were given it there in the wilderness world.
The deer singers, the tampaleo, even the pahkolam
    were given it and got it there.
That is why they are able to dance and to play instruments well.
They didn't do it for God like we do now.
They started it long ago before the time of the Talking Stick.
Long ago.
All is there in the enchanted home.
Like the raspers, they are there.
All of these things are there: the tampaleo's flute and drum, the
    water drum, the drumstick, the harp, the violin, the pahkolam's
    regalia,
All is there.
Who ever wanted it would go to get it, to borrow it there.
Those who went were given years—three, four,
Up to any amount, or even just one year.
When their years were up, they say they seemed to die.
They didn't really die.
Then they went there to live and they sit in there.
Like that it was given to the ones who asked for it.
They live there in a little hole like the ants.
Many Yaquis have entered there.
It is much the same as here they say,
The ones who visit over there.
But nobody can see them, the ones who live there.
All of them there are like the people here,
But they are enchanted.
There it is just like in a dream.

Don Jesús talked of enchanted homes in several specific places in the wilderness world of the Río Yaqui area: in caves on the mountains called *Sikil Kawi* and *Yasikwe,* and at a rock formation called *Pilem* near Ortiz where a numinous warrior José Kukut presides.[26]

Don Jesús' descriptions of cave visitations are strikingly similar to those reported by Ralph Beals after talking with Yaquis in the 1920s. It seems likely that many of the accounts of experiences in the *yo ania* become a part of Yaqui tradition. Soldiers, marksmen, hunters, cowboys, and others may attribute their abilities to such encounters in the *yo ania*. But it is the *pahko* performers—the deer dancer, the deer singers, the *pahkolam*, and their musicians—who bring the experience of the *yo ania* into public view in the villages most dramatically with their music and their dance.[27]

Tu'ik Memoriakame Vea A Hahamne: One with a Good Memory Will Catch On

The wilderness worlds of flowers and enchantment are the wellsprings of Yaqui deer songs, but the continuance of Yaqui deer songs today depends as much on an alert ear and a good memory, long practice sessions with peers, and very likely an apprenticeship with an older deer singer. While he regarded the *yo ania* as *the* source for deer songs, Don Jesús was emphatic that the songs continue today in other ways.

There are still many things in the enchanted world,
But now, we Yaquis, we do not teach ourselves that way.
Now we teach ourselves.
The violin players, the harp players, the tampaleos,
*   the deer singers,*
All have taught themselves.
We don't enter the mountains, into the enchanted
*   homes to learn.*
Now we learn in God's truth.
One with a good memory will catch on.
It will arrive in his head in that way.
And one will get the knowledge.
We have received it from our elders in that way,
*   through memory,*
And now we work with what we have received from them.

Don Jesús told how he learned deer singing through an apprenticeship with an established singer, working his way through all the arts of the *pahko* until finally he "sat down to these raspers and stayed with them."

I first started to sing at Vicam on San Juan fiesta,
In 1918 or 1919,
When I was about the age of my son here,
I started to sing.
But before that I started with the water drum,
The water playing,
When I went to work with the elders.
After I learned the water drum with them,
Then I danced deer and after that I started dancing
    pahkola.
They had me do it all.
Then when the elders died,
I sat down to these raspers and stayed with them.
After the elder deer singers died.
And I have stayed with it until now.
I can still dance though,
But the body is heavy.
One who is called Antonio Potakovanao,
He was an elder who lived in Potam
And he sang well.
I danced to him and he taught me to sing.
He was old, eighty, maybe even ninety years old
    when he taught me.

All the songs he knew, Don Jesús maintained, he learned from this teacher and from other deer singers he sat down with over the last sixty years. Don Jesús said that he did not compose any deer songs himself, nor did he know anyone who did.[28] The songs were all passed down from the elders.

Reporting on a visit to Arizona in the 1920s, the ethnomusicologist Frances Densmore tells of walking through the Yaqui village of Guadalupe early one morning and hearing "concerted music" of the deer and the *pahkolam* pouring from one of the houses. "It's only the young men playing," her Yaqui host assured her, "they often play like that all day."[29] Don Jesús remembered many such sessions from the days of his youth, when he and his peers gathered to sing the songs they learned from older singers. The sessions became so formalized among them as to be called *ehkwelam*, schools.

There in Potam we had a school.
We would get together on Saturday evening,

And go to school and practice.
We would lay out the raspers and dance deer.
Most of the quick ones there would catch on,
And in this way we taught each other.
As I have said, I first heard it from the elders,
I learned it from them.
When I traveled with them from pahko to pahko.
So when we got together like this on Saturdays,
I was often their teacher.

One contemporary deer singer in southern Arizona tells of standing in the grave-yard and "hearing" the songs of the elders which have been lost there. But most contemporary Yaqui deer singers, in Arizona and in Sonora, continue to learn in much the same way as did Don Jesús. Younger singers sit down with older ones during *pahkom*, and it is not at all uncommon to see groups of young men making *pahko* music to pass the time in both Sonora and southern Arizona. Those who have been practicing the music in this way are given an opportunity to perform in public during the final hour of most *pahkom*. Just after the *maehto* has said his final prayers in the hour before the dawn near the end of *pahko,* the deer singers offer their place and their instruments to those who would like to try singing or dancing. During this "amateur hour," as it is called in southern Arizona, young singers are given the opportunity to practice the songs they have been learning and to try out new ones.

The technologies of our time make other possibilities available as well. The grave-yards of academic publications and archives yield songs to some singers. Federally funded "culture" programs provide occasional opportunities for younger Yaquis to study deer singing and other traditional Yaqui skills with older Yaqui teachers. And perhaps most importantly there are sound recordings. It is a rare Yaqui singer in Sonora or Arizona who does not have access to a cassette tape recorder on which to listen to commercial or home-made recordings of deer songs and other *pahko* music. More than once we have passed the heat of the afternoon under a house *ramá* dubbing cassette tapes and trading.

✠ As an eighth grade student, I was interested in deer songs. I remember that I made my first rasper and rubber at that time. I made them from a chinaberry tree branch. The notches were about a quarter of an inch apart. I used to walk alone to the desert and sing some songs that I had heard during recent *pahkom*. I never knew all the words but, if I didn't know the words, I would just hum the melody. I was thirteen years old then.

Actually my first real interest in deer dancing and singing came about when I was taken to *pahkom* as a young boy, starting when I was about five. My grandfather was a *pahkola* dancer, and I lived with my grandparents. So when my grandfather was asked to dance at a village *pahko* or a household *pahko*, my grandparents would take me along. They thought I was too young to stay home alone. I was always happy to be able to go with them. After the *pahkom* my brother and my cousin usually came over to my house and we danced deer and tried to sing songs to entertain each other. I don't remember much about this playing, but I remember it was always after a *pahko* and that we always danced under a big tamarisk tree by the house.

Later when I became a high school student I had less interest. Not that I had less interest for Yaqui ways, but I was very interested in my school work. I worked hard at my school work so that I could get on the honor roll. So as a high school student I sang less. Later I even dropped out of the *fariseo* society in which I had been a sergeant. I had been initiated into the *fariseo* society when I was nine years old. My grandparents worried a lot about me because I didn't

fulfill my obligations to Jesus through the society. During my high school years I went to the Easter ceremonies to watch as a spectator, never as a participant. I felt bad for a while and finally I forgot completely about it, and I have never participated as a *fariseo* again.

After my grandmother died in 1975, I began to take my grandfather to the *pahkom* because he enjoyed them so much. It was about that time I became interested in deer songs again. We had a record album produced by Canyon Records in Phoenix. I began to pay more attention to the rhythm of the songs as I listened to it. My brother also enjoyed the music. Another Canyon record of Yaqui music came out in 1976, and this time we could hear the words clearly on the album. My brother asked me if I wanted to try to sing the songs on the record. I said I would like to try. We borrowed my Uncle Juan's raspers and bought a big gourd from my Uncle Pete and sawed it in half to make a water drum. The first song we started out with was from the Canyon record. The song is *Tosali Wikit*, White Bird. It sounded okay, but at first we were shy and would start laughing at each other. It continued like this for maybe half a dozen sessions and finally we got used to singing. To make things easier my brother requested that I write out the words to the songs on the Canyon record. That way he said he would learn the songs better. I wrote all the three songs on the second Canyon record album and tried to write out the words to the first one but many of them were unclear. In this way we started to sing together. My brother sang much better than I because he had a better voice.

14. *Practicing at Yoem Pueblo ...*

15. *Joaquin "Bumper" Garcia dances the words ...*

About the same time I started working for the Marana Schools in their bilingual education program, so I wrote to Dr. Spicer for some Yaqui materials. To my amazement, he sent a Yaqui dictionary by Jean Johnson and some deer songs from a book by Carleton Wilder. My brother and I were so happy that we immediately tried to sing all of those songs, except we didn't know what rhythm the songs had so we sang them our own way. So that added more songs to our practice sessions. At the end of that school year the Marana bilingual program decided to hold a program in connection with the Mexican Cinco de Mayo celebration. The director asked us if we would sing. So that was our first performance for the public. Later in the fall we performed in Gallup and again in Window Rock.

My godfather Anselmo Valencia, who is chief of the village of New Pascua, became aware of our singing and right away he said that we must participate in Yaqui *pahkom* if we wanted to sing at other places. So during the next Easter week I sat down with my godfather Anselmo and sang. My brother couldn't sing because he couldn't get a leave from his job. Because of his job and because he got married, my brother was not available to sing from that time until now. I hope that he will begin to sing at *pahkom* sometime in the future.

So this is the way I began to sing. Now I participate in village *pahkom* and household *pahkom* in the Yaqui villages of Arizona and also during the tribal fairs and ceremonials of other tribal groups. At this time I am still learning new songs here in Arizona and down in the Yaqui country in Sonora. I have now even learned some Mayo deer songs.

Here in our little village in Marana which we call Yoem Pueblo I have started teaching the young boys to sing and dance the deer. The young boys are interested somewhat, but I can never tell how much. They were very curious and interested when Larry and I worked with Don Jesús' songs. My godson is very interested and always wants to learn more deer songs, and our young deer dancer is more interested in singing than dancing. He has a good memory and remembers many songs and learns a lot from them. Some of the other boys probably just come because they want something to do. But the boys must like it because they are the ones who come to me to hurry me up to get the practice sessions going. In this way we entertain ourselves and learn while doing it. I don't know how long we'll keep it up, but we've been practicing regularly for quite a while now. In this way a part of our Yaqui heritage will continue into the twenty-first century.

There remains a very strong sense of continuity which stretches back through all these sources in Yaqui communities to a beginning in the time before the talking tree. Whether they are learned from an elder singer, a school playmate, a record, an old thesis, or a videotape, when Yaqui singers give voice to deer songs they become the enchanted speech of *saila maso*, little brother deer, continuing a language as old as Yaqui habitation in this desert world. As he concluded a conversation about deer songs and deer singing with us, singer Loretto Salvatierra expressed this continuity and its responsibilities, succinctly:

In the beginning, like this,
Our grandfathers,
The ones who are grandfather Surem,
The ones that first appeared here,
They left this inheritance.
Then the Baptized People received it
And were given it.
Like this, now, it is continued in the songs.
It is known like this.
This is all the knowledge that was told to us,
But we still work poorly with it.
Perhaps we are not taking care of it like the ones
    who stood up to it in the beginning.
But for the births that are coming,
The people you are going to talk with about it,
Like this the inheritance is left.
This is cherished and respected.
This is all the truth you asked for.
Like this it stays in your hands.

MAISO YOLEME

Ala inikun maiso yoleme
  hunu kun maiso yoleme
    ini kun tua maiso yolemeee

Ala inikun maiso yoleme
  hunu kun maiso yoleme
    ini kun tua maiso yolemeee

Ala inikun maiso yoleme
  hunu kun maiso yoleme
    ini kun tua maiso yolemeee

Ayaman ne seyewailo
  fayaliata naisukuni
    weyekai
      im ne yo siali vata paku
        weyekai
Hunu kun maiso yoleme
  hunu kun tua maiso yolemeee

DEER PERSON

So now this is the deer person,
  so he is the deer person,
    so he is the real deer person.

So now this is the deer person,
  so he is the deer person,
    so he is the real deer person.

So now this is the deer person,
  so he is the deer person,
    so he is the real deer person.

Over there, I, in the center
  of the flower-covered opening,
    as I was walking,
      here in the open green water,
        as I was walking,
So he is the deer person,
  so he is the real deer person.

Felipe Molina
Yoem Pueblo
August 21, 1984

16. At the center of the kolensia …

3

SENU TUKARIA BWIKAM
ONE NIGHT OF SONGS

DEER SONGS may be sung by almost anyone—man, woman, or child—in informal settings in Yaqui communities. In this way, although they may never perform them at a *pahko*, some women become known for their ability to sing deer songs. Especially among children and young men, these informal performances often take on the mood of practice sessions. Giddings writes that "in Sonora, not only the deer-singers, but also various individuals (including members of the younger age groups) know and sing deer-songs for pleasure."[1]

But within Yaqui communities, deer songs are most often performed during a *pahko*, a ceremonial occasion when Yaquis gather to perform religious observances and to celebrate. Most Yaquis translate the word as "fiesta," but others object that a *pahko* is not the same kind of event that the Mexican term implies.[2] Therefore, we use the Yaqui word throughout. Don Jesús and other singers we talked with remembered the *pahko* was originally a part of a ritual carried out before the hunting of deer, and, for that reason, they pointed out that the deer singers have a central place in most *pahkom*. During a *pahko*, the deer singers must create, in Don Jesús' phrase, "one night of songs."

The mood of the *pahko* is festive, as Yaquis gather to eat and drink, visit and worship. The pace of performances during the *pahko* is oceanic, ebbing and cresting throughout the long night. Each time the deer dancer explodes out of the swell of the *pahkolam*'s dance into the center of the *ramá*, he carries the *pahko* to a crest, and it foams with his color, sound, and motion. Dipping delicately as if to drink; erect, curious, then bounding with the *pahkolam* in their play; or suddenly motionless and coiled with tension, alert to some new movement in the darkness—the dancer's ability to suggest the movements of a deer can be astonishing and mesmerizing. But the dancer can only move to the music of the deer singers. Their water drum is said to represent his heartbeat, their raspers his breathing, their words his voice. Through their song he becomes the real deer person.

The role the words of the deer songs play in dictating the movement of the *maaso* has not been widely recognized outside Yaqui communities. Wilder writes that "regardless of the song being sung, [the *maaso's*] dance does not vary."[3] This is true of *lutula weme bwikam*, straight-going or "regular" songs. But there are other kinds of songs, and in some of them the dancer must interpret the words being sung in his dance. *Wikit bwikam*, bird songs are an example. *Wikit bwikam* are always *yeu bwikam*, play songs. When they are sung, the *maaso* must interpret the words in his dance. The hovering of a buzzard in a deer song may in this way become a sweeping whirl by the *maaso* with his arms outspread. Anselmo Valencia, a deer singer in southern Arizona, describes the relation of the dance to the song in this way: "The best deer dancer will follow the beat of a song with his feet, the raspers with his hands and waist, and his deer head will do what the words of the song call for whether it is a bird or an insect, or an animal."[4] Deer singer Loretto Salvatierra put it this way: "That animal *[saila maaso]* walked around in the wilderness world in the beginning, that the people put into a song, so that now the animal is able to play with the song with his body, with the birds and the other things of the wilderness world."[5]

A *pahko* may be held at the household of an individual family on such occasions as the anniversary of the death of a relative, called a *lutu pahko*; the funeral of a child, a *usi mukila pahko*; the observance of the ritual for the Departed Souls on November 1, an *animan pakoriawa*; or to mark the completion of a special vow made in thanksgiving, a *manda pahko*. The whole village gathers for a *santo* or *pweplo pahko* to celebrate the Saint's Day of the village patron. *Santísima Trinidad*, Holy Trinity, is, for example, the Saint's Day celebrated as a *pweplo pahko* at Potam, while at Yoem Pueblo, a *pweplo pahko* is held on San Juan Day.

There is a provocative mention of another formal occasion when deer songs may have been sung in Yaqui communities. Lucas Chavez, a *maehto* from the village of Pascua in the 1940s, remembered some details of an early, formalized context for telling *etehoim*—stories in which deer songs were sung to punctuate the storytelling. Ruth Giddings reports that Chavez recalled that, in Sonora, gatherings were held three times a year when people from neighboring rancherias would gather at the house of a leader. Yaqui governors and soldiers would come too, and they would be greeted formally by the group. None of the religious aspects of the *pahko* were present, nor were there *pahkolam* to entertain the people. Special food was served unlike that usually prepared for a *pahko*. Chavez recalled that "five wise old men spoke alternately from dusk until dawn. They spoke of the past, told stories, and discussed the future. These men were skilled in the magic uses of smoking native cigarettes *(hiak' vivam)* and, by their use, were said to be able to receive messages from people who were in distant pueblos." At intervals throughout the night, in between the talk of the old men, "a deer dancer and his musicians would perform."[6] Gatherings of this sort have not been held in Sonora or Arizona in recent times.

The usual setting for a *pahko* is within the village in a *ramada*, a shelter with a flat roof and one or more open sides. The place is called *heka* or *ramá* in Yaqui, and is divided not by any walls but by the way in which the space is used. On one side, the *maehto* and other Baptized Ones worship before an altar covered with statues and other holy church objects which are transferred from the church for the event. This side is sometimes referred to as the *santo heka*, holy canopy. The *pahkolam* and their musicians, the deer dancer and the deer singers, together with their respective managers, hold forth on the other side, which is often referred to as the *kolensia*, a word from the Spanish *querencia*, a favorite place or haunt. Thus under the single roof of the *pahko ramá* Yaqui priests and performers give voice to the two strands of their tradition which they carried away from the encounter with the talking stick. The *maehto* and his assistants voice the words of the Baptized Ones in Yaqui, Spanish, and Latin; the deer singers and the *pahkolam* bring the traditions of the wilderness world into Yaqui words with such force that the whole *pahko ramá* is said to become the flower world during their performances. The people gather around both sides to witness and to celebrate.

17. *Angel Duarte anticipates ...*

18. *Pakola Francisco Alame'a dances ...*

❋ The crowd settles in after 2 A.M. From where I stand leaning against the side of a house not far from the front of the *ramá*, I can see the deer dancer and the deer singers without obstruction. Felipe has gone off to visit someone in the kitchen. I watch the dancers and singers and think over what he has told me about how they work together. Two Yaqui men come slowly across the plaza and stand in front of me. They look me over, then ask the Yaqui leaning on the wall next to me if he knows me. He says no, then turns to introduce himself: I'm Joe, this is my friend Mr. Matus. The third pushes closer to touch my hand. His name is Chuy. Chuy really wants to talk and to explain things to me. This is what we used to do before we went after deer, it's our religion, we may look poor, but . . . like that, he continues with help from Joe. I tell them I'm from Tucson and have been to a *pahko* there. Joe wants to know where I learned to call it that. I tell him Felipe is my friend, and he has taught me a few things. Mr. Matus announces that Larry is *his* friend and that he wants to talk to me. Joe shuts up. Chuy keeps babbling, more insistent all the time.

Mr. Matus is telling me that he is blind. I hadn't noticed the closed eyes behind his dark glasses. White goatee, hair swept back, navy blue warm-up jacket, suede boots, he looks like I think a '50s hipster should. He's telling me something about the dancing. They are all dancing the same thing he says. What do you mean? I don't get what he is saying. Chuy is continuing to talk into my left ear, whole left side really, on and on. He begins to tug my arm. Something about Joe. Joe tries to explain. He is going to marry Chuy's daughter, so Chuy is explaining that he will be Joe's father-in-law. They teach me the words for the relationship. I forget when they try to test me. My head is over on the right side with Mr. Matus. I try to turn that way, then realize that the visual cue is wasted.

Joe tells Chuy to back off. Chuy comes on stronger, talking steadily now, not fast but faster than before. I nod, grunt now and then. Mr. Matus says Larry is my friend. Joe puts his arm around Chuy and says Chuy is going to be his father-in-law. Mr. Matus begins to talk again about the dancers. Look, he says, look. If you don't know what the song says just watch the way they dance. First the violin will play a song and then the flute will play the same one and then the deer singers on the ground over there will play the same one. They all play the same song and the *pahkolam* and the deer will just dance what the song says. Look, just look. See, watch them, they are birds.

The *pahkola* is spreading his arms like a bird in his dance. I remind myself that Mr. Matus is blind. I ask if he can see it in his mind. Chuy has got something to say about women, Joe takes him by the arm and says let's us go to the weeds. Mr. Matus says Larry is my friend. I want to tell him how the Yaquis could get the hostages out of Iran.

We settle back against the wall and I listen to Mr. Matus describe old and exotic weapons as I watch the deer dancer whirl and glide through the song.

Masobwikame: The Deer Singers

The deer singers occupy a space near the center of the *ramá* throughout the *pahko*. Usually there are three, and they sit together in a row facing the *kolensia*, the area where the deer dancer performs. Some say that they should face the east as they sing, but the singers we have seen seem to sit on one side or the other of the *ramá* according to village, family, or even personal custom. The *hipetam* (bamboo mat, a blanket, or an old piece of carpet) gives them a little cushion and a place to stretch out and rest between songs during the night.

The *masobwika yo'owe*, lead deer singer, sits in the middle. He chooses the songs to be sung and begins each one. The other singers follow along. As they sing, each plays an instrument which rests on the ground in front of him. The lead singer and the singer on his left play *hirukiam*, wood raspers, which rest on *bweheim*, half-gourd resonators. The third singer plays a steady beat with a *hiponia*, a drumstick wrapped with corn husks, on another half-gourd which he floats in a *soto'i*, basin of water. The instrument is called a *va kuvahe*, water drum, and the singer is known as the water drummer. It is common for three men to make a regular group and always perform together. The three deer singers and the *maso* are in the care of a manager known as the *maso moro*. He makes arrangements for them to perform and sees that they are cared for during the *pahko*.

Deer singers usually make their own instruments, but some buy them from other singers or craftsmen. The *hirukiam* are carved from pieces of hardwood. *Huchahko*, Brazil wood, is a preferred material, but *hu'upa*, mesquite, and other hardwoods from the desert may be used. The choice of material seems largely based on availability. "When I can go to the mountains, I use *huchahko*," Don Jesús told us, "if I don't want to go to the mountains, I use *hu'upa keka'a*." Two raspers are carved. One, long and flat, is cut with shallow notches at regular intervals perpendicular to its length. It is called *hirukia*, rasper.[7] A second shorter length is smooth, narrow, and rounded. It is called *hirukia aso'ola*, baby rasper, or just the rubber. The number of notches a singer cuts into his *hirukia* is variable. Don Jesús told us that "the elder people say that there should be the same number of notches as the mysteries of the rosary," that is, as the number of beads on the Yaqui rosary. "Those people," Don Jesús went on, "say that there are prayers in there, that each of the notches has a prayer. That is why we put a cross on each end." He cautioned us, though, that the custom is not always observed: "The elder Yaqui singers speak about it like that, but we just make the raspers and don't worry too much about it."

Pahko Vichame: Those Who See the Pahko

Don Jesús believed that *pahko vichame*, those who see the *pahko*, the audience, could affect the deer singers greatly. If someone in the audience had bad thoughts or hatred in their heart for the singers, the singer might make mistakes in the songs or even forget them completely. To protect himself from these *erim*, bad thoughts, Don Jesús believed that a deer singer should carry a small cross carved from Brazil wood, a piece of blessed palm, and a seed pod from a plant called *tamkokochi*, a variety of Devil's claw, all in a pouch.

Before a singer began to sing, Don Jesús said he should pray to God for guidance, and then to past deer singers, asking their permission to sing their songs once again. In this way, a deer singer would more easily remember the deer songs throughout the night. In the morning, at the end of the *pahko* as the raspers and gourds are being picked up, the deer singers of the past should be thanked for their help during the *pahko*.

The relationship which the deer singers have with the audience at a *pahko* is significantly different from that of the other performers with whom they work. The *pahkolam* are literally "the old men of the *pahko* " and functionally ceremonial hosts and clowns. In their expansive way, they are always interacting with the audience which is drawn to them. During their joking and repartee, they constantly play to their audience and expect laughter and verbal response. Even when the eldest *pahkola* delivers the opening and closing sermons, he expects the audience to respond with the formulaic affirmative "*heewi.*" By contrast, the deer singers never call for, nor do they expect, any verbal response from the audience at a *pahko*. Their single interest is to attend to the rhythms and words they provide for the *maaso's* dance. In fact, they have a special kind of deer song called *tohakteme*, bouncing ones, which they can use to protect themselves from those in the audience who want to get too participatory and join the dance. A *tohakteme* is a kind of song with a rhythm that is more difficult to dance to. Don Jesús explained: "It is a deer song, but not a dance song. It is some-thing we hit them with, the ones who want to be proud of themselves and show off by dancing. Some of them [in the audience] always want to borrow the gourd rattles and dance. When they do that, we hit them with this kind of song."

Being too proud of one's abilities is something to be avoided not only by the audi-ence but by both the *maaso* and the deer singers themselves. "The deer, too," Don Jesús told us, "can like himself too much. He too can be too proud. When we see that, we hit him with the *tohakteme* too. And he will roast." In the same way, a deer singer should not call attention to himself by singing too well. Those who do so run the risk of losing their voices. At the same time a singer should not be sloppy or slovenly about his singing either. As an example of a poor performance, Don Jesús spoke of a singer who was so drunk for one of the *pahkom* that he just sang the following fragment over and over:

sewata tuleka sewata tuleka	loving the flower, loving the flower
ai la la la la la la	ai la la la la la la
sewata tuleka	loving the flower,
ai la la la la la la	ai la la la la la la

A good singer, according to Don Jesús, concentrates on his songs. He sings with a high voice. He can take his voice up to a high pitch and carry it through the longest lines of the song without pausing. This is especially important in the performance of the first part of the *tonua*, the concluding stanza, which may be very long in some songs. Of one such song Don Jesús said: "It has a long *tonua*. It is beautiful only if you have a *tuik kutanak*, good throat." Don Lupe told Felipe to pay attention to the end of the song: "When it ends with "aa" or "ee" the sounds should be carried out. Don't cut it short. Carry it out."

Wilder writes that "a good deer singer is one who sings with much gusto, and can make his song carry over the combined noise of the rasps, water drum, *maso* gourd rattles, rustling of the *tenevoim* of the *maaso*, pounding of his feet, as well as over the various accompanying musical sounds of the pascola dance which is performed at the same time as the deer dance."[8] To this litany of sounds we should add others. It is likely that as the deer singers begin their song, the *maehto* and the *kopariam* will be chanting out their prayers before the altar just behind the deer singers and that the *matachinim* will be diligently working through the rustle of their dance just in front of the altar side of the *ramá* to the stringed harmonies of their own musicians. On some occasions in Sonora, the distant rhythm of the flat drum and the sounds of a coyote song may be heard as members of the Coyote Society perform in the area out beyond the *matachinim* as well.

Amid all the other sounds coming out of the *pahko ramá* during the time the deer singers perform, the words of the deer songs are sometimes difficult to hear. Amos Taub, a commentator on the literary value of the words of deer songs, found them "practically incomprehensible in actual performance."[9] Yet, given the kind of vigorous singers described above, that part of the audience who is actually interested in listening to the words of the deer songs usually has little trouble. These people gravitate to the areas close to the singers.

✠ Whenever I am invited to sing I think about what songs I will be using. I don't worry about anything but getting sick. When the *pahko* is a few days away, the songs will be running through my head. A deer singer plays with his mind. He picks out his songs and arranges them. We do this when we are working in the fields or somewhere else. Sometimes I may be thinking about songs and arranging them when I am around my house relaxing or working. Sometimes when I am thinking this way a song may come out, and others may hear it. I have fun doing this, because I am getting excited about the up-coming *pahko*, and I just can't wait to sing for the crowd and the dance group inside the *ramá*.

On the actual day of the *pahko*, I must be ready to go with the *moro* at a set time. Usually we all are taken together to perform at an hour that the *moro* chooses. Down in Río Yaqui country, the *moro* comes on foot, while here in Arizona he may have a pickup truck to haul all his people. People want it to work this way but sometimes it doesn't. Sometimes some of the performers aren't ready, and sometimes the *moro* doesn't pick up everybody. This holds up the *pahko* and keeps it from starting at the appointed hour.

When we all arrive with the *moro* at the *pahko*, we are greeted by the ones who are giving the *pahko*, the *pahkome*. They give us a place to rest. If we bring wives or children, they are asked to rest too in any *ramá* that is available. After a while the *pahkome* get a table set, and they invite the whole group with wives and children and anyone else we brought along to move to the table and eat.

Usually they give us *waka vaki*, Yaqui beef stew, with tortillas and coffee. Everybody eats with much enjoyment, and there is much joking around among the men at the table. People must not laugh out loud. They are supposed to suppress their laughter when a good joke is told. "Long time ago," one of the deer singers might say, "there was a time when the Yaquis were very poor, but being Yaquis they always had their *pahkom* anyway. Well, anyway, when they had a *pahko*, they usually borrowed cow bones from each other to throw into the *waka vaki*. If somebody threw one of these bones away by mistake, somebody else would run over to pick it up and put it away for the next *pahko*." Then the deer singer might take some of the *waka vaki* he is eating in his spoon, maybe some with a little bone in it. "That is why these bones are so white and shiny," he might say. Usually the kitchen ladies will overhear the conversation and will laugh, but the people at the table must not. "I am irrigating sugar," says a deer singer as he stirs his coffee. "You must be melting and washing it away," says another deer singer. "No. Not that kind of sugar, sugar beets," says the first one. We may make fun of each other, too, at the long table, but only because all should have a good sense of humor and be in a good mood before we start the *pahko*. All the joking around helps us to not be nervous before we start singing.

After everybody finishes eating, the kitchen helpers remove the dishes. If any food is left over, usually the people at the table send it home, or they have it sent to a friend who is close by somewhere. Then the eldest *pahkola* gives a talk of thanksgiving, thanking God, the kitchen people, and the *pahkome* for the food and for allowing us to come together for this *pahko*. After this we will go out and sit down in our place in the *ramá* with the other musicians, the violin and the harp and the *tampaleo*. When they are ready, the *pahko* starts with the song called the *kanariom* which is played by the harp and the violin; then the *kanariom* moves to the *tampaleo*, and then to us and we sing our first deer song. The deer dancer is not supposed to come into the *ramá* until the third song. That is when he begins to dance.

In the early evening or the afternoon, when the *pahko* is getting started, usually there are many people around. They are anxious to see the deer dancer and the *pahkolam* dance. Everybody seems excited. There is happiness in the air while the people talk and socialize and watch the other people at the *pahko*. During this time, we try to sing our loudest, so that the people can enjoy the songs. People who understand the Yaqui language try to stand close to us to listen to the words of the songs and to watch to see if the deer dancer dances the meaning of the songs. Some people like the songs so much they just stand there behind us all night. Some of them record the songs on their cassette machines so they can listen to the songs later in their houses. Yaquis admire a good deer dancer and we tend to criticize a bad dancer. A dancer needs good, loud singers and good songs to dance well.

19. The pahkome, those who sponsor the pahko, serve ...

U Masobwikame Weiyawa: Carrying Out the Deer Singing

Deer singers may know as many as three hundred or more deer songs; however, during a *pahko* they will only have an opportunity to perform a fraction of their repertory, perhaps eighteen or twenty, certainly no more than fifty.[10] The choice of which songs to sing is restricted by Yaqui tradition in a number of ways, but finally it is the lead deer singer who decides.

It is not the deer singers but the *pahkolam* who are the first performers as the *pahko* opens, however. Wearing their masks, stumbling, their *moro* leads them into the *pahko ramá* as the violin and the harp play the first of three opening songs. During the first song they perform a ritual which is said to purify the space where they and the deer will spend the night dancing. At the conclusion of this first song, which is called the *kanariom*, the eldest *pahkola* delivers a sermon in which he talks about the inheritance he and the other *pahko* performers have received from God and how they will be working with it during the *pahko*. He asks the permission of those present to begin. They answer with the formulaic Yaqui affirmative "*heewi.*" The antiphonal traditions of the *pahko* require the deer singers to answer each of these three songs with one of their own. Don Jesús said that he always sang the same three songs during this opening part of the *pahko*. He called these *naate bwikam*, beginning songs. According to Don Jesús, it is during the third beginning song that the deer dancer comes into the *ramá* to dance for the first time. However, at *pahkom* in southern Arizona it is common for the deer dancer and the *pahkolam* to come into the *ramá* together without observing any special opening ritual. When they do that, the deer dancer will dance from the first song on.

20. Leonardo Bultimea's water drum …

✠ Nowadays, some of the old customs are changing or being neglected. One place where change has occurred is in the opening ritual of the *pahko*. The last time I saw a complete opening ritual at a *pahko* was in *Se chopoi* (Sand Hill), near Chandler, Arizona. My grandfather was invited to dance at a *lutu pahko* (death anniversary fiesta). I was about eight years old at the time. Much later, when I was about fifteen, my grandfather explained everything I had seen. At the time I was too young to understand what was going on and, besides, I had my mind on other things like playing with the children. However, I vividly remember my grandpa, Luis Ka Tomela, and Cipriano as *pahkolam*, and Juan María Maso as the *maso*.

The *moro* led the *pahkolam* from the bushes that were south of the southward-facing *pahko ramá*. The *moro* leads the *pahkolam* like this because they are not humans at this time. He finally took them into the ramada, where he walked them around three times in a circle and then stood them in front of the *labaleo* and the *aapaleo*. While the *pahkolam* stood there, they started to swing their hips so that the bells were constantly ringing to the music of the violinist and the harpist, who were playing the *kanariom*, or opening piece. They started to say things that popped into their minds—crazy things, because they were still on the side of the Devil. Things like: "With this nose I can smell great distances"; "With these ears I can hear far away"; "I am a baker"; "I am a farmer." I also noticed that they made the sign of the cross awkwardly, sometimes touching their heads all the way down to their knees. Grandpa told me they said and did these things because they were still confused and still people of the Devil. Then they said: "Watch out harp player, these legs have killed many harp players," and then they named dead harpists that I knew, and others from before my time. "Prepare yourself, because they will constantly want to dance."

After this confusing routine they turned around and shouted. Grandpa told me that this was because they were trying to scare and frighten away the Devil, who was lurking in the area around the fiesta ramada. At this time I pictured the Devil standing back and starting to run away from the *pahko ramá*, falling and tripping clumsily.

After the *pahkolam* had finished with that ritual, they started all together to dance to the *kanariom* that the musicians were playing. As soon as the *labaleo* and the *aapaleo* had finished their tune, the *tampaleo* began to play his *kanariom*. As they had done to the other music, the *pahkolam* all danced to the *tampaleo* at the same time.

When they had finished dancing to the *tampaleo* they started to bless the ground. They stood toward the east, home of the Texans, and they asked for help from *santo mocho'okoli* (holy horned toad). Each *pahkola* marked a cross on the ground with the bamboo reed with which the *moro* had led him into the ramada. Then they stood toward the north and said: "Bless the people to the north, the Navajos, and help me, my *santo vovok* (holy frog), because they are people like us," and they marked another cross on the ground. Still they stood toward the west and said: "Bless the *Hua*

Yoemem (Papagos) and help me my *santo wikui* (holy lizard)," and they marked another cross on the ground. Finally they stood toward the south and said: "To the south, land of the Mexicans, bless them and help me my *santo vehori* (holy tree lizard)," and they marked the last cross on the ground. The head *pahkola* said: "My holy crosses, we have marked you on the ground so that you can protect us from all evil that might harm us."

Putting the bamboo reeds away, the *pahkolam* said to them, "Wait here for me until the *aki* (organ pipe cactus) fruit have ripened. I will use you to *hiabwa* the *aki takam* (pick the cactus fruit)." Finally they put their reeds among the ceiling beams of the *pahko ramá*. Now that the ground had been blessed and purified, the *pahko* was ready to begin. The deer dancer would arrive shortly, and the people were ready to enjoy and be blessed by the *pahko.*

After the beginning songs are sung, the *maehto* and the other church people come and get the deer dancer and the *pahkolam* to accompany them in a formal procession which brings the saints and other holy objects from the village church to the *pahko ramá*, where they are placed on a small table which serves as an altar. At the end of the *pahko* in the morning, the holy objects are returned in another procession. During these two processions the deer singers must sing what Don Jesús called *kaminaroa bwikam*, procession songs. They are deer songs which often incorporate Christian references or themes within the standard deer-song format. These two processions frame the *pahko*, and they are notable as the only times during the *pahko* when the deer singers and the *maehto* coordinate their singing in a formal way. Between the two processions, the deer singers and the other performers who share the *kolensia* go their own way, while the *maehto* and the church people go theirs before their altar on the other side of the *ramá*.

The hymns which the *maehto* sings during the *pahko* are called *alavansam*, and those *bwikam* which the deer singers sing as the *maehto* is singing take the same name. When we asked Don Jesús what the difference was between *alavansam* (hymns) and *bwikam* (songs), he replied, "They are *bwikam*, just *bwikam*. The violin player has his *alavansam*. The harp player has *alavansam*. The *tampaleo* has *alavansam*. And the deer singers too have *alavansam*. They are just *bwikam*." Yet while both the songs of the deer singers and those of the *maehto* are commonly known by the same term, there seems to be no formal effort between the two sides to coordinate who sings what when. And sometimes the *maehto* and the deer singers end up singing at the same time. One woman from Potam, a veteran of a lifetime of *pahkom*, pined to us at length how she loved to listen to *all* of the *alavansam*, those of the *maehto* and those of deer singers. Because their performance so often overlapped, however, she felt it was impossible to give a good hearing to both.

By contrast the performances of the deer singers are very consciously orchestrated with the other musicians who share the *kolensia*, their side of the *ramá*. The *pahko* proceeds in repeated sequences of music and dancing. The violin and the harp players play together and begin each sequence, and, when they do, each *pahkola* takes a turn dancing to their stringed music. There is a break during which the *pahkolam* may joke with the crowd or among themselves; then, one of them may call for the *tampaleo*, the flute and drum player, to begin. A small bed of mesquite coals is kept at the side of the *tampaleo*. He uses these coals to heat and tune the head of his drum. The sharp distinctive sound of the *tampaleo* searching for the right tuning on his drum is a signal that a deer song will soon be sung. And when they hear it, the audience concentrates around the edge of the *ramá*. Once the *tampaleo* has begun his song, the *pahkolam* each take a turn dancing to his music, this time with their masks covering their faces. It is as the *pahkolam* begin to dance to the music of the *tampaleo* that the deer singers finally begin. Usually a deer song is sung two or three times. When the deer dancer has performed and the deer song is over, everything stops. There is a more extended break. The violin and the harp players begin a new song and the sequence is begun again. So it goes throughout the *pahko*.

As it is the violin and the harp players who begin each of these sequences, they are said to *vata weiya*, carry it first. In addition to the temporal order of the sequence, this means that the violin player chooses the songs, the *alavansam*. If the violin player chooses an *alavansa* titled, say, *wichalakas*, cardinal, then the *tampaleo* is supposed to follow with a cardinal song on his flute and drum, and the deer singers in their turn should choose a cardinal song from their own repertory as well. Only the deer songs have words, but the *alavansam* of both of the other sets of musicians are known by titles.

In addition to choosing the songs, the violinist "carries it first" in another way. The violin and the harp use three different tunings during the *pahko*.[11] Felipe, from conversations with both Don Jesus and Don Lupe, identifies the following names and associated times: *alavansa:* from the beginning of the *pahko* until an hour or so before midnight; *partiyo:* the hours around midnight when it is said "the world turns"; and *kompania:* from around 1 A.M. until the close of the *pahko*. It is said that certain kinds of *alavansam* are traditionally performed during each of these portions of the *pahko*. This appears to be a general pattern which individual singers interpret and define in their own ways over the course of their careers.

Don Jesús talked about his choices of deer songs in the following way. He began a *pahko* with a sequence of three *naate bwikam*, beginning songs, which he referred to as the *kanariom, kanariom saila,* and *maso yeu weye* (the deer comes out). Always, he said, he sang the same three songs to begin. Similarly, he always closed the *pahko* with two songs which were always the same: a *hilukiam tovoktane bwikam* (pick up raspers song) and a *sakawame bwikam* (a leaving song). A *kaminaroa bwikam* (procession song) always followed the beginning songs and followed the closing songs. Within this frame, Don Jesús felt a great latitude of choice. Any *alavansam* could be used there he told us: "After the procession song, we can sing anything." However, he then went on to say that he usually began with a sequence of songs about *saila maso*, little brother deer, followed these with songs about the flowers in the wilderness world, moved in the middle of the *pahko* to songs about animals, and finally to bird songs as dawn approached. He named these groups as *hubwa kupteo bwikam* (early evening songs), *nasuktukaria bwikam* (middle of the night songs), and *matchuo vicha bwikam* (toward the morning songs).[12]

Don Jesús and other deer singers we talked with preferred to discuss the sequence of deer songs they sang during a *pahko* not as a taxonomy but as a narrative. Don Jesús consistently returned to the idea that the deer songs represent the voice of *saila maso*. At the same time the songs describe him, they describe what he sees and encounters as he goes out into the wilderness world. Deer singer Loretto Salvatierra describes the way he thinks about the sequence of deer songs during a *pahko* in this way:

When we are moved, we sing the beginning songs. Three songs there must be. In the yard that is made ready, the animal that has come will start to move around. With the movements it has while it is alive and walking, it will start sounding and it will have the hour.

Then during the hours of the dusk, all the wilderness flowers will be sung. When it falls to night, the animals in the wilderness: the mountain lion, a little cottontail or a jackrabbit, even a little rat, all the ones that are alive and walk around, they will start to sound. The animal that has come sees them and they will be sung about from there until the world turns.

From where the world turns until the dawn wind, the ones you see when you are walking in the wilderness will be said, and the birds will also be imitated. They will be known and can be said.

Toward the morning the song is said of the animal, the one that loves the dawn wind and is walking, the animal that stands under the palo verde. Under it he will stand and rub his antlers with that wind. He loves it so, that dawn wind.

From there we will sing the morning service song, and then the procession song, and it will end. Yes, that is it. All that he should talk about, that is what we sing, that is it. He does not talk, but he talks in an enchanted way.

Sewau Hotekate: We Sit Down to the Flower

Deer songs are most commonly performed within Yaqui communities, then, not individually but as a part of sequences that individual singers create, sequences which each fill one *pahko* with songs. Accordingly, we believe the most appropriate way to present deer-song words for appreciation is not in a catalogue but in such sequences.

During the time we worked recording songs and talk about songs, Felipe was increasingly invited to perform as lead deer singer at both family and community *pahkom*, as well as at various functions outside the Yaqui community.[13] During these performances he began to incorporate the songs we were recording into his own repertory.

What follows is one sequence of songs which Felipe Molina, Timothy Cruz, and Felipe Garcia sang at a *pahko* held at Old Pascua in 1984. Many of the songs which Felipe chose to sing were learned from Don Jesús, Don Lupe, and other singers we worked with in Potam, Sonora. The sequence thus indicates one way in which their songs continue in contemporary Yaqui tradition. From this perspective it is a living anthology of their work. Out of respect for the *pahkome*, we did not record the songs that night, but sat down together to write down the songs and work out these translations later. We repeat the first part of each song the same number of times Felipe remembers singing them, and after each song we give the comments which Felipe made on the songs as we wrote them down. These glosses may be viewed as a step toward the oral literary criticism for which many have called.[14] They seemed to both of us an inseparable part of the songs as soon as they were said.

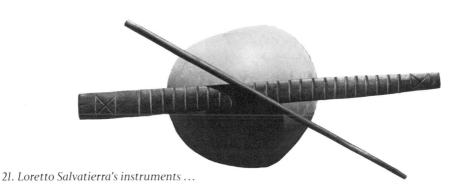

21. Loretto Salvatierra's instruments ...

SEWAILO MALICHI

Aa sewailo malichi yewelu sika
  yo chikti yo sea
    huya aniwapo
      yeulu sika
sewailo malichi yewelu sika
  yo chikti yo sea
    huya aniwapo
      yeulu sikaaa

Aa sewailo malichi yewelu sika
  yo chikti yo sea
    huya aniwapo
      yeulu sika
sewailo malichi yewelu sika
  yo chikti yo sea
    huya aniwapo
      yeulu sikaaa

Ayamansu sewailo
  yo fayaliasu
    weyekai
      yeulu sika
Sewailo malichi yewelu sika
  yo chikti yo sea
    huya aniwapo
      yeulu sikaaa

FLOWER-COVERED FAWN

Aa flower-covered fawn went out,
  enchanted, from each enchanted flower
    wilderness world,
      he went out.
Flower-covered fawn went out,
  enchanted, from each enchanted flower
    wilderness world,
      he went out.

Aa flower-covered fawn went out,
  enchanted, from each enchanted flower
    wilderness world,
      he went out.
Flower-covered fawn went out,
  enchanted, from each enchanted flower
    wilderness world,
      he went out.

Over there, in the flower-covered
  enchanted opening,
    as he is walking,
      he went out.
Flower-covered fawn went out,
  enchanted, from each enchanted flower
    wilderness world,
      he went out.

This is always the first song of the pahko. *In it we talk about* saila maaso, *little brother deer, as a young deer, a fawn. During the night of the* pahko, *he will grow up. In this song we talk about him coming out to walk around and to play in an enchanted opening in the flower world. When I sing, my mind is always in the flower world. That is where I think the songs take place. There must be an opening in the wilderness over there in the flower world. The fawn comes out into that to dance and to play.*

I learned this song from Miki Maaso. He always begins the first part of his songs with an "aa" to carry him into the song. So when I sing his songs I do that too. Chikti *means each. I am not sure just what it means in this song, but when I sing it I think about Don Jesús. He talked about* chikti huya, *meaning each and every tree and bush in the wilderness world. The fawn must go out from each and every part of the wilderness world.*

During this song the deer dancer will be getting ready to come out from where he is dressing, but he is not in the pahko ramá *yet. We sing this song after the violin and the harp begin with a song about the canaries which they call the* kanariom. *So we call our song the* kanariom *too.*

ELAPO YEU WENE

Elapo yeu wene
   vae tatakalim awakame
Elapo yeu wene
   vae tatakalim awakameee

Elapo yeu wene
   vae tatakalim awakame
Elapo yeu wene
   vae tatakalim awakameee

Elapo yeu wene
   vae tatakalim awakame
Elapo yeu wene
   vae tatakalim awakameee

Ayaman ne seyewailo yevuku
   yolemta sea tevatchiapo
     sewa lilihti awakai
Elapo yeu wene
   vae tatakalim awakameee

LET THE ONE GO OUT

Let the one go out,
   with the three-pointed antlers.
Let the one go out,
   with the three-pointed antlers.

Let the one go out,
   with the three-pointed antlers.
Let the one go out,
   with the three-pointed antlers.

Let the one go out,
   with the three-pointed antlers.
Let the one go out,
   with the three-pointed antlers.

Over there, I, in Yevuku Yoleme's
   flower-covered, flower patio,
     I have sparsely flowered antlers.
Let the one go out,
   with the three-pointed antlers.

This is trying to say that the little deer's antlers are barely growing. He just has three little points on his antlers. Maybe as he is walking out he snags a few flower blossoms on his antlers, maybe he has rubbed his antlers against some branches and some flowers stuck. When he comes out, he just has a few flowers on his antlers. Lilihti, *sparsely, is the opposite of* yuin, *abundant. Maybe because there are so many flowers in the flower world the fawn can't help but get a few on his antlers.*

Yevuku Yoleme *is someone who lives entirely in the wilderness world, someone who doesn't live in the village at all. He has a special feeling for the animals and the other things out there. "You can still be a* Yevuku Yoeme *if you are willing to go out and live that way," my uncle told us. There is a* Yevuku Yoeme *in the old stories too. He is the one who is in charge of everything in the flower world. That is why the song says the patio in the flower world belongs to* Yevuku Yoleme. *We add the "l" to his name to show affection. It is song language, but sometimes we use it in our conversation too.*

I learned this song from Don Jesús. It is always the second song we sing. We call it the kanariom saila. *The deer dancer is still not out when we sing it. We are waiting for him. This tells those in the flower world to let him come out to dance.*

WANA YEU WEYEMA

Wana yeu weyemai
   wana yota karipo
      yeu ne weyekai
Wana yeu weyemai
   wana yota karipo
      yeu ne weyekaiii

Wana yeu weyemai
   wana yota karipo
      yeu ne weyekai
Wana yeu weyemai
   wana yota karipo
      yeu ne weyekaiii

Ayaman ne seyewailo yevuku
   yolemta tevatchiapo
      sewa lilihti awakai
Wana yeu weyemai
   wana yota karipo
      yeu ne weyekaiii

THERE HE COMES OUT

There he comes out,
   there from the enchanted house,
      I come out from there.
There he comes out,
   there from the enchanted house,
      I come out from there.

There he comes out,
   there from the enchanted house,
      I come out from there.
There he comes out,
   there from the enchanted house,
      I come out from there.

Over there, I, in Yevuku Yoleme's
   flower-covered, flower patio,
      I have sparsely flowered antlers.
There he comes out,
   there from the enchanted house,
      I come out from there.

This is the song when the deer dancer comes into the ramá *from where he gets ready. First he goes to the patio cross, then he starts walking in toward the* ramá *like a deer. But this song is saying that he comes from the yo* kari, *enchanted house. When I learned this song from Don Jesús, I asked him about this enchanted house. He said, "The enchanted house, well, yes, somewhere in the mountains there are enchanted homes. From the enchanted home, he will come out." Another time Don Jesús told us that the deer songs and the ability to sing and to dance can come from these yo* hoaram, *enchanted homes.*

   Many deer singers begin the tonua, *concluding stanza, with* ayamansu, *a word that means the same thing as* ayaman, *over there. Don Jesús usually began his* tonua *with* ayaman ne. Ne *means "I." I think Don Jesús liked to use it in his songs because he always said that it was the deer who was speaking in them. "U maso hunen hia/the deer is saying that," he said after teaching us this song. But there can be other voices in there too. In this song we are describing the deer, and then he talks back to us.*

SEATA VALUMAI

Tane seata valumai
  sea mochala awaka
    weyekai
Kiane seata valumai
  sea mochala awaka
    weyekaiii

Tane seata valumai
  sea mochala awaka
    weyekai
Kiane seata valumai
  sea mochala awaka
    weyekaiii

Ayaman ne seyewailo
  huyatanaisukuni
    machiau kuaktekai
Sea mochala awaka
  weyekai
Tane seata valumai
  sea mochala awaka
    weyekaiii

WASH THE FLOWER

But I am washed by the flower,
  with a cluster of flowers in my antlers,
    I walk.
I am just washed by the flower,
  with a cluster of flowers in my antlers,
    I walk.

But I am washed by the flower,
  with a cluster of flowers in my antlers,
    I walk.
I am just washed by the flower,
  with a cluster of flowers in my antlers,
    I walk.

Over there, I, in the center
  of the flower-covered wilderness
    I turned toward the dawn.
With a cluster of flowers in my antlers,
  I walk.
But I am washed by the flower,
  with a cluster of flowers in my antlers,
    I walk.

After the deer has danced we take a little break. Then the pahkome, *the sponsors of the* pahko, *say that they are ready for the procession. The* moro ya'ut, *our manager, comes to us deer singers and asks our permission to take the deer dancer along with the* pahkolam *and the* tampaleo *to the church. He makes a formal speech, and then he takes them over there, and they lead the procession with the holy figures back to the* ramá. *When the deer gets back to the patio cross we start to sing this song for him. It is a procession song, a flower song.*

In the song the deer is telling us that he is being washed by the flowers. Don Jesús said, "he is washing his face, brushed by the flowers, he is washing his face with them." Maybe as he walks in through the wilderness some flowers are hitting his face. During the procession the church ladies will throw confetti or flowers whenever the deer stops. I think that the song refers to this too.

The deer's place is the flower world, in the east, beneath the dawn. So when he stops, he looks back that way, the way he comes from. Yaquis think of the west as the place of death. Maybe as he is walking in toward death, he is looking back to the east, trying to decide if he wants to go on. You have to think about that in the song.

I learned this song from Don Jesús. He called it a kaminaroa bwika *(a road song or procession song). He said, "there are many* kaminaroa bwikam, *but they all must be flower songs."*

SEWAU HOTEKATE

Vasate sewau hotekate
  sewa valikai
    sewau hotekateee

Vasate sewau hotekate
  sewa valikai
    sewau hotekateee

Vasate sewau hotekate
  sewa valikai
    sewau hotekateee

Ayaman ne seyewailo
  yevuku yolemta sea tevatchiapo
Sewa valikai
  sewau hotekateee

WE SIT DOWN TO THE FLOWER

Already we sit down to the flower.
  To receive the flower,
    we sit down to the flower.

Already we sit down to the flower.
  To receive the flower,
    we sit down to the flower.

Already we sit down to the flower.
  To receive the flower,
    we sit down to the flower.

Over there, I, in Yevuku Yoleme's
  flower-covered, flower patio,
To receive the flower,
  we sit down to the flower.

This song tells that we are ready to sit down to the flower to receive the flower. This means we are going to sit down to our holy obligation, to our holy instruments, our raspers and our water drum. It tells the people that we are starting. We do this to begin to complete their sacred request. This is the first one we sing after the procession song.

Everything is flowers in the deer songs. The sewa, flower, is our deer singing instruments: the raspers, the gourds, the water drum. The sewa also is grace, the blessing or the benefit we singers will receive by bringing the songs from the flower world. The sewa is also the song itself. The deer dancer is sometimes called sewata ye'eme, *he who dances the flowers.*

I learned this song from Don Jesús.

MAISO YOLEME

Ala inikun maiso yoleme
  hunu kun maiso yoleme
    ini kun tua maiso yolemeee

Ala inikun maiso yoleme
  hunu kun maiso yoleme
    ini kun tua maiso yolemeee

Ala inikun maiso yoleme
  hunu kun maiso yoleme
    ini kun tua maiso yolemeee

Ayaman ne seyewailo
  fayaliata naisukuni
    weyekai
      im ne yo siali vata paku
      weyekai
Hunu kun maiso yoleme
  hunu kun tua maiso yolemeee

DEER PERSON

So now this is the deer person,
  so he is the deer person,
    so he is the real deer person.

So now this is the deer person,
  so he is the deer person,
    so he is the real deer person.

So now this is the deer person,
  so he is the deer person,
    so he is the real deer person.

Over there, I, in the center
  of the flower-covered opening,
    as I was walking,
      here in the open green water,
      as I was walking,
So he is the deer person,
  so he is the real deer person.

Maiso is a word for a mature deer, but early in the evening this deer is still a malichi, *a fawn. Maybe here he is in between, like a teenager, between being a child and an adult.*

    The deer dancer is in between in other ways too. He is between this world and the flower world. He is both a yoeme, *a person, and a* yoawa, *an animal. So that is how he can be the deer person. When he is called* tua maiso yoleme, *the real deer person, I think about the way Don Jesús named our ancestors. He called them* tua vat hiakim: *the first real Yaquis. I learned this song from Don Jesús.*

AWA HISA MOELAM	OLD ANTLER CROWN

In awa hisa molewaim
    nane kovate
In awa hisa molewaim
    nane kova kovateee
	My old antler crown,
	    I move my head around.
	My old antler crown,
	    I move my head, head around.

In awa hisa molewaim
    nane kovate
In awa hisa molewaim
    nane kova kovateee
	My old antler crown,
	    I move my head around.
	My old antler crown,
	    I move my head, head around.

In awa hisa molewaim
    nane kovate
In awa hisa molewaim
    nane kova kovateee
	My old antler crown,
	    I move my head around.
	My old antler crown,
	    I move my head, head around.

Ayaman ne seyewailo yevuku yoemta
    sea tevatchiapo
      sea mochala awa
        wainase vuite
In awa hisa molewaim
    nane kova kovateee
	Over there, I, in Yevuku Yoleme's
	    flower-covered, flower patio,
	      with a cluster of flowers on your antler,
	        you come running from that side.
	My old antler crown,
	    I move my head around.

Hisa is the word we use for a headdress. We call the ceremonial headdress of the Coyote Society dancers a hisa. *The quail have their little* hisa, *their topknot, the feathers on the top of their heads. The Plains Indians' long headdress of feathers we call a* hisa *too. And the comet, we call the comet* choki hisa, *star headdress. When it is a verb,* hisa *may describe the growth of the deer's antlers. "Maso awam hisane/the deer's antlers will unfold," we say in one song. Usually when we talk about the deer dancer's headdress we call it* masokova, *deer head. This song just talks about the top, the antlers as the* hisa.

It is the deer speaking. I don't know why he says his antler crown is old. The antlers of a deer change every year, but the deer dancer's antlers stay the same year after year. So the headdress that the deer dancer uses is old, but Don Lupe Molina told me that everything in deer songs is not in reality, not in this moment. Maybe there is a reason the antler crown is old in the flower world.

I learned this song from Don Jesús.

SEWA HUYA

Sewa huya
yeu ne wevalika
sewa huya
Sewa yo huya aniwapo
yeu ne sika
sewa huyaaa

Sewa huya
yeu ne wevalika
sewa huya
Sewa yo huya aniwapo
yeu ne sika
sewa huyaaa

Sewa huya
yeu ne wevalika
sewa huya
Sewa yo huya aniwapo
yeu ne sika
sewa huyaaa

Ayaman ne seyewailo
kaila vetukuni
enchi vivichaka
Sewa yo huya aniwapo
yeu ne sika
sewa huyaaa

FLOWER WILDERNESS

Flower wilderness,
as I want to go out,
flower wilderness.
In the enchanted flower wilderness world,
I went out,
flower wilderness.

Flower wilderness,
as I want to go out,
flower wilderness.
In the enchanted flower wilderness world,
I went out,
flower wilderness.

Flower wilderness,
as I want to go out,
flower wilderness.
In the enchanted flower wilderness world,
I went out,
flower wilderness.

Over there, I,
under the flower-covered brightness,
I see you.
In the enchanted flower wilderness world,
I went out,
flower wilderness.

The deer is talking to the wilderness world in this song. The kaila *is the brightness of the light before dawn. At Yoem Pueblo and around the Marana area, we use that word for Tucson.* Kala solai, *you can see the brightness, is what we call it. I learned this song from Don Jesús.*

SEMALULUKUT

Aa semalulukut taka huni
  toloko huapo sika
    huapo sewa luute
Semalulukut taka huni
  toloko huapo sika
    huapo sewa luuteee

Aa semalulukut taka huni
  toloko huapo sika
    huapo sewa luute
Semalulukut taka huni
  toloko huapo sika
    huapo sewa luuteee

Aa semalulukut taka huni
  toloko huapo sika
    huapo sewa luute
Semalulukut taka huni
  toloko huapo sika
    huapo sewa luuteee

Ayaman ne seyewailo
  saniloata naisukun
    weyekai
      sanilo huapo sika
        huapo sewa luute
Semalulukut taka huni
  toloko huapo sika
    huapo sewa luuteee

HUMMINGBIRD

Aa the hummingbird, also,
  in the light blue wilderness went,
    in the wilderness he is using up the flower.
The hummingbird, also,
  in the light blue wilderness went,
    in the wilderness he is using up the flower.

Aa the hummingbird, also,
  in the light blue wilderness went,
    in the wilderness he is using up the flower.
The hummingbird, also,
  in the light blue wilderness went,
    in the wilderness he is using up the flower.

Aa the hummingbird, also,
  in the light blue wilderness went,
    in the wilderness he is using up the flower.
The hummingbird, also,
  in the light blue wilderness went,
    in the wilderness he is using up the flower.

Over there, I, in the middle
  of the flower-covered grove,
    as I am going,
      in the wilderness grove I went
        in the wilderness he is using up the flower.
The hummingbird, also,
  in the light blue wilderness went,
    in the wilderness he is using up the flower.

When the flowers are open, the hummingbird goes from flower to flower. He sucks out the nectar; that uses up the flower. Luute *means to use up. We say* apo vam luuta, *he is using up the water. This is different from two other words in Yaqui:* chupa *and* ansuwa. *We say* apo a tekilwa chupa, *he is completing his work, and* pahko ansuwa, *the* pahko *is ending.*

Luute *is more like "running out of " or "using up." We say* apo tomita luuta, *he is using up the money, or* tomi luute, *he is running out of money.*

The song tells what the deer sees. He is looking at what the hummingbird is doing in the wilderness world. The flowers are open, and the hummingbird is flying through the light blue sky, going from flower to flower.

I learned this song from Tani Masobwikame in Potam.

EMPO KA YO KAUSI WOLEKAME YOU WHO DO NOT HAVE ENCHANTED LEGS

Empo ka yo kausi wolekame
  hitasa haliwa
    hitasa haliwa
Empo ka yo kausi wolekame
  hitasa haliwa
    hitasa haliwaaa

Empo ka yo kausi wolekame
  hitasa haliwa
    hitasa haliwa
Empo ka yo kausi wolekame
  hitasa haliwa
    hitasa haliwaaa

Empo ka yo kausi wolekame
  hitasa haliwa
    hitasa haliwa
Empo ka yo kausi wolekame
  hitasa haliwa
    hitasa haliwaaa

Ayamansu seyewailo
  huyata naisukuni
Empo ka yo kausi wolekame
  hitasa haliwa
    hitasa haliwa
Empo ka yo kausi wolekame
  hitasa haliwa
    hitasa haliwaaa

You who do not have enchanted legs,
  what are you looking for,
    what are you looking for?
You who do not have enchanted legs,
  what are you looking for,
    what are you looking for?

You who do not have enchanted legs,
  what are you looking for,
    what are you looking for?
You who do not have enchanted legs,
  what are you looking for,
    what are you looking for?

You who do not have enchanted legs,
  what are you looking for,
    what are you looking for?
You who do not have enchanted legs,
  what are you looking for,
    what are you looking for?

Over there, in the middle
  of the flower-covered wilderness,
You who do not have enchanted legs,
  what are you looking for,
    what are you looking for?
You who do not have enchanted legs,
  what are you looking for,
    what are you looking for?

When someone has ability from the enchanted homes and the enchanted world, he can dance well. I am not sure what this song means, but I think of the deer walking around in this song—maybe he has lost his enchantment, maybe he is a little clumsy, maybe he is looking for his enchantment, his ability to dance again. I learned this song from Tani Masobwikame.

SEWAILO WESIME

Sewailo wesime
  sewailo vosime
    seyewailo yo satemali
    aman te yaine
Sewailo wesime
  sewailo vosime
    seyewailo yo satemali
    aman te yaineee

Sewailo wesime
  sewailo vosime
    seyewailo yo satemali
    aman te yaine
Sewailo wesime
  sewailo vosime
    seyewailo yo satemali
    aman te yaineee

Sewailo wesime
  sewailo vosime
    seyewailo yo satemali
    aman te yaine
Sewailo wesime
  sewailo vosime
    seyewailo yo satemali
    aman te yaineee

Ayamansu seyewailo
  huyata naisukuni
Sewailo wesime
  sewailo vosime
    seyewailo yo satemali
    aman te yaine
Sewailo wesime,
  sewailo vosime,
    seyewailo yo satemali
    aman te yaineee

FLOWER-COVERED, GOING

Flower-covered, going,
  flower-covered, crawling,
    flower-covered, enchanted, mountain lizard,
    there we will arrive.
Flower-covered, going,
  flower-covered, crawling,
    flower-covered, enchanted, mountain lizard,
    there we will arrive.

Flower-covered, going,
  flower-covered, crawling,
    flower-covered, enchanted, mountain lizard,
    there we will arrive.
Flower-covered, going,
  flower-covered, crawling,
    flower-covered, enchanted, mountain lizard,
    there we will arrive.

Flower-covered, going,
  flower-covered, crawling,
    flower-covered, enchanted, mountain lizard,
    there we will arrive.
Flower-covered, going,
  flower-covered, crawling,
    flower-covered, enchanted, mountain lizard,
    there we will arrive.

Over there in the middle
  of the flower-covered grove,
Flower-covered, going,
  flower-covered, crawling,
    flower-covered, enchanted, mountain lizard,
    there we will arrive.
Flower-covered, going,
  flower-covered, crawling,
    flower-covered, enchanted, mountain lizard,
    there we will arrive.

The deer and the lizard are going along together in this song, and the deer is saying that they will arrive in the flower world. He is trying to encourage the lizard.

The mountain lizard is a big lizard, not like the little ones you see around the village here in Marana. But it is not an iguana. That one we call kuta wikui. *This is a different one, a mountain lizard. In the song it says he is* vosime. *That is not exactly like crawling in English. In Yaqui we say that babies or even drunks* wakate, *crawl. They can't walk, so they crawl. But* vosime *means that you are lying, moving, or crawling because you want to be, because you have the ability. I learned this song from Don Lupe.*

SEWA HUYA ANIWA

Empo sewa yo huya aniwa
  empo yo huya aniwa
    vaewa sola voyoka
Empo yo huya aniwa
  vaewa sola voyoka
    huya aniwaaa

Empo sewa yo huya aniwa
  empo yo huya aniwa
    vaewa sola voyoka
Empo yo huya aniwa
  vaewa sola voyoka
    huya aniwaaa

Empo sewa yo huya aniwa
  empo yo huya aniwa
    vaewa sola voyoka
Empo yo huya aniwa
  vaewa sola voyoka
    huya aniwaaa

Ayamansu seyewailo
  huyata naisukunisu
    yo huya aniwapo
      usyoli machi hekamake
        usyolisi vaewa sola voyoka
      huya aniwaaa
Empo yo huya aniwa
  vaewa sola voyoka
    huya aniwaaa

FLOWER WILDERNESS WORLD

You are an enchanted flower wilderness world,
  you are an enchanted wilderness world,
    you lie with see-through freshness.
You are an enchanted wilderness world,
  you lie with see-through freshness,
    wilderness world.

You are an enchanted flower wilderness world,
  you are an enchanted wilderness world,
    you lie with see-through freshness.
You are an enchanted wilderness world,
  you lie with see-through freshness,
    wilderness world.

You are an enchanted flower wilderness world,
  you are an enchanted wilderness world,
    you lie with see-through freshness.
You are an enchanted wilderness world,
  you lie with see-through freshness,
    wilderness world.

Over there, in the center
  of the flower-covered wilderness,
    in the enchanted wilderness world,
      beautiful with the dawn wind,
        beautifully you lie with see-through freshness,
      wilderness world.
You are an enchanted wilderness world,
  you lie with see-through freshness,
    wilderness world.

I learned this song from Don Lupe Molina who lives at Vicam. The song reminds me of the flower world in the early morning hour when the sun is coming out. It is talking about the dew. The dew is on the blades of grass and the many leaves on the different plants in the wilderness world. Animals of the wilderness are just becoming active at this hour. In this song the deer sees the peaceful and quiet morning. He sees the freshness, the dew on the ground, when he looks toward the east where the sun is rising over the mountains.

SEWA YOTUME

Sewa yotume sewa yotume
  sewa yo machi hekamake sika
Machi hekamake hekawapo chasime
  yo yo machi hekamake sikaaa

Sewa yotume sewa yotume
  sewa yo machi hekamake sika
Machi hekamake hekawapo chasime
  yo yo machi hekamake sikaaa

Sewa yotume sewa yotume
  sewa yo machi hekamake sika
Machi hekamake hekawapo chasime
  yo yo machi hekamake sikaaa

Ayamansu seyewailo
  vetana yo aniwata vevepa
    mekka hikat chasime
      ta'ata aman weche vetana
        usyoli kala lipapati ansime
Empo yo machi hekamake sikaaa

GROWING FLOWER

Growing flower, growing flower,
  flower, with the enchanted dawn wind, went.
With the dawn wind's air, you are flying,
  with the enchanted, enchanted dawn wind you went.

Growing flower, growing flower,
  flower, with the enchanted dawn wind, went.
With the dawn wind's air, you are flying,
  with the enchanted, enchanted dawn wind you went.

Growing flower, growing flower,
  flower, with the enchanted dawn wind, went.
With the dawn wind's air, you are flying,
  with the enchanted, enchanted dawn wind you went.

Over there, along side the flower-covered,
  on top of the enchanted world,
    far, on the top, you are flying,
      on the side, where the sun falls,
        beautifully, endlessly, sparkling, you go.
With the enchanted dawn wind, you went.

When I look at the sky in the morning before dawn after a pahko, *I think of this song. The growing flower is the light of the sun pushing back the darkness of the night until it disappears to the west. Don Lupe taught me this song.*

SEWAILO SEVOLI

Sewailo sevoli sevoli
  awane hisane
Sewailo sevoli sevoli
  awane hisaneee

Sewailo sevoli sevoli
  awane hisane
Sewailo sevoli sevoli
  awane hisaneee

Sewailo sevoli sevoli
  awane hisane
Sewailo sevoli sevoli
  awane hisaneee

Ayamansu seyewailo
  huyata naisukuni
    tevulia yukuta wecheko
     sewaheka mak ne
      awane hisane
Sewailo sevoli sevoli
  awane hisaneee

FLOWER-COVERED FLY

Flower-covered fly, fly,
  my antlers, I will unfold.
Flower-covered fly, fly,
  my antlers, I will unfold.

Flower-covered fly, fly,
  my antlers, I will unfold.
Flower-covered fly, fly,
  my antlers, I will unfold.

Flower-covered fly, fly,
  my antlers, I will unfold.
Flower-covered fly, fly,
  my antlers, I will unfold.

Over there, in the center
  of the flower-covered wilderness,
    when the summer rains fall,
    with the flower wind, I,
     my antlers, I will unfold.
Flower-covered fly, fly,
  my antlers, I will unfold.

When the summer rains come in late June or July everything begins to grow and there are more flies around then. In this song the deer is talking to the flower-covered fly and telling him that his antlers are growing, or unfolding. In Yaqui yotune *means to grow.* Hisane *means to unfold.*

Yaquis talk about many different flies, special flies, in the songs and in our culture. There is a yoko sevo'i, *spotted fly, who has a part in the killing the deer ceremony. And the* teka sevo'i, *heaven fly, is believed to bring bad news or to foretell disaster. Teka sevo'i is a large fly that is called the horsefly.*

I learned this song from Don Lupe.

TOLO PAKUNI	TO THE LIGHT BLUE OUTSIDE

Aa yeweli hiweka
    tolo pakuni
        tolo pakun hikawi
Yeweli hiweka
    tolo pakuni
        tolo pakun hikawiii

Aa yeweli hiweka
    tolo pakuni
        tolo pakun hikawi
Yeweli hiweka
    tolo pakuni
        tolo pakun hikawiii

Aa yeweli hiweka
    tolo pakuni
        tolo pakun hikawi
Yeweli hiweka
    tolo pakuni
        tolo pakun hikawiii

Aa wainavo su
    itou weyekai
Wainavo su
    itou vuitema
Yeweli hiweka
    tolo pakuni
        tolo pakun hikawiii

Aa look out,
    to the light blue outside,
        up to the light blue outside.
Look out,
    to the light blue outside,
        up to the light blue outside.

Aa look out,
    to the light blue outside,
        up to the light blue outside.
Look out,
    to the light blue outside,
        up to the light blue outside.

Aa look out,
    to the light blue outside,
        up to the light blue outside.
Look out,
    to the light blue outside,
        up to the light blue outside.

Aa from that side,
    to us, as he is walking,
From that side,
    to us, as he is running,
Look out,
    to the light blue outside,
        up to the light blue outside.

Some deer songs I like just for the way they sound. I heard this one from Miki Maaso and learned it from him. When tolo pakuni *is repeated, it is very beautiful to hear. When we sing this song, the deer dancer goes out to look at the sky. He goes out of the* ramá *and looks up.*

TUKA YOLEMEM

Tukawa yolemem
  hainhuni ka howaka
    hiokot sem hiusaka
Tuka tukawa yolememmm

Tukawa yolemem
  hainhuni ka howaka
    hiokot sem hiusaka
Tuka tukawa yolememmm

Tukawa yolemem
  hainhuni ka howaka
    hiokot sem hiusaka
Tuka tukawa yolememmm

Ayaman ne seyewailo
  naiyoli yo tuka aniwapo
    chewa yolemem
Hainhuni ka howaka
  hakun kukusiata
    hiokot sem hiyawa
Tuka tukawa yolememmm

NIGHT PEOPLE

Night people,
  though nothing is done to them,
    they go sounding pitifully.
Night, night people.

Night people,
  though nothing is done to them,
    they go sounding pitifully.
Night, night people.

Night people,
  though nothing is done to them,
    they go sounding pitifully.
Night, night people.

Over there, I, in the flower-covered,
  cherished, enchanted night world,
    I am more human.
Though nothing is done to them,
  somewhere, loudly,
    they go sounding pitifully.
Night, night people.

Don Jesús said that the night people in this song were bats. They make a sound like a cry or a whine as they fly around at night. Don Jesús said that it is Yevuku Yoleme *speaking in this song. He says that the bats are* yolemem, *people, but that he is* chewa yolemem, *more people or more human.* Yevuku Yolemem *had the ability to communicate with birds and animals.*

    An evaluator came to talk with us about our Yaqui bilingual program at Richey School. She was a Pueblo Indian woman from Denver. I think about her when I look at the concluding stanza of this deer song because she said, "Indians don't have adjectives. Only white people use a lot of adjectives. Indians get right to the point." The beauty of the tonua, *final stanza, is how all the adjectives pile up. Usually the* tonua *begins with aya-man or ayamansu, words that mean "over there." Then in most of Don Jesús' songs comes ne, I, usually referring to the deer or to Yevuku Yoleme. Then there is always a phrase which describes a place over there in the flower world. In that phrase the adjectives pile up like clouds against a mountain. In this song there are three:* seyewailo, *flower-covered;* yo, *enchanted; and* naiyoli, *cherished. When there is a long* tonua *and a singer has a strong voice to sing it all in one breath, the song sounds very beautiful.*

SIKILI SUVA'I

Siali vakata weyekapo ne su
    siali vaka heka vetukun
        ni kateka
Sikili suvawi sikili suvawiii

Siali vakata weyekapo ne su
    siali vaka heka vetukun
        ni kateka
Sikili suvawi sikili suvawiii

Siali vakata weyekapo ne su
    siali vaka heka vetukun
        ni kateka
Sikili suvawi sikili suvawiii

Ayaman ne seyewailo
    naiyoli yo huya aniwapo
        chewa yolemem
Siali vaka heka vetukun
    ni kateka
Sikili suvawi sikili suvawiii

RED QUAIL

Where the green bamboo stands,
    under the green bamboo breeze,
        I sit.
Red quail, red quail.

Where the green bamboo stands,
    under the green bamboo breeze,
        I sit.
Red quail, red quail.

Where the green bamboo stands,
    under the green bamboo breeze,
        I sit.
Red quail, red quail.

Over there, I, in the flower-covered,
    cherished, enchanted wilderness world,
        I am more human.
Under the green bamboo breeze,
    I sit.
Red quail, red quail.

"Who is more human?" I asked Don Jesús after he taught me this song. "Well, he is the same *Yevuku Yoeme, Yevuku Yoeme,*" he told me. If he would not have told me that, I would have thought that the song was talking about the deer, but I guess it is the *Yevuku Yoeme sitting out there talking to the red quail.*

Red quail are called bobwhite quail in English. Don Jesús said that the red quail live up in the mountains, in the Vakateteve Mountains east of the Yaqui villages. Vakateteve means tall bamboo in Yaqui. There is tall bamboo that grows by the springs up in the Vakateteve Mountains.

KAU SATEMA

Kau satema
  kowema
    kowema
      koyowe
Kau satema
  kowema
    kowema
      koyoweee

Kau satema
  kowema
    kowema
      koyowe
Kau satema
  kowema
    kowema
      koyoweee

Kau satema
  kowema
    kowema
      koyowe
Kau satema
  kowema
    kowema
      koyoweee

Ayaman ne seyewailo
  teweli kauta heheka vetukun
    koyowe
Kau satema
  kowema
    kowema
      koyoweee

MOUNTAIN BUZZARD

Mountain buzzard,
  hover,
    hover,
      hovering.
Mountain buzzard,
  hover,
    hover,
      hovering.

Mountain buzzard,
  hover,
    hover,
      hovering.
Mountain buzzard,
  hover,
    hover,
      hovering.

Mountain buzzard,
  hover,
    hover,
      hovering.
Mountain buzzard,
  hover,
    hover,
      hovering.

Over there, I, under the shadow
  of the flower-covered, deep blue mountain,
    I am hovering.
Mountain buzzard,
  hover,
    hover,
      hovering.

Yaquis call all vultures wirum. Kau satema *is one kind that we call mountain buzzard. They say that mountain buzzards were very big, but that they haven't seen them for a long time. Perhaps they were condors.*

I learned this song from Don Jesús. It is a tohakteme, *a bouncing one. I can sing a* tohakteme *to give a deer dancer a chance to show off his ability to dance, or we can use it to show a dancer he should not be too proud. The* tohakteme *has a special rhythm that is hard to dance to.*

These bird songs usually come late during the night. When we sing them, the pahkolam *and the deer dancer will play with them and act out the words. The dancer will put his arms out and whirl like a vulture in this one.*

CHUKULI POUTELA

Aa tolo bwiapo yeyewe
  chukuli yo poutela
Saniloapo yeyewe
  chukuli yo poutelaaa

Aa tolo bwiapo yeyewe
  chukuli yo poutela
Saniloapo yeyewe
  chukuli yo poutelaaa

Aa tolo bwiapo yeyewe
  chukuli yo poutela
Saniloapo yeyewe
  chukuli yo poutelaaa

Ayamansu seyewailo
  yoyo kauta vepa
    yeyewe
Tolo bwiapo yeyewe
  chukuli yo poutela
Saniloapo yeyewe
  chukuli yo poutelaaa

BLACK COWBIRD

Aa upon the light blue earth, you play,
  black, enchanted cowbird.
Within the grove, you play,
  black, enchanted cowbird.

Aa upon the light blue earth, you play,
  black, enchanted cowbird.
Within the grove, you play,
  black, enchanted cowbird.

Aa upon the light blue earth, you play,
  black, enchanted cowbird.
Within the grove, you play,
  black, enchanted cowbird.

Over there, upon the top
  of the flower-covered, enchanted mountain,
    you play.
Upon the light blue earth, you play,
  black, enchanted cowbird.
Within the grove, you play,
  black, enchanted cowbird.

The poutela *is a small black bird that sounds in the early morning hours before dawn. The deer must be talking to the* poutela. *The* poutela *is called the brown-headed cowbird by English speakers. I learned this song from Miki Maaso.*

MALISU KA SEATENE

Inika tae valita yeu yumako
   u malisu ka seatene
Inika tae valita yeu yumako
   u malisu ka seateneee

Inika tae valita yeu yumako
   u malisu ka seatene
Inika tae valita yeu yumako
   u malisu ka seateneee

Inika tae valita yeu yumako
   u malisu ka seatene
Inika tae valita yeu yumako
   u malisu ka seateneee

Iyikaine seyewailo machilo aniwata
   kalasoita hikausu chatuko
      im yo bwiapo naikim am mamachiasu
         u malisu ka seatene
Inika tae valita yeu yumako
   u malisu ka seateneee

THE FAWN WILL NOT MAKE FLOWERS

This daytime coolness reaches out,
   the fawn will not make flowers.
This daytime coolness reaches out,
   the fawn will not make flowers.

This daytime coolness reaches out,
   the fawn will not make flowers.
This daytime coolness reaches out,
   the fawn will not make flowers.

This daytime coolness reaches out,
   the fawn will not make flowers.
This daytime coolness reaches out,
   the fawn will not make flowers.

This flower-covered dawn world rises up brightly,
   here when they divide
      the enchanted earth with light,
         the fawn will not make flowers.
When this daytime coolness comes out,
   the fawn will not make flowers.

This is an alva bwikam, *a morning service song, which I learned from Don Lupe. It is say-
ing that the* pahko *will soon be over and then the deer, the fawn, will be gone back to the
flower world. The song talks about the way the rays of the dawn sun fan out to divide up
the earth with lines of light.*

*During this song the deer dancer blesses the ground. When he is dancing in front of us
in the* ramá *he will dance first to the east, then to the north, then to the south, and finally
to the west. He does this to bless the four directions and all the earth. At the same time the*
maehto *will be saying his morning service prayers. Sometimes he will say a prayer called
the* alavalo. *When he does, the* moro *takes candles from the altar and puts one in front of
each of us in the* kolensia. *He puts one in front of each musician and dancer. After the
deer dancer and the* pahkolam *finish dancing, they take their candles out to the patio
cross and leave them there.*

Seatene, *make flower, is like other Yaqui verbs such as* katene, *make a house.*

TOSALI WIIKIT

Tosali wiikit, tosali wiikit,
  haisempo auka witosalita
    kala witwitti wikema
Tosali wiikit, tosali wiikit,
  haisempo auka witosalita
    kala witwitti wikemaaa

Tosali wiikit, tosali wiikit,
  haisempo auka witosalita
    kala witwitti wikema
Tosali wiikit, tosali wiikit,
  haisempo auka witosalita
    kala witwitti wikemaaa

Tosali wiikit, tosali wiikit,
  haisempo auka witosalita
    kala witwitti wikema
Tosali wiikit, tosali wiikit,
  haisempo auka witosalita
    kala witwitti wikemaaa

Ayamansu seyewailo
  huyata naisukuni
    senu yo huya aniwapo vai vakuliapo
      kala witwitti wikema
Tosali wiikit, tosali wiikit,
  haisempo auka witosalita
    kala witwitti wikemaaa

WHITE BIRD

White bird, white bird,
  what happened to you that
    you are endlessly pulling the web straight?
White bird, white bird,
  what happened to you that
    you are endlessly pulling the web straight?

White bird, white bird,
  what happened to you that
    you are endlessly pulling the web straight?
White bird, white bird,
  what happened to you that
    you are endlessly pulling the web straight?

White bird, white bird,
  what happened to you that
    you are endlessly pulling the web straight?
White bird, white bird,
  what happened to you that
    you are endlessly pulling the web straight?

Over there, in the center
  of the flower-covered wilderness,
    upon one cool enchanted wilderness world branch,
      you are endlessly pulling the web straight.
White bird, white bird,
  what happened to you that
    you are endlessly pulling the web straight?

This song is about a spider. People ask us to sing it. That is why I put it here in the amateur hour. During this time after the morning service anyone can come and ask us to use our instruments to sing with or they can ask us to sing something for them so that they can try to dance deer or pahkola dances. We call these songs limohnaim *(donated ones). Maybe they ask for this one a lot now because there is a record out with a deer song by this title on it. During the amateur hour is a time when I might hear a new deer song that I hadn't heard before. I enjoy the chance to take a break and listen to those who have learned songs from somebody somewhere else.*

I learned this song from a singer they call Hopom *who is from Loma Vahkom.*

ILI MASO

Ili maso
    huyapo bwiapo
        komsu sika
Ili maso
    huyapo bwiapo
        komsu sika

Ili maso
    huyapo bwiapo
        komsu sika
Ili maso
    huyapo bwiapo
        komsu sika

Ili maso
    huyapo bwiapo
        komsu sika
Ili maso
    huyapo bwiapo
        komsu sika

Matchuka teweli bam
    yoko bampo se heka
        notteka toloko bwiapo komsu sika
            sewa hekapo komsu hiyawa
Ili maso
    huyapo bwiapo
        komsu sika

LITTLE DEER

Little deer,
    within the wilderness, upon the earth,
        down, he went.
Little deer,
    within the wilderness, upon the earth,
        down, he went.

Little deer,
    within the wilderness, upon the earth,
        down, he went.
Little deer,
    within the wilderness, upon the earth,
        down, he went.

Little deer,
    within the wilderness, upon the earth,
        down, he went.
Little deer,
    within the wilderness, upon the earth,
        down, he went.

Morning came, dark blue water,
    in the spotted water, you drank,
        returning on the light blue earth, down, you went,
            on the flower dawn wind, down, you are sounding.
Little deer,
    within the wilderness, upon the earth,
        down, he went.

In this song I see a little fawn walking down the slope of a mountain. The song says that the fawn is sounding, making a sound. Maybe it has lost its mother and is crying for her.

The tonua, *concluding stanza, of this song does not begin with* ayaman ne *or* aya-mansu *like most of the others I sing. When I have one that is like this, I tell the deer dancer to listen. I tell him the first word of the* tonua, *and I tell him to listen for that.*

Yoko means spotted in English, but it is talking about the way the water looks to the little deer. The water is clear but it has patches of green suspended in it, so the deer says that it is spotted.

I heard Marcos Savivae from Potam sing this song.

SEWA HULI

Sewa huli
  haikunsa usyolisi sewa temula
    ne se muteka teki
Haikunsa usyolisi sewa temula
  ne se muteka teki
    sewa huliii

Sewa huli
  haikunsa usyolisi sewa temula
    ne se muteka teki
Haikunsa usyolisi sewa temula
  ne se muteka teki
    sewa huliii

Sewa huli
  haikunsa usyolisi sewa temula
    ne se muteka teki
Haikunsa usyolisi sewa temula
  ne se muteka teki
    sewa huliii

Ayamansu seyewailo
  saniloata naisukunisu
    masa'asai sewata
      sewa nat se weche vetuku
        uyolisi sewa temula
          ne se muteka teki
Haikunsa usyolisi sewa temula
  ne se muteka teki
    sewa huliii

FLOWER BADGER

Flower badger,
  where have you placed me,
    a beautiful, rolled, flower pillow?
Where have you placed me,
  a beautiful, rolled, flower pillow,
    flower badger?

Flower badger,
  where have you placed me,
    a beautiful, rolled, flower pillow?
Where have you placed me,
  a beautiful, rolled, flower pillow,
    flower badger?

Flower badger,
  where have you placed me,
    a beautiful, rolled, flower pillow?
Where have you placed me,
  a beautiful, rolled, flower pillow,
    flower badger?

Over there, in the center
  of the flower-covered grove,
    under the masa'asai flower,
      where the flower falls,
        a beautiful, rolled, flower pillow,
          you placed me.
Where have you placed me,
  a beautiful, rolled, flower pillow,
    flower badger?

Deer songs are sometimes difficult to understand unless they are explained by the singer. When I asked Don Lupe about this one after he taught it to me, he told me it was about a badger and a sidewinder snake. The badger grabbed the sidewinder and killed it. Then the badger tossed the snake among the falling blossoms under the masa'asai. *The* masa'asai *is called Queen's Wreath by some people here in Arizona. I guess that the sidewinder was coiled up, that's why the song says it was* temula, *rolled up in a ball. When I first heard the song I thought* temula *was a form of* tetemula, *to kick. But when I talked with my aunt in Potam, she told me* temula *means balled up or rolled up in a ball.* Teki *means "laid," but in this translation that doesn't come out right, so we decided to translate it "placed."*

HILUKIAM TOVOKTIANE

Imete itom sea hilukiam
  tovoktiane saila
Imete itom sea hilukiam
  tovoktiane sailaaa

Imete itom sea hilukiam
  tovoktiane saila
Imete itom sea hilukiam
  tovoktiane sailaaa

Imete itom sea hilukiam
  tovoktiane saila
Imete itom sea hilukiam
  tovoktiane sailaaa

Ayaman ne seyewailo
  yevuku yolemta sea tevatchiapo
    yeuwatuko lutine
      chaiwatuko lutine
Imete itom sea hilukiam
  tovoktiane sailaaa

PICK UP RASPERS

These our flower raspers,
  let us pick up, little brother.
These our flower raspers,
  let us pick up, little brother.

These our flower raspers,
  let us pick up, little brother.
These our flower raspers,
  let us pick up, little brother.

These our flower raspers,
  let us pick up, little brother.
These our flower raspers,
  let us pick up, little brother.

Over there, I, in Yevuku Yoleme's
  flower-covered, flower patio
    what was played will end,
      what was shouted will end.
These our flower raspers,
  let us pick up, little brother.

This song tells the deer that we are ready to stop singing. It tells him that the songs and the games are over for this pahko. *Don Jesús taught me this song.*

SEA YOLEME HUYA SIKA

Sea yoleme
  sea yo huyawi sika
    sea yo huyawe sika
Sea yoleme
  sea yo huyawi sika
    sea yo huyawe sikaaa

Sea yoleme
  sea yo huyawi sika
    sea yo huyawe sika
Sea yoleme
  sea yo huyawi sika
    sea yo huyawe sikaaa

Sea yoleme
  sea yo huyawi sika
    sea yo huyawe sika
Sea yoleme
  sea yo huyawi sika
    sea yo huyawe sikaaa

Ayaman ne seyewailo
  huyata naisukuni
    seata yosi wechepo
      seata yosi hekapo
Sea yoleme
  sea yo huyawi sika
    sea yo huyawe sikaaa

FLOWER PERSON IS GOING TO THE WILDERNESS

Flower person,
  to the enchanted flower wilderness is going,
    to the enchanted flower wilderness is going.
Flower person,
  to the enchanted flower wilderness is going,
    to the enchanted flower wilderness is going.

Flower person,
  to the enchanted flower wilderness is going,
    to the enchanted flower wilderness is going.
Flower person,
  to the enchanted flower wilderness is going,
    to the enchanted flower wilderness is going.

Flower person,
  to the enchanted flower wilderness is going,
    to the enchanted flower wilderness is going.
Flower person,
  to the enchanted flower wilderness is going,
    to the enchanted flower wilderness is going.

Over there, I, in the center
  of the flower-covered wilderness,
    where the flower falls with enchantment,
      where the flower blows with enchantment,
Flower person,
  to the enchanted flower wilderness is going,
    to the enchanted flower wilderness is going.

I learned this procession song from Don Jesús. While it is being sung the deer dancer and the pahkolam *will go with the* maehto *and the church people in a procession to take the holy figures back to the church. When the deer dancer gets to the patio cross, we stop the song. This is the last deer song of the* pahko.

  The song talks about the deer, the flower person. He is going back to the flower world, to the place of enchantment, back to his enchanted home.

22. To celebrate the blessing of the village grounds ...

24. After months of practice ...

23. *Yoem Pueblo residents and visitors crowd …*

25. *The altar is ready …*

4

Ka ne huni
  into ne inia aniat
    ne na ne welamsisimne
Kia ne ka ne huni
  into ne inia aniat
    ne na ne welamsisimne

Kia ne ka ne huni
  into ne inia aniat
    ne na ne welamsisimne
Kia ne ka ne huni
  into ne inia aniat
    ne na ne welamsisimne

Ayaman ne
  seyewailo saniloata fayalikun
    weyekai
Kia ne yevuku yolemta wikoli
  ne yo yumatakai
Yevuku yolemta vaka hiuwai
  ne yo yumatakai
Ka ne huni
  into ne inia aniat
    ne na ne welamsisimne

Never again I,
  will I on this world,
    I, around will I be walking.
Just I, never again I,
  will I on this world,
    I, around will I be walking.

Just I, never again I,
  will I on this world,
    I, around will I be walking.
Just I, never again I,
  will I on this world,
    I, around will I be walking.

Over there, I,
  in an opening in the flower-covered grove,
    as I am walking,
Just I, Yevuku Yoleme's bow
  overpowered me in an enchanted way.
Yevuku Yoleme's bamboo arrow
  overpowered me in an enchanted way.
Never again I,
  will I on this world,
    I, around will I be walking.

Don Jesús Yoilo'i
Yoem Pueblo
May 9, 1981

26. Summer rain clouds gather over Yoem Pueblo …

4
MASO ME'EWA
KILLING THE DEER

CONTEMPORARY YAQUIS often interpret the deer dancer as gathering the wilderness world into a symbol of earthly sacrifice and of spiritual life after death. Explaining the *maaso's* regalia in 1979, Felipe wrote:

Everything the deer dancer uses in his dance has held life. The cocoon rattles around his legs were once homes of the butterflies. As we dance we want the butterfly to know that, even if he is dead, his spirit is alive and his house is occupied. The gourd rattles in the dancer's hands give life to the plant world. The rattles around the dancer's waist are deer hooves. They represent the millions of deer who have died so that men might live.[1]

And there is the story of Victor Flores, a seventeen-year-old Yaqui, who died in 1984 of leukemia. During the weeks of hospitalization before his death, Victor inspired the medical staff and other patients. "Even though he hurt and he suffered, he did not fight it," a medical social worker said of Victor's approach to death, "it was just total acceptance of the reality." During this period of suffering, Victor carved a clay figure of a Yaqui deer dancer. He requested that his parents give the statue to the pediatrics unit of the hospital so that "other sick children could see it and perhaps draw strength from it." Yaqui religious leader Anselmo Valencia spoke at the hospital during the dedication of the statue six months after Victor's death. He explained that "to the Yaquis, the deer dancer symbolizes the rebirth of the soul after earthly death," and, after he blessed the statue, he said, "Victor knew he would be born again."[2]

Parallels between the *maaso* and the sacrificial victim Christians call the lamb of God have been noted by non-Yaqui interpreters. But, in our understanding, contemporary Yaqui culture brings the figure of the deer dancer together with the figure of Christ only implicitly and very tentatively.

We have reported earlier how the epithet "flower person," when it is used in a deer song sung on Holy Saturdays, seems to allude not only to the *saila maso* of aboriginal Yaqui belief but to the risen Christ as well.[3] As an instance of the reverse, we note the paintings of the *maaso* that Yaqui artist Danny Leon created on stoles in the early 1980s so that, in the spirit of Vatican II, Catholic priests could allude to the image of *saila maso* in their ministry. Such interplay is complex and reciprocal, and, according to Edward H. Spicer, over the long years of contact it has resulted in "a conjunction of world views" that cannot be explained by simplistic models of culture change. We agree. In the present instance we note that after more than three and one-half centuries of dialogue with Catholicism, not to mention various other versions of Christianity in this century, Yaquis continue to hold the figures of Christ and the *maaso* explicitly apart in their ceremonies.

The best-known Yaqui ceremony is the village drama carried out each spring during the Easter season. This Yaqui version of the passion and death of Christ is enacted in all of the Sonoran Yaqui towns and at least four Yaqui communities in Arizona as well. Characterized by Spicer as "the tragedy of the Chapayekas," it stretches across the forty days of Lent to a climactic ritual battle in which the Chapayekas are defeated on Holy Saturday morning.[4] Several explicit representations of Jesus Christ are employed by Yaquis during this extended drama. They include a statue, which is called "the Nazarene"; a candle, referred to as "the Light of the World"; and one of the masked Chapayekas, who, as he takes on the additional role of Jesus Christ as a very old man for a brief period on Holy Thursday, is called "*O'ola*, old man."[5] The deer dancer and the deer singers play a role in the defense of the church during the Gloria, as we explained earlier when we gave translations of the three deer songs Don Jesús traditionally sang on that occasion. However, they have only a very peripheral role in the whole of this great Lenten drama, and the *maaso* stands significantly apart from the representations of Christ which we have mentioned.

Rather, the *maaso*'s role as a figure of spiritual life after death is realized in another Yaqui dramatic tradition that is no less important to Yaquis for being less known to the world beyond their villages. This other drama of suffering, life, death, and spiritual continuance relates not to the realm of the church and heaven that so dominates "the tragedy of the Chapayekas," but rather to the realm of the *pahko ramá* and the wilderness world of aboriginal Yaqui belief. Yaquis call this drama *maso me'ewa:* killing the deer.

Pahkolam

As we have seen, when the deer singers perform at a *pahko*, their singing is always surrounded by the varied performance of the *pahkolam*. Like the deer singers, the *pahkolam* are men of words. The eldest *pahkola* opens and closes the *pahko* with sermons of great dignity and solemnity. Throughout the *pahko*, the *pahkolam* serve as ceremonial hosts, maintaining an on-going verbal exchange with each other and the crowd as they pass out water and cigarettes. In these exchanges, "the passing stream of [community] activities is commented on, twisted into odd forms through the license accorded them, and tossed back for comment to the more articulate persons in the crowd."[6] During such exchanges the *pahkolam* avoid smiling or looking directly at anyone. Usually they gaze off into the distance as they speak in high-pitched voices. The voice quality they use has a very distinctive timbre, and they consistently "misuse" everyday Yaqui speech in a special way. When they tell stories, they may imitate the speech of the characters in the stories as well. As their deer singers complete a song, it is not unusual to hear the *pahkolam* giving a whining, sing-song parody as an echo.

The *pahkolam* are also accomplished dancers and masters of mime. They are the first to dance at every *pahko*. Initially, they dance to the stringed music of the violin and the harp; then, after a break, they move their masks around to cover their faces and dance to the *tampaleo*'s flute and drum. During both performances they dance one at a time, usually in order, youngest to eldest. Both kinds of *pahkolam* music are purely instrumental, but the tunes are named, often for birds, animals, and other living things in the wilderness world, but sometimes for domestic animals as well. There are songs for the badger, the rat, the turtle, various snakes, horses, and others. *Wikit bwikam* (bird songs) are considered *yeu bwikam* (play songs), and the *pahkolam* are expected to imitate the bird named in the song in the dance. During these songs they are also expected to mime or mock the deer dance. Don Jesús' son Aleho, who has been a *pahkola* as well as a deer dancer, told us: "You don't play when it is not a game song. If it is not a game song and the *pahkolam* approach the deer to play, the deer may kick at them."

The dancing of the *pahkolam* alternates with that of the deer throughout the night, and the *pahkolam* rarely miss the opportunity during the play songs to counterpoint the dance rhythms of the evening by mimicking the movement of the deer. The mimicry may grow into outright pantomime and slapsticks, and late in the night it may flower into more elaborate farces. Yaquis often refer to these as "skits" in English. In their own language they are called *yeuwame*, games. Several of these make up *maso me'ewa*.

❋ The corner I come into is small and packed with men. Their hats bob before me as they strain to see into the *ramá*. It is decorated with fresh, green cottonwood boughs hung over every surface. That and the single bulb hanging from the ceiling are about all I can see. I find a milk crate, and step up over the hats. The deer dancer stands just beyond the light, arms crossed, staring off into the night, totally removed from the mayhem that is being played out around him.

A tall, young Yaqui crowds up beside my milk crate: hey man, you look like John Denver. How you doing, John?

Fine, what's happening?

They're hunting, he says, they're crazy and they're hunting for a raccoon. Crazy as a coon. I'm an Aggie, that's what the Aggies say. Have a beer, John. See my hat, I'm an Aggie.

Sure enough, his feed-store hat says Texas A&M. Off behind the deer dancer on the other side of the *ramá*, a priestly old man and women in shawls appear before the altar and begin to sing slow polyphonic chants from books. The *matachinim* dance back and forth out in the plaza, the streamers on their crowns fluttering as they work methodically through their line dance steps to the lilting melody of violins and guitars. All around the edges of the plaza people laugh and talk. Behind us in the darkness, pop-tops snap. It's Saturday night, party night, Aggie tells me, and before us the *pahkolam* have center stage.

There are four, and, from where Aggie and I stand, I can only see their heads. They all wear straw hats. Not Yaqui straws, but the tourist kinds. Each one is different: one has a brown plastic inset

along the front of the brim, another looks like a golf hat with a flashy fan of feathers on the side, a third has a pelt on it. The tail trails off the back, Davy-Crockett style. Each of the hats is torn open on top so that the *pahkola*'s topknot stands up through. One of the hats is opened up like a can of beans, another is pulled open from a cross-shaped cut so that it looks like a ragged four-petaled flower, another one is just bashed open, as if someone shoved a fist through it.

Two of the *pahkolam* get the crowd around us going with their hat routines. One pulls his all the way past his chin, down onto his shoulders, the other does the same. They gag and choke and whine for the crowd. They play with the chin straps, pulling them up so tight around their straw hat collars that their tongues are forced out. Any excuse to grimace at the crowd seems good enough. What one tries, the other imitates.

One *pahkola* has a very round face and can do things with his eyes and eyebrows. His face is wide-open, lost, bewildered, an innocent fallen into a confusing situation. The other has a little mustache which wiggles knowingly through all the parodies he gives of his partner's faces.

There is scuffling. The Davy-Crockett *pahkola* shoots up onto a folding chair in the corner of the *ramá*. He has a very long face and, as he climbs around on the chair and tries to get higher up the corner post among the cottonwood leaves, he whines and whimpers like a treed animal and plays to the crowd for mercy. The deer dancer stands statuesque, still gazing off into the night.

The other *pahkolam* have come up

with little bows and arrows tipped with corn cobs. The long-faced *pahkola* jumps down from the folding chair and suddenly pops up in our corner, first jumping around on a bench, then, after a well-advertised but daring leap, he hangs high from the corner post of the *ramá*. From there he plays to the crowd of men around us frantically. Arrows fly. Finally a couple bounce off the back of the treed *pahkola* and down he goes. The others pounce on him growling and howling.

They got him, I say to Aggie, hoping for an explanation. But Aggie admires my running shoes. Did I know that he works with Yaqui athletes? Some of the best runners in Phoenix, man. He goes on to rip off a litany of accomplishments: high school marathons, state track meets, like that. I've been a *pahkola*, he says suddenly at the end of his list.

The *pahkolam* are back up and showing off the "skin" of the raccoon, offering it for sale by auction. The eldest *pahkola* has come up with a stenographer's pad and directs the affair. He wears a pair of huge, oversized sunglasses, lenses the size of cantaloupes. They are perched on the tip of his nose, upside down, of course. The bids roll in, going from little numbers to great big ones. The *pahkola* records them laboriously in his pad, muttering jokes in Yaqui that have the crowd going all the while.

"If you white people could understand them you'd put them on 'Saturday Night Live,' " Felipe's brother told me late one night as we watched the *pahkolam* at Yoem Pueblo. Here at Guadalupe, Aggie starts to explain something the *pahkola* has said, then he wants to tell me about his studies in landscape architecture at Texas A&M. Gonna be a Yaqui architect, John Denver, a *pahkola* architect.

Sweat is running down the faces of the *matachinim* as they dance on. The eldest *pahkola* adjusts those enormous sunglasses professorially, to the very tip of his nose, grasps his pencil ever so thoughtfully. Then he announces another bid. Aggie interrupts his report of how he will do a better job landscaping desert development to laugh appreciatively. The deer dancer rubs his arms and shifts his gaze to another part of the night.

Yeuwame: Games

A number of writers have described games that the *pahkolam* and the *maaso* enact. G. Montell writes of a "juego del venado y los coyotes" which he observed in Tlaxcala in the 1930s. Ralph Beals reports a dramatization he calls the "Play of the Deer" from his early Sonoran Yaqui research. Writing in *Pascua* (1940), Spicer says that Yaquis "speak of a mock deer hunt which took place at dawn or shortly after, in which the *pascolas* acted as hunters and went through an elaborate hunting scene, eventually catching the deer dancer, pretending to skin him, and carrying him home to their wives." At that time it was reported to Spicer that the mock deer hunt was "no longer carried out, although . . . it should be."[7] Not surprisingly, the most detailed description of such games comes from a Yaqui author.

In 1935–36, Refugio Savala gave Dr. John Provinse, a University of Arizona professor, a portfolio of writing which Savala had done at the urging of his teacher, Miss Thamar Richey. Included in this portfolio are narrative accounts of several of the *pahkolam*'s games. The accounts are early student writing by a young man working with his teacher to learn a third language. Perhaps for that reason they were not included in Savala's *Autobiography of a Yaqui Poet*, a memoir that demonstrates how well Savala eventually mastered the English language. We have edited the following accounts from the Provinse portfolio lightly, inserting some punctuation and changing spellings.

The Deer Hunt

The ground is prepared. Green brush is planted to give the scene of a forest. The deer hunt is played by the pahkolam *and the deer singers and dancer.*

The hunter has two sons. He sends the oldest to his neighbor to borrow the instruments with which they will perform the satirical songs for the hunting dance.

"Go into the forest to the camp where my friend is and give him this canteen of sweet water. Tell him this is from the stream on the border of which we are camping, so he may also taste it. After he has tasted the water, tell him that I sent you to borrow the hirukiam.*"*

The boy is so cowardly he is almost crying. He is afraid to go into the forest, because he knows that coyotes are abundant. Finally he departs.

When he arrives, he salutes them in a way of respect: "Dios em chania, achaim." When he was received, he began to tell the old men these things: "My fathers, your friend has the need of this errand and to you sent me. This canteen of water contains the sweet water from the stream that flows near our camp. My father desires that you should taste it, so that you may know that we are in a choice country. This one thing he also did. My father desires that you may let him know if by any chance in your family there is a girl that I could take in marriage." The old man answers him smiling.

"There are three girls in my family which I also desire to give in marriage, but tell your father to come here and select the one he likes most for you."

The boy returns to his father and merrily explains everything the old men told him. But his father did not send him for this purpose, and he gets so angry that he whips the boy. When the younger son was sent, he does the same thing in the end. Then their fathers goes to explain everything and to borrow from the old men the hirukiam. When he brings them, he and his two sons begin to sing a spring song. Their father says these words: "The cool eastern wind brings the spring blossom perfume to the shanty where I live." The two boys leave the hirukiam and look around and sense the wind. In the meantime, the man in charge of the deer dance [the moro] steals the hirukiam, and their father again whips them and makes them find the hirukiam. This happens until at last the singing is finished and the hirukiam are taken back to their owner.

In preparing for the hunt, they gather up some spicy weeds and burn them. With it they fume up their body all over so the deer won't sense them. The father and his older son dress in full hunt costume with bow and arrows. The younger son is a skillful dog "pochee" who helps them in the search of the game.

The hunt begins in the ramada where the deer and the pahkolam dance. The deer is chased out into the patio. The man in charge of the deer dance is with the deer. It hides behind him. Everytime the deer is found it sounds the rattles and runs. The boy is frightened by this and also runs, throwing his bow and arrow and hat away. Then his father whips him and makes him find the things he has lost. The dog runs about and barks. The hunter will shoot any person who happens to be near. In the ground the hunters dig, and water is found after a great deal of search. Then the deer is found and killed.

Sometimes the hunters carry the game on their shoulders and sometimes a burro carries it into the ramada. They get the skin, and they go into the woods and find tanning post. This is also a pahkola who stands among the crowd. The other pahkolam cut the post. When it is falling and someone is near, it happens that he or she gets a hard slap in the face from the pahkola who acts as the post. It is done even when it is cold in winter. Now when it is made into a good pelt the pahkolam begin to peddle it. After the measurement is figured out, it is bought with liquor. All the "water" that the pahkolam drink during the deer hunt is pure liquor.

The Rain

In the morning the pahkolam borrow the drum from the tampaleo. They begin to rumble with it, striking lightly the beams of the ramada with it. This is to produce the noise of the thunder, and the pahkolam make the lightning by sticking their tongues out. After this is done the three get all the gourd cups of the deer singers and get water from the big pan which is also the deer singers' instrument.

27. *Playing with the deer ...*

Then the pahkolam *will throw water on anyone who happens to be near, just like the rain. Many people run away and they chase them far out of the* ramá. *Sometimes people who fall asleep near the dance are awakened with the last, heaviest shower, which is the big pan of water. It is said that it is good luck to get soaked by this play rain, but the majority run away for shelter especially in winter.*

After the rain, again the pan of water is filled, and the dance continues for a short time with funny deer songs which the pahkolam *dance. When the deer hunt is going to be danced, it is begun after "The Rain."*[8]

These extraordinary narratives surely describe the burlesques of the deer hunt by the *pahkolam* mentioned by the scholars we quote above. When Spicer returned to this subject in 1965, as a part of his discussion of contexts for deer dancing in the culture of Mexico, he observed that many variations of such games existed. He also argued that they were a part of "the absurd world of the *pahkolam*" and not a part of what he thought of as the ritual of the deer dance itself.[9] We do not agree. Neither the scholars, who have mentioned the *pahkolam*'s games, nor Savala, who described them so vividly, note that they accompany the singing of fixed sets of deer songs. While these songs are not "scripts," they have an intimate relation to the *pahkolam*'s games. Indeed, the *pahkolam*'s burlesques and the deer singers' song sets come together to provide an expression of the very core of the ritual of the deer dance that is as powerful as any we know.

Maso Me'ewa: Killing the Deer

In January 1981, Felipe heard that a special ceremony he called *maso me'ewa*, killing the deer, would be held in the Yaqui village of Guadalupe, just south of Phoenix, Arizona. We attended that *pahko* Saturday night and Sunday morning, January 17 and 18, as a part of a large audience who enjoyed a series of *yeuwame*. These culminated in an elaborate parody of a deer hunt Sunday morning just after dawn. The absurd slapstick of the *pahkolam*, as they worked through parodies much like those described by Savala, captured the major attention of the audience. But through many of the plays, including the dawn deer hunt, the deer singers remained seated before their instruments, absorbed in performances of their own that attracted an equally attentive, if not large, audience. We did not have an opportunity to talk with the deer singers who performed on that occasion nor to record any of their songs. But later in the month, when we were in Potam for the weekend, we asked Don Jesús if there were special deer songs that went along with the *maso me'ewa*. "Of course," he replied.

We arranged to bring Don Jesús to Marana in May 1981 for a week. During that time we recorded the three song sets which, in Don Jesús' understanding, comprised all the deer songs sung during a *maso me'ewa*.[10]

According to Don Jesús, the games which make up a *maso me'ewa* are performed only during a *pahko* held to mark the first anniversary of the death of a relative, a *lutu pahko*. This ceremony is held to release the family from their year of mourning and to release the spirit of the departed from its final year of bondage on "this weeping earth."

The *lutu pahko* begins during the evening of the first day with an event called *vantea velaroawa*, flag vigil, which includes the singing of three deer songs. These three, according to Don Jesús, are the three that are normally used to open a *pahko*. Black yarn known as the *lutu* is tied around the neck of the family members signifying that the year of mourning is still in effect. Around noon on the second day this yarn, the *lutu*, is cut off. The *ramá* is decorated with cottonwood boughs so that it suggests a dense thicket in the wilderness world. Then the deer and *pahkola* dancing begins and continues into the evening with a sequence of songs such as we have given in the last section. Later in the night, "when the world turns," a series of *yeuwame* begins. Don Jesús described four: the first in which the *pahkolam* take on the role of Yaqui farmers who are bothered by a raccoon, the second in which they enact a hunt by mountain lions, a third in which they are hunters who pursue and kill a deer, and a fourth, which he considered optional, in which the *pahkolam* and the deer dancer enact the drama of rain. The final three have deer songs.

The literary power that Yaqui song words can create when they appear singly or in sequences is considerable. Their images are often vivid and evocative of the world they describe, even to an audience with a minimal experience with that world. What gives those individual songs and song sequences a greater power is the perception of the narrative coherence they realize by being an expression of the equation upon which the aboriginal part of Yaqui religion is based. That equation links the gritty world of the *pahko ramá* with the ethereal flower world, a world seen with one unseen, a world that is very much here with one that is always over there. Within this equation of worlds, we can perceive deer songs as sequences of scenes that have the unity of the flower world they depict. In the statements of deer singers, we are told that *saila maso* is always at the center of those sequences. As Loretto Salvatierra explained, deer songs tell what "the animal that has come sees." It is only when they come into *saila maso*'s view that the subjects of the deer songs "will be known and can be said."

The sequence of deer songs that we translated in the previous section demonstrates that other points of view can be and are represented. *Yevuku Yoleme*, the sidewinder snake, and others with whom *saila maso* shares the flower world are given a voice in the songs. There is, too, the omniscient voice of the deer singers themselves, describing *saila maso* in the third person, talking to him in the second, and, sometimes, pushing against the limits of the equation that encloses their art with unmistakable irony:

> So now this is the deer person,
> > so he is the deer person,
> > > so he is the real deer person.

But always the voices of the deer singers return to represent the definitive persona of *saila maso*. There are many voices in his one, and it is his perspective that gives coherence and continuity to the story deer singers put together in their sequences in a loose and episodic way.

As we discussed *maso me'ewa*, Don Jesús taught us that deer singers use more structured combinations of songs. We call these combinations song "sets," in order to contrast them with the song "sequences" we have described thus far. When they appear in song sets, Yaqui deer-song words achieve an even greater literary power. What we say here parallels the case and the thesis proposed by Donald Bahr with regard to Pima and Papago song texts. He writes that "among the Pimans song becomes a powerful literary form through the use of multisong sets," and continues to argue that "the study of isolated songs would miss the power of the literature."[11] One reason, then, that the *maso me'ewa* song sets Don Jesús recorded for us take on an imaginative power greater than that represented in songs sung individually or in sequences during a *pahko* is that they have a closer and more fixed relation to one another. But there are other equally important reasons.

One is the dramatic context in which the song sets are performed. While they clearly are not what we would call scripts, the words to these song sets have a very close relation to the burlesques which the *pahkolam* perform as they are sung. We do not know enough about the relationship to detail it much beyond the comments we quote from Don Jesús. But it seems likely that the relationship between song words and dance act is an extension in kind of that which we discussed in connection with individual *yeu bwikam* (play songs). That is, the deer singers create a verbal image, and the *pahkolam* are expected to give a kinetic interpretation of it in their absurd mode.

A third reason the song sets we recorded from Don Jesús achieve a literary power extraordinary even in Yaqui tradition is that they are *his*. That is, they were the performances of a mature, accomplished verbal artist who, over the course of his long association with the arts of the *pahko*, developed a repertory of songs that were uniquely his own, even as they satisfied the traditional conventions of the genre. It should be evident, by contrast, that the sequence of songs that Felipe recorded in the last section is stylistically eclectic. He draws on the styles of the many singers he has worked with in putting together his own performances. This is how it should be. It is the way "one with a good memory will catch on." With more experience, and the gift of a long life, it seems inevitable that Felipe's own style will emerge. When we recorded him, Don Jesús was already at the end of such a long life. We comment on some aspects of his style as we introduce our translations of his song sets.

U Choparao: The Raccoon

The *maso me'ewa* begins with a farce that does not have deer songs. Rather it is performed to the accompaniment of the *pahkolam*'s violin and harp players. So far as we know there are no deer songs about domestic animals or crops. However, the violin and the harp players, as well as the *tampaleo*, who plays the flute and drum songs, have melodies that are named for cows, horses, and other domestic animals. This burlesque is as much about agriculture as it is about hunting. It seems to us, in fact, to be a kind of agriculturalists' parody of a hunt. The deer singers indulge the *pahkolam*/farmers by lending their advice and instruments, but they and the deer remain aloof from any active participation. We are tempted to see this as an expression of the vaunted disdain of some native hunting peoples for the agriculture introduced to them by Europeans, but, of course, Yaquis practiced a successful floodplain agriculture with corn, squash, beans, pumpkins, amaranth, and other crops, long before they invited the Jesuits onto their lands with other grains and a complete barnyard in 1617.[12] With regard to the Papago deer-hunting ritual, Underhill, Bahr, and their Papago collaborators report that "the overall explanation is that the deer was killed to make the new farm crops nourishing."[13] We have not heard any Yaquis make this connection, and our question about it to Don Jesús did not make any sense to him. Nevertheless, in the context of *maso me'ewa*, the hunt of the raccoon by farmers serves as an effective foreshadowing of the greater hunts in the wilderness world that are to come later.

Don Jesús gave the following description of the raccoon hunt. As he recorded it, he illustrated the dialogue of the *pahkolam* by shifting into their high, whining tone. Don Jesús made a very convincing bark out of the phrase "*um katek, um katek*," which we translate as "there he is, there he is."

That is the violin player's part. He will play the raccoon song. He will start the raccoon song. The deer singers will not sing anything. The violin and the harp will work with that.
    When the raccoon song begins, the pahkolam *will start. Three* pahkolam *will be oxen.*

The oxen will be sent outside. They themselves will be sent outside. Then the elder pahkola will remain. He will arrive to the deer singers. He will ask them for the oxen.

"There I have a little irrigated land," he will say. "Narrow it is, but wide," he will say. "There I want to plant a little corn," he will say. "Fathers, I want to borrow the oxen," he will say to the deer singers.

"Oh, yes, they are somewhere out there walking, lying in the shade of some ironwood trees picnicking," they will say. "One might be called Alasan, one Hohko, and one Vayu. They walk over there. Look for them over there," they will say to him.

Later from there he will guide them back. Then when the cows arrive at the water [the water drummer's basin], they will let them drink. After giving them some water, they will put on the yoke. Then they will plow. They will just be poking with a bamboo cane or something. Then they will rake with an old burlap sack. Then they will plant with just a bucket of dirt. And after they plant, they will let them go outside again.

Then the elder pahkola will go to the tampaleo and borrow the drum. "Here we are going to stay up all night with the little corn we planted," he will say. "The raccoons will eat our corn." Then he will borrow the raspers, and the three will sit together and play. They'll say just anything. They are just playing around. Then they will sleep.

Then one will be made into a dog. The dog, the one who is made into a dog, will walk around the others. Then the one who is going to be a raccoon will be sent outside. When they have fallen asleep again, the raccoon will enter and will dig around. Then he will grab the asses of the ones who are sleeping. "The dog, the sleepy dog! He did not sense it," they will say. Then they will look for the raccoon.

Three times they will look, three times. The last time the raccoon will climb to the top of one of the ramá posts. The dog will look for it. "Look for it, man, Pochi," they will say to him.

The dog will find it there and will bark at it. "There he is, there he is!" barking, he will say to them, almost talking. Then down, as he barks, down it will fall.

Then they will skin the raccoon and sell the skin. It is just a burlap sack that they have, but they say it is the skin. They will just ask for some wine for it. "Four thousand or five thousand," they will say. When that is done, the drum will be returned, given back to the tampaleo.

"You see, father, we have finished. It almost ate up all our corn. There are just little ones standing here and there," they say.

That is all the raccoon does. It all comes out from the violin player. The tampaleo doesn't start it. Only the violin players do that.

Ousei Bwikam: Mountain Lion Songs

This set of four songs presents tableaus from the drama of mountain lions stalking and killing a deer. The four each create a vivid single image that is allusive to the worlds of Yaqui belief we have discussed and directly evocative of great emotion. In the first, someone with ears like the large, round leaves from the *ho'opo* tree [*Jatropha cinera?*] stalks the wilderness world listening in vain for the sound of "the animal of this enchanted grove." In the second, a "flower lion" is described walking the same wilderness world, not listening for sounds, but rather making them: "*tomtomti,* thump, thump." The third image pictures the final moment of the stalk as a "mad" mountain lion is poised threateningly in a stand above the edge of a watering place, "the flower-covered enchanted water" in which the little fawn comes out to play in so many versions of the opening song of every *pahko.* And in the final song of the set, a buzzard hovers and a big coyote howls at the place "where the enchanted spotted mountain lion ate" and "a fawn's head was found."

The object of the hunt, *malichi,* the little fawn, is represented only by indirection in the song words: in the first song by the epithet "*yoawa,* the animal," and in the last by the metonomic "*malichi kovasu,* fawn's head." Nor, contrary to predominant deer-song practice, does *malichi* speak. The absence of his persona in the song words in this set in the *maso me'ewa* builds anticipation for the next song set in which *malichi* speaks so movingly in the final moments of the hunt and at the very moment of his death. In anticipation, here, we sense his presence more acutely in his absence. The same may be true of the absence of the mythic deer hunter *Yevuku Yoleme.*

A major stylistic feature of Yaqui deer songs on every level, from individual sound through lines and stanzas on to the most encompassing themes, is repetition. Often such repetition is used to create an effect of balanced opposition.[14] This stylistic feature reflects the balanced equation of worlds that generates all deer songs. Like other singers, Don Jesús uses antithesis often in his songs. In this set, for example, the buzzard, who was not hovering in the first stanza of the final song, hovers in the concluding stanza. More subtly, at the level of the song set, a deaf lion is contrasted with a sounding one, a female lion with a male, the Spanish *liowe* with the Yaqui *ouseli,* a placid "flower" lion with a menacing "mad" lion, and the tense, solitary moment just before the kill with the anticlimactic, howling convergence of carrion eaters just after. These and other oppositions bind the four images which make this song set as surely as the implied narrative they illustrate and the burlesques of the *pahkolam* which they accompany.

Before we compare specific song words too closely, however, it is important to recognize that Don Jesús could sing these songs in different ways. On April 15, 1980, we recorded the following deer song about a mountain lion from him at his home in Potam:

Ouseli kun omte 　ouseli Ouseli kun omte 　ouseli	Mountain lion may be mad, 　mountain lion. Mountain lion may be mad, 　mountain lion.
Ayaman ne seyewailo 　yo va bwibwikola 　　senu kuta huya tosali 　　ne hikat husama 　　　waiwanola chaka 　　　omte ouseli Ouseli ma omte 　ouseli	Over there, I, at the edge 　of the flower-covered enchanted water, 　　on top of one white wood branch, 　　I am brown, 　　　dangling, hanging, 　　　mad mountain lion. Mountain lion really is mad, 　mountain lion.

After we had recorded and translated the four mountain lion songs we give below, we noted the very close resemblance between the words of the third song in the set and the song we recorded earlier. When we asked Don Jesús about the differences, he said not to worry about it: "*Sime nanana tavesa tabwisi bwika,* they are the same, but just sung differently." Neither Don Jesús nor Felipe felt that one version was better or worse than the other. Perhaps this points to a fundamental difference Mark Booth notes between the experience of song and that of a printed poem. "A song fulfills its potential in significant part according to what it shares with other similar good songs," Booth writes, not in being innovative.[15] But it points, too, toward a cross-cultural value shift that occurs when we call song words a poem. Evers feels that as words on the page, as a "poem," the 1980 version, with its antithesis *ma*, may be/*kun*, really is, creates a sense of discovery within the portrayal of the song's single image that is not present in the other. Moreover, the image of the lion in the tree itself is made much more vivid by the additional, and antithetical, color contrast of the white branch and the brown mountain lion.

Molina believes that such variation is characteristic of the work of mature singers and notes that, until they develop a real confidence in their abilities, younger singers try to sing their songs exactly in the same way, word for word. His comment suggests that deer singers' concepts of song identity shift from "verbal" to "thematic" as they develop.[16] More importantly for our present purpose is the *caveat* this example suggests. The song words printed here are based on performances that are each an original. Until they became written literature here, there was no fixed text. These considerations do not diminish the beauty or the importance of any of the texts, but they do suggest the peril in comparisons to the model of written literature with its great emphasis on *the* text and *the* original and correct version.[17] Moreover they suggest an equal danger in the assumption sometimes made in folklore studies that the first-collected version is some sort of "original."

The following versions were recorded at Yoem Pueblo May 9, 1981. We give the same number of repetitions of the first stanza as did Don Jesús when he recorded them. Don Jesús used the song titles we give here. The commentary after each translation is from his talk about each song as we played them back for him to review. In addition to clarifying song words and suggesting links between them and the burlesques of the *pahkolam*, the comments hint at the remarkable kinship Don Jesús felt with the personae he created: "That deaf mountain lion . . . well, he is just like me, a little deaf."

OUSEI NAKAPIT

Hopomoila mulati weyekai
  huyawi nakaka weyekai
Hopomoila mulati weyekai
  huyawi nakaka weyekai

Hopomoila mulati weyekai
  huyawi nakaka weyekai
Hopomoila mulati weyekai
  huyawi nakaka weyekai

Hopomoila mulati weyekai
  huyawi nakaka weyekai
Hopomoila mulati weyekai
  huyawi nakaka weyekai

Ayaman ne seyewailo
  huyatanaisukunisu
    ikane yo huya saniloata
      yoawa hikkaipelaka weyekai
Hopomoila mulati weyekai
  huyawi nakaka weyekai

DEAF MOUNTAIN LION

Like a ho'opo, nodding as I am walking,
  I have ears to the wilderness, as I am walking.
Like a ho'opo, nodding as I am walking,
  I have ears to the wilderness, as I am walking.

Like a ho'opo, nodding as I am walking,
  I have ears to the wilderness, as I am walking.
Like a ho'opo, nodding as I am walking,
  I have ears to the wilderness, as I am walking.

Like a ho'opo, nodding as I am walking,
  I have ears to the wilderness, as I am walking.
Like a ho'opo, nodding as I am walking,
  I have ears to the wilderness, as I am walking.

Over there, I, in the center
  of the flower-covered wilderness,
    the animal of this enchanted wilderness grove,
      I want to hear, as I am walking
Like a ho'opo, nodding as I am walking,
  I have ears to the wilderness, as I am walking.

The ho'opo *is a tree. It has big leaves. Well, there are some of them over at* Tetaviakti. *The tree is big. It has big leaves. Here along the river there are none. Over there in the mountains there are* ho'opom. *It does not sing. There are no songs about it, but this deaf lion talks about the* ho'opo. *It has big leaves, like his ears.*

That deaf mountain lion is walking, and he cannot hear. Well, he is just like me, a little deaf. Walking, going, he cannot hear, as he is walking with his ears to the wilderness.

"Over there, in the center of the wilderness grove, as I am walking, the animal of this wilderness grove I want to hear, as I am walking," it says. "I have ears to the wilderness, as I am walking," he says that, the deaf mountain lion.

OUSEI HAMUCHIA   FEMALE MOUNTAIN LION

Sewa liowe, sewa liowe,   Flower lion, flower lion,
  huyapo weama, sewa liowe.   walking in the wilderness, flower lion.
Sewa liowe, sewa liowe,   Flower lion, flower lion,
  huyapo weama, sewa liowe.   walking in the wilderness, flower lion.

Sewa liowe, sewa liowe, sewa liowe,   Flower lion, flower lion, flower lion,
  huyapo weama, sewa liowe.   walking in the wilderness, flower lion.
Sewa liowe, sewa liowe, sewa liowe,   Flower lion, flower lion, flower lion,
  huyapo weama, sewa liowe.   walking in the wilderness, flower lion.

Sewa liowe, sewa liowe, sewa liowe,   Flower lion, flower lion, flower lion,
  huyapo weama, sewa liowe.   walking in the wilderness, flower lion.

Ayaman ne seyewailo   Over there, I, in the center
  huyatanaisukunisu   of the flower-covered wilderness,
    ikane yo huya saniloata   through this enchanted wilderness grove,
      tomtomti weama   thump, thump, I am walking.
Sewa liowe, sewa liowe, sewa liowe,   Flower lion, flower lion, flower lion,
  huyapo weama, sewa liowe.   walking in the wilderness, flower lion.

It is the female mountain lion, they say. She is just walking in the wilderness. Thump, thump, she sounds, going around the wilderness, female mountain lion.

OUSELI OMTEKAI

MOUNTAIN LION IS MAD

Ouseli omtekai
  wana huyapo
    omtekai
Ouseli omtekai
  wana huyapo
    omtekai

Mountain lion is mad,
    there in the wilderness,
      is mad.
Mountain lion is mad,
    there in the wilderness,
      is mad.

Ouseli omtekai
  wana huyapo
    omtekai
Ouseli omtekai
  wana huyapo
    omtekai

Mountain lion is mad,
    there in the wilderness,
      is mad.
Mountain lion is mad,
    there in the wilderness,
      is mad.

Ouseli omtekai
  wana huyapo
    omtekai
Ouseli omtekai
  wana huyapo
    omtekai

Mountain lion is mad,
    there in the wilderness,
      is mad.
Mountain lion is mad,
    there in the wilderness,
      is mad.

Ayaman ne seyewailo
  yo va bwibwikola
    senu kuta huyachi
      ne husama
        waiwanola chaka
          omte ouseli
Ouseli omtekai
  wana huyapo
    omtekai

Over there, I, at the edge
    of the flower-covered enchanted water,
      on one wood branch,
        I am brown,
          dangling, hanging,
            mad mountain lion.
Mountain lion is mad,
    there in the wilderness,
      is mad.

Here, during the concluding stanza, the deer will put down his headdress. The mountain lion sitting there will jump down on it, will pounce on it. He will drag the head around, and when he arrives there in front of us he will lay brush, dry branches, and leaves on it.

Then a coyote will arrive and will walk around him, and the mountain lion will punch him. It goes like that.

OUSEI O'OW

Yolko ouselita yo hibwakaposu
  malichi kovasu teuwakai
Yoyo wilu
  ka amani koyowe
Yoyo hunama wo'i
  amani hiyawa

Yolko ouselita yo hibwakaposu
  malichi kovasu teuwakai
Yoyo wilu
  ka amani koyowe
Yoyo hunama wo'i
  amani chayevu

Yolko ouselita yo hibwakaposu
  malichi kovasu teuwakai
Yoyo wilu
  ka amani koyowe
Yoyo hunama wo'i
  amani chayevu

Yolko ouselita yo hibwakaposu
  malichi kovasu teuwakai
Yoyo wilu
  ka amani koyowe
Yoyo hunama wo'i
  amani hiyawa

Ayaman ne seyewailo
  saniloata naisukunisu
    isu yoyo wilu
      amani koyowe
Yoyo hunama wo'i
  amani chayevu

MALE MOUNTAIN LION

Where the enchanted spotted mountain lion ate,
  a fawn's head was found.
An enchanted, enchanted buzzard
  was not hovering there.
An enchanted, enchanted big coyote
  was sounding there.

Where the enchanted spotted mountain lion ate,
  a fawn's head was found.
An enchanted, enchanted buzzard
  was not hovering there.
An enchanted, enchanted big coyote
  was howling there.

Where the enchanted spotted mountain lion ate,
  a fawn's head was found.
An enchanted, enchanted buzzard
  was not hovering there.
An enchanted, enchanted big coyote
  was howling there.

Where the enchanted spotted mountain lion ate,
  a fawn's head was found.
An enchanted, enchanted buzzard
  was not hovering there.
An enchanted, enchanted big coyote
  was sounding there.

Over there, I, in the center
  of the flower-covered grove,
    this enchanted, enchanted buzzard
      was hovering there.
An enchanted, enchanted big coyote
  was howling there.

This song comes after the mountain lion kills. That spotted mountain lion wants to eat the deer. When the lion puts brush on the deer over here in front of us, the deer singers will start this song. Then it will eat.

"Where the spotted mountain lion ate, the head was found," it says. There is a buzzard hovering there, and there is this hunama coyote howling there, where the mountain lion ate. Wanting to eat, the hunama coyote is howling. He is howling around by it, that hunama coyote. He is about this size, big, with a white-striped tail. He is much bigger than the coyote. The hunama coyote is big. That one is a killer. He kills deer.

That is all. There is nothing else. There are only four songs.

Maso Nehhawa Bwikam: Running the Deer Songs

When the mountain lion game has ended, "the story will go toward running the deer," Don Jesús told us. This third and climactic *yeuwame* accompanies a set of eighteen deer songs. Don Jesús called these *maso nehhawa bwikam* (running the deer songs). The words of these songs describe the drama of a deer hunt using points of view of both the hunters and the hunted. But more, they go beyond earthly death with the deer *saila maso* to describe how he "becomes flower" and is received back into the sentient wilderness world from which he was taken. The extraordinarily powerful portrait of life and death created by the song words is linked to one of the most extended and rollicking of the *pahkolam*'s games.

We relate this combination of the farcical and the serious to other dramatic traditions of native America, most especially the Yaquis' Uto-Aztecan relatives the Hopis, who create a similar combination each time they bring their clowns and *katsinam* into the same plaza. Barbara Tedlock suggests that "the ability of American Indian religions to allow room for the disruptive, crazy, but creative power of the clown is perhaps their greatest strength."[18] Emory Sekaquaptewa sketches a powerfully particular instance in "One Last Smile for a Hopi Clown."[19] There he tells how one Hopi man "respected for his resourcefulness and performance as a clown" arranged to make a burlesque of his own burial in order to keep the memory of his death within the memory of his most creative role in life. "Translation between the realms of the living and the dead, between the visible and invisible worlds . . . is but one form of dialogue in which the clowns engage," writes Barbara Babcock. "Clowns are mediators par excellence between all types of cosmic, natural, and social dualities, between inside and outside, self and other, creation and destruction, order and chaos."[20]

When the Yaqui *pahkolam* clown their exuberant slapsticks, they open the audience with laughter and lift away any hint of sentimentality from the song words of the deer singers. In this way the absurd burlesques of the *pahkolam* provide a context in which deer-song words can achieve an emotional intensity that is rare in any poetic tradition. At the same time, they mediate the stark dualities inherent in this native drama of life and death.

Don Jesús' description of the running-the-deer game parallels that we have quoted from Refugio Savala above. Don Jesús explained that it takes place just after dawn on the final morning of a *lutu pahko*. One of the *pahkolam* takes the part of a hunting dog, while the other three become *masoreom*, deer hunters. The eldest *pahkola* is called "father"; the other two "sons."

The decorative style of the *ramá* is carried out into the plaza. Fresh bamboo canes are cut, gathered into bundles, and planted in the plaza in front of the *ramá* in pairs. Then the two bundles are bent together and tied to form leafy arches. A number of these arches are constructed so that there is a long path, an arcade, out of the *ramá* into the village.

When they are ready to begin the hunt, the *pahkolam* come to the deer singers to request the use of their instruments. They are going hunting, they say, and they need to sing to prepare themselves for the hunt. "They want to speak about the wilderness world. They are singing for the wilderness world, to enter the wilderness world, to purify themselves," Don Jesús' son Aleho told us. Of course, as *pahkolam* they turn their preparations as deer hunters into an elaborate parody. They hold their borrowed instruments upside down and with the wrong hands, play awkward rhythms, and, as Don Jesús put it, "*vempo hanahunibwikne*/they sing in an incorrect way."

With the instruments back in the hands of the deer singers, the *pahkolam* begin their hunt. They discover the tracks of a deer which lead out of the *ramá* toward the long pathway of bamboo arches beyond. Armed with their little bows and arrows and led by their "dog," they go out. Their quarry is the deer dancer who is always just beyond them as they hunt from arch to arch out into the village. Corncob-tipped arrows fly all around, the crowd shrieks, the jabber is constant as they track, catch sight of the deer, only to lose him again. The "dog" follows a false scent and is punished, then discovers a "water hole," a buried bottled of tequila, and is rewarded.

Finally the deer is wounded. The *maso moro* fixes an arrow in the deer dancer's headdress and he staggers on. The hunters discover the trail of blood and close in quickly to find that the deer has died under the last bamboo arch, the one most distant from the *ramá*. They celebrate; then, one is made into a "burro" to carry the deer back to the *ramá*. The "burro" is stubborn, there are other difficulties, the jokes continue. After some time, the deer is finally laid out, "skinned," then "butchered" by the *pahkolam* under the *ramá*. The *pahkolam* feast on a tortilla which they call the deer's brains as they pull it from the headdress. Then they go to lengths to tan the deer hide, a burlap sack, beating it against the ground and each other, as well as some unlucky ones in the crowd, after they have soaked it in the water drummer's basin. When the deer hide is cured in this way, the *pahkolam* announce an auction and sell it.

All the while this extended burlesque unfolds, Don Jesús said, "we just sit and sing for the deer."

Don Jesús' songs create images of eighteen moments during the hunt. These images accumulate, as much as they develop, within a pattern of journey and return.[21] During the first three songs, the deer remains within the *ramá*, his home, his *kolensia*. The hunters remind themselves of the rules of the hunt:

> First you just look,
>   later you will find, find.

and again:

> Around there,
>   look for tracks,
>   go get him for me.

Between these two songs introducing the hunt is a more allusive image foreshadowing its conclusion. Two vultures, each a different kind, meet "where the white wood stands." There they "will talk about this animal." "These are the ones who are going to eat him," Don Jesús tells us in his commentary. The setting is potent with allusions to that impending death. The "white wood," a dead tree, repeats the setting used in the song just before the killing of the deer in the mountain lion game. Similarly, the mention of the place "where the mescal agave like mescal agave stands" may echo another of Don Jesús' songs in which that plant speaks for itself:

> Still I am beautiful,
>   with green leaves,
>   sitting.
> Toward the top,
>   I have black fruit,
>   standing.

Just as it bears fruit, Don Jesús explained, "the mescal agave talks like that. The mescal is almost dying."

During the third song in the set, the deer bolts from the *ramá*. The next ten songs describe his journey toward a death in the wilderness world. For the first time in the *maso me'ewa*, the deer speaks and foreshadows his own death:

> Toward a place where
>   I could not find safety I went.

and again:

> Although unseen in the wilderness
>   I am just running,
> My antler crown with these three branches
>   is showing, moving.

and yet again:

> Flower-covered grove, as I am walking to you
>   I am talking to you, flower-covered grove.

The use of the first person in these songs builds pathos for the deer, but what seals that response to the song words are Don Jesús' glosses: "Well, he isn't sure of himself"; and "The poor thing wants someone to talk for him. Not wanting to die, the deer himself says that in the song."

Don Jesús suspends this response with the next two songs, in which he shifts from the point of view of the deer to that of the hunters again: from intimate revelations of the deer's thoughts to a celebration of the exuberance of the hunt and the joy of the hunters as they run "in the flower fawns's flower dust." When again we return to the point of view of the deer for the final scenes of the hunt, we experience first the frenzy:

> Not wanting to die,
> dodging through the wilderness.

and then the exhaustion:

> with my head hanging down toward the ground,
> as I am walking,
> with foam around my mouth
> as I am walking.

and finally the resignation of the moment just before death seems inevitable:

> Never again I,
> will I on this world,
> I, around will I be walking.

As before, it is Don Jesús' very personal identification with the deer that pushes the emotion these words evoke to a greater intensity: "just as all will say 'yes,' while being taken somewhere to a war, they will be walking there to die ... like that, this deer speaks in the song." This from a man who was wounded fighting in his homeland during the Mexican Revolution.

Don Jesús' use of the first person singular pronoun *ne* in his songs is an important aspect of the style of his song words. It is most prominent in the *tonua*, the concluding stanza, which, in almost all of the songs we recorded from him, Don Jesús began *ayaman ne. Iyiminsu* and *ayamansu* are two locatives that many other singers use in the same position; *Iyiminsu* seems characteristic of the oldest generation of singers of whom we have recordings. When we asked Don Jesús about his use of *ayaman ne*, he told us that it was used "during the run in the deer chase," but that he used it other times because he liked it. Other singers use the form but none, in our experience, quite so pervasively. Don Jesús' use of *ne* at the beginning of his concluding stanzas provides a constant personal presence in his songs. We wonder if he felt a special affinity near the end of his own life with the persona of the deer he perpetuated. By the time we thought to ask that question he was gone. In any case, what Don Jesús accomplishes through the use of this "I" is not the celebration of his individual ego but rather an identification with the persona that has endured as long as any other in Yaqui culture. He accomplishes what Kenneth Burke calls a rhetoric of identification: "Only those voices from without are effective which can speak in the language of a voice within."[22]

It is at this point in the song set, after an intense emotional climax as the deer is "overpowered," that we would expect his point of view, his "I," to disappear. Yet, incredibly, the deer continues to speak in two songs as he is carried back to the *kolensia*, his favored haunt, and laid out there on a bier of branches gathered from each plant in the wilderness world. The transmogrification of the deer that occurs there as his physical body is divided is imaged in the final five songs of the set. A tree asks for the deer's tail:[23]

> Put a flower on me
> from flower-covered person's flower body

As his flesh is roasted, his hide tanned, and his innards thrown to glisten in the patio, no doubt awaiting the vultures who gathered to talk about him earlier, the deer speaks:

> I become enchanted
> . . . .
> I become flower.

This graphic sequence of images of death and rebirth indicates, in the words of Don Jesús, that "the deer's spirit stays in the wilderness." Performed on the occasion of the anniversary of the death of a loved one, during the Yaqui ceremony that releases the family from mourning even as it releases the spirit of the departed from this world, these song words must provide a powerful articulation of the sorrow and the joy of the community.

The last image is one of a stick standing in the wilderness. It is called *kutataka* in the song, and, in the context of the accompanying dramatic action, has more the sense of a post, one which the *pahkolam* imitate and one which in their imitation serves as the place where the deer's "hide" is "tanned" in their final burlesque. Yet, surely, the *kuta* mentioned in this last song evokes those other sticks we have discussed earlier: the fawn stick of the deer singers through which they give voice again to the deer, thereby continuing the language of the stick that spoke when the world was becoming new here. In part, because these were the last things we talked about with Don Jesús, we have his own death in mind in our reading of his song words.

Kialem vata hiwemai
    chukula hubwa teune teunevu
Kialem vata hiwemai
    chukula hubwa teune teunevu

Kialem vata hiwemai
    chukula hubwa teune teunevu
Kialem vata hiwemai
    chukula hubwa teune teunevu

Ayaman ne seyewailo
    saniloata fayalikun
        yeulu siko
            hunak hubwa teune teunevu
Kialem vata hiwemai
    chukula hubwa teune teunevu

First you just look,
    later you will find, find.
First you just look,
    later you will find, find.

First you just look,
    later you will find, find.
First you just look,
    later you will find, find.

Over there, I, in an opening
    in the flower-covered grove,
        I went out,
            then you will find, find.
First you just look,
    later you will find, find.

"First, just take a look for him," it says. "When he goes out in an opening of the grove, then you will find him," it says. "First you just look, while later you will find him," the deer hunters, the pahkolam, they are the ones who are speaking in it.

Then, then the pahkolam will go out. Somewhere in the wilderness they will look for the tracks. Yes, in the wilderness. Well, not really in the wilderness, but just around there in front of the ramá they will walk, walk. Later they will really look for him out there. But like that they look, and like that they will come back inside the ramá again. Like that the song goes.

Imte kuyutai
  kuyuliti weyekapo
    naute yayaine
Imte kuyutai
  kuyuliti weyekapo
    naute yayaine

Imte kuyutai
  kuyuliti weyekapo
    naute yayaine
Imte kuyutai
  kuyuliti weyekapo
    naute yayaine

Emposinto yoyo wilutakaine
Emposinto yoyo tekoyelikaine
Imte tosali kutata weyekapo
  naute yahakai
    inikate yowata naute etehone
Imte kuyutai
  kuyuliti weyekapo
    ka naute yayaine

Here, we, where the mescal agave
  like mescal agave stands,
    together we will meet.
Here, we, where the mescal agave
  like mescal agave stands,
    together we will meet.

Here, we, where the mescal agave
  like mescal agave stands,
    together we will meet.
Here, we, where the mescal agave
  like mescal agave stands,
    together we will meet.

And you are an enchanted, enchanted black vulture,
And you are an enchanted, enchanted turkey vulture,
Here, we, where the white wood stands,
  together we meet,
    together we will talk about this animal.
Here, we, where the mescal agave
  like mescal agave stands,
    together we will not meet.

The black vulture and the turkey vulture will meet where the white wood is standing. "When we meet we will talk about the animal," it says. They will talk together, the turkey vulture and the black vulture, about the deer. The black vulture wants to say that. The deer will dance with that. The turkey vulture and the black vulture want to talk together themselves where there is white wood standing.

They come out here when they see something lying dead like cows or horses. They live somewhere here on top of us. They live on top of us. They want to come down here to eat. That turkey vulture, that black vulture. The song says that.

The black vulture and the turkey vulture want to hunt, want to eat there. That's why they say this. Over there they say they will meet where the white wood is standing. Maybe it is a dead tree. Sitting together there, the sun hits them, warms them. They will talk about the animal, where they are going to overpower him. So these are the ones who are going to eat him. They are sitting somewhere out there.

Ayatemawoki
  haliwaka
    nechem a nuriavo
Ayatemawoki
  haliwaka
    nechem a nuriavo

Ayatemawoki
  haliwaka
    nechem a nuriavo
Ayatemawoki
  haliwaka
    nechem a nuriavo

Ayatemawoki
  haliwaka
    nechem a nuriavo
Ayatemawoki
  haliwaka
    nechem a nuriavo

Ayaman ne seyewailo
  saniloata fayalikun
    ne yeulu siko hunak hubwa
      nechem a nuriavo
Ayatemawoki
  haliwaka
    nechem a nuriavo

Around there,
  look for tracks,
    go get him for me.
Around there,
  look for tracks,
    go get him for me.

Around there,
  look for tracks,
    go get him for me.
Around there,
  look for tracks,
    go get him for me.

Around there,
  look for tracks,
    go get him for me.
Around there,
  look for tracks,
    go get him for me.

Over there, I, in an opening
  in the flower-covered grove,
    I go out, then
      you will get him for me.
Around there,
  look for tracks,
    go get him for me.

"Around there, look for tracks. After a while we will get him," it says. "Toward the flower opening, when he goes out there, we will get him," the pahkolam say that. Then, when he has gone out, they will get him. He will run out with this song, run out.

The deer will stand at the patio cross there. And these who wait for him will sit here. All four of them will sit behind some brush. When they are out there, the deer singers will start this song. When the song is starting, the deer will run toward them in the brush. They will fall backward and knock each other down. They will tell each other not to make noise. The pahkolam will joke around.

Then during the concluding stanza, the deer will push aside the one sitting there and run out. Then that pahkola will fall over backward. When he shoots, when he shoots, he will shoot upward, up into the air, and he will throw his bow.

Then the pahkolam who are the sons, they will say: "As an elder, why did you do that, father, papa?" They will start spanking him. They will spank their father!

"Where is my wiko'i (bow)?"

"He is at Vicam Switch."

"There at Potam is another."

In that way the pahkolam will joke among themselves. But then one will say, "No, not the men named Wiko'i but the wooden bow." Then they will look for it.

"Here it lies, the one that belongs to you."

That is after the deer has already run out of the ramá. There at the patio cross, the pahkolam will make a round looking for him. The dog will already be there with them. The dog will look for tracks. After he finds them, the dog will bark loudly.

"The dog found it over there," they will say. And again the dog will chase the deer out. The dog will take off after him. The song goes like that.

Hakunhunine ka ama
  yoliwau vichaka sika
Hakunhunine ka ama
  yoliwau vichaka sika
Hakunhunine ka ama
  yoliwau vichaka sika

Hakunhunine ka ama
  yoliwau vichaka sika
Hakunhunine ka ama
  yoliwau vichaka sika
Hakunhunine ka ama
  yoliwau vichaka sika

Ayaman ne seyewailo
  saniloata fayalikun ne su
    ime yo wikoyolim
      na katepo
Hakunhunine ka ama
  yoliwau vichaka sika
Hakunhunine ka ama
  yoliwau vichaka sika

Toward a place where
  I could not find safety I went.
Toward a place where
  I could not find safety I went.
Toward a place where
  I could not find safety I went.

Toward a place where
  I could not find safety I went.
Toward a place where
  I could not find safety I went.
Toward a place where
  I could not find safety I went.

Over there, I, in an opening
  in the flower-covered grove, I am
    here where these enchanted
      bow people are walking about.
Toward a place where
  I could not find safety I went.
Toward a place where
  I could not find safety I went.

Like that the deer ran out, went out in the world, saw the grove and went out. "Nowhere could I find safety," it says. "Well, here where the bow people are, toward them I went," it says.

Well, he isn't sure of himself. That is why he went toward where they were. "Toward a place where there is no safety, I went," it says, toward the wilderness grove and the wilderness world. The deer talks about that. The deer himself says that. He ran out to the wilderness world. The song says that.

Kiane huyapo ka yeu machiata
vuite oyoven
Humesu im awa hisam vae vakuliam
yeu machiata ansime

Kiane huyapo ka yeu machiata
vuite oyoven
Humesu im awa hisam vae vakuliam
yeu machiata ansime

Kiane huyapo ka yeu machiata
vuite oyoven
Humesu im awa hisam vae vakuliam
yeu machiata ansime

Kiane huyapo ka yeu machiata
vuite oyoven
Humesu im awa hisam vae vakuliam
yeu machiata ansime

Ayaman ne seyewailo
saniloata naisukuni
weyekai
Humesu im awa hisa vae vakuliam
yeu machiata ansime

Although unseen in the wilderness
I am just running,
My antler crown with these three branches
is showing, moving.

Although unseen in the wilderness
I am just running,
My antler crown with these three branches
is showing, moving.

Although unseen in the wilderness
I am just running,
My antler crown with these three branches
is showing, moving.

Although unseen in the wilderness
I am just running,
My antler crown with these three branches
is showing, moving.

Over there, I, in the center
of the flower-covered grove,
I am walking,
My antler crown with these three branches
is showing, moving.

The deer is hiding, running. In a desert like this, he is running out. But his antlers are seen moving. That is what tells on him. That is why it says this. "Although unseen in the wilderness, I am just running," it says. "But my antlers are out. They are seen moving," it says. The deer himself says that. He has big antlers. The song goes like that.

Sewailo saniloa eu ne weyekai
  eu ne noka sewailo saniloa

Flower-covered grove, as I am walking to you,
  I am talking to you, flower-covered grove.

Sewailo saniloa eu ne weyekai
  eu ne noka sewailo saniloa

Flower-covered grove, as I am walking to you,
  I am talking to you, flower-covered grove.

Sewailo saniloa eu ne weyekai
  eu ne noka sewailo saniloa

Flower-covered grove, as I am walking to you,
  I am talking to you, flower-covered grove.

Sewailo saniloa eu ne weyekai
  eu ne noka sewailo saniloa

Flower-covered grove, as I am walking to you,
  I am talking to you, flower-covered grove.

Ayaman ne seyewailo
  saniloata fayalikuni
    weyekai
      imene yo wikoyolim
      in amau vichakane
Imene vichaka eu ne noka
  sewailo saniloa

Over there, I, in an opening
  in the flower-covered grove,
    as I am walking,
      these enchanted bow people,
      behind me I see.
These I see,
  I am talking to you, flower-covered grove.

The deer will be running during this song. As he is running, he is talking to the wilderness world. As he is going, he is talking to the wilderness world. "Flower-covered grove," it says. "As I am walking to you, I am talking to you," it says.

He wants someone to talk for him. He wants the wilderness world to talk for him. How will it talk for him? The song, the song just says that. The poor thing wants someone to talk for him. Not wanting to die, the deer himself says that in the song. The song goes like that.

Eme emo ow sailakame
　tui tulisi nawem chaisaka
Tui tulisi nawem chaisaka
　tulisi nawem chaisaka

Eme emo ow sailakame
　tui tulisi nawem chaisaka
Tui tulisi nawem chaisaka
　tulisi nawem chaisaka

Eme emo ow sailakame
　tui tulisi nawem chaisaka
Tui tulisi nawem chaisaka
　tulisi nawem chaisaka

Ayaman ne seyewailo
　fayaliata naisukun
　　tennekai
Kiane sea malitta
　sea tolochiapo
　　tennekai
Tui tulisi nawem chaisaka
　tulisi nawem chaisaka

You who are each other's brothers
　are shouting well, beautifully together,
Shouting well, beautifully together,
　shouting beautifully together.

You who are each other's brothers
　are shouting well, beautifully together,
Shouting well, beautifully together,
　shouting beautifully together.

You who are each other's brothers
　are shouting well, beautifully together,
Shouting well, beautifully together,
　shouting beautifully together.

Over there, I, in the center
　of the flower-covered opening,
　　we are running,
Just I, in flower fawn's
　flower dust,
　　we are running,
Shouting well, beautifully together,
　shouting beautifully together.

The deer hunters, the pahkolam.

Well, this song is the four pahkolam *chasing the deer, running, shouting, chasing the deer. It is like when the children chase and shout at something. They are running that way.*

"Running there in an opening in the grove," it says. "Running in flower person's, flower fawn's dust," it says. "Shouting well, beautifully together," it says. "You who are each other's brothers," it says. The four pahkolam, *the deer hunters,* pahkolam. *The song says that.*

Hakuni chaiwame	Where is the shouting?
fayaliata pakun chaiwame	Outside in the opening is the shouting.
Hakuni chaiwame	Where is the shouting?
fayaliata pakun chaiwame	Outside in the opening is the shouting.

Hakuni chaiwame	Where is the shouting?
fayaliata pakun chaiwame	Outside in the opening is the shouting.
Hakuni chaiwame	Where is the shouting?
fayaliata pakun chaiwame	Outside in the opening is the shouting.

Hakuni chaiwame	Where is the shouting?
fayaliata pakun chaiwame	Outside in the opening is the shouting.
Hakuni chaiwame	Where is the shouting?
fayaliata pakun chaiwame	Outside in the opening is the shouting.

Hakuni chaiwame	Where is the shouting?
fayaliata pakun chaiwame	Outside in the opening is the shouting.
Hakuni chaiwame	Where is the shouting?
fayaliata pakun chaiwame	Outside in the opening is the shouting.

Ayaman ne seyewailo
  saniloata fayalikunisu
    sea malitta sea tolochiapo
      tennekai
Hakuni chaiwame
  fayaliata pakun chaiwame

Over there, I, in the opening
  in the flower-covered grove,
    in the flower fawn's flower dust,
      we are running.
Where is the shouting?
  Outside in the opening is the shouting.

The pahkolam *will be running and shouting after the deer. "Where is the shouting?" it says. "Well, outside in the opening is the shouting," it says. The* pahkolam *are running after the deer, while we are inside singing. "Over there in an opening in the grove, in flower fawn's flower dust, they are running," it says. "The shouting is outside in an opening," it says. The song says only that.*

Kauni mukivalekai
   huyata nanale
Kauni mukivalekai
   huyata nanale
	Not wanting to die,
	   dodging through the wilderness.
	Not wanting to die,
	   dodging through the wilderness.

Kauni mukivalekai
   huyata nanale
Kauni mukivalekai
   huyata nanale
	Not wanting to die,
	   dodging through the wilderness.
	Not wanting to die,
	   dodging through the wilderness.

Kauni mukivalekai
   huyata nanale
Kauni mukivalekai
   huyata nanale
	Not wanting to die,
	   dodging through the wilderness.
	Not wanting to die,
	   dodging through the wilderness.

Kauni mukivalekai
   huyata nanale
Kauni mukivalekai
   huyata nanale
	Not wanting to die,
	   dodging through the wilderness.
	Not wanting to die,
	   dodging through the wilderness.

Kauni mukivalekai
   huyata nanale
Kauni mukivalekai
   huyata nanale
	Not wanting to die,
	   dodging through the wilderness.
	Not wanting to die,
	   dodging through the wilderness.

Ayaman ne seyewailo
   sanilomak lolopola
      weyekai
         chikti yo huyata
            nanaleka wesime
Kauni mukivalekai
   huyata nanale
	Over there, I, alongside
	   the flower-covered grove,
	      as I am walking,
	         each enchanted thicket,
	            dodging, moving.
	Not wanting to die,
	   dodging through the wilderness.

Toward the wilderness, he is walking. The deer himself, to save himself there, he wants to enter the wilderness. "I want to enter the wilderness," it says. "Not wanting to die, I want to enter the wilderness," the deer himself says that. The deer himself, while he is walking, he is saying that in that way.

Vuiti yumilata ke wesime
  vuiti yumilata ke ansime
    vuiti yumilata ke wesime

Vuiti yumilata ke wesime
  vuiti yumilata ke ansime
    vuiti yumilata ke wesime

Vuiti yumilata ke wesime
  vuiti yumilata ke ansime
    vuiti yumilata ke wesime

Vuiti yumilata ke wesime
  vuiti yumilata ke ansime
    vuiti yumilata ke wesime

Ayaman ne seyewailo
  saniloata fayalikun
    weyekai
  kiane seyewailo
    saniloa lolopola
      weyekai
  kiane bwiapo
    komne kovaka
      weyekai
  kiane somochia
    bwibwikola teneka
      weyekai
Vuiti yumilata ke wesime
  vuiti yumilata ke ansime

Exhausted from running, you are walking;
  exhausted from running, you are moving;
    exhausted from running, you are walking.

Exhausted from running, you are walking;
  exhausted from running, you are moving;
    exhausted from running, you are walking.

Exhausted from running, you are walking;
  exhausted from running, you are moving;
    exhausted from running, you are walking.

Exhausted from running, you are walking;
  exhausted from running, you are moving;
    exhausted from running, you are walking.

Over there, I, in an opening
  in the flower-covered grove,
    as I am walking,
  alongside
    the flower-covered grove,
      as I am walking,
  with my head hanging down
    toward the ground,
      as I am walking,
  with foam
    around my mouth,
      as I am walking,
Exhausted from running, you are walking;
  exhausted from running, you are moving.

"Exhausted from running, you are walking," it says. "Exhausted from running, you are walking," it says. Tired, walking, moving, there at the edge of the grove, the deer is walking. With his head hanging down to the ground, with foam around the mouth, he is walking. Tired, walking, the deer himself says that in that way.

Ka ne huni
    into ne inia aniat
        ne na ne welamsisimne
Kia ne ka ne huni
    into ne inia aniat
        ne na ne welamsisimne

Kia ne ka ne huni
    into ne inia aniat
        ne na ne welamsisimne
Kia ne ka ne huni
    into ne inia aniat
        ne na ne welamsisimne

Ayaman ne
    seyewailo saniloata fayalikun
        weyekai
Kia ne yevuku yolemta wikoli
    ne yo yumatakai
Yevuku yolemta vaka hiuwai
    ne yo yumatakai
Ka ne huni
    into ne inia aniat
        ne na ne welamsisimne

Never again I,
    will I on this world,
        I, around will I be walking.
Just I, never again I,
    will I on this world,
        I, around will I be walking.

Just I, never again I,
    will I on this world,
        I, around will I be walking.
Just I, never again I,
    will I on this world,
        I, around will I be walking.

Over there I,
    in an opening in the flower-covered grove,
        as I am walking,
Just I, Yevuku Yoleme's bow
    overpowered me in an enchanted way.
Yevuku Yoleme's bamboo arrow
    overpowered me in an enchanted way.
Never again I,
    will I on this world,
        I, around will I be walking.

This is where he falls. "Never again, I, will I here, around will I be walking," it says. The deer himself is going to be killed, going to die. "Yevuku Yoleme's wooden bow," it says. It means with a wooden bow I am overpowered in an enchanted way. "With Yevuku Yoleme's bamboo arrow I am overpowered in an enchanted way. Never again, I, will I on this world, I around will I be walking," it says.

*   The deer himself says that like that. He talks like that. As he is going to die, while dying, as he is going to die, he says that like that. Just as all will say "yes," while being taken somewhere to a war, they will be walking there to die. As if to say, "never again are we going to walk about on this earth." Like that, this deer speaks in the song. "Never again, I, will I on this earth, I around will I be walking." The deer says that like that. He is talking about himself.*

Haisa ne auka ne in awa hisa
   vepa mamsime
Haisa ne auka ne in awa hisa
   vepa mamsime

Haisa ne auka ne in awa hisa
   vepa mamsime
Haisa ne auka ne in awa hisa
   vepa mamsime

Haisa ne auka ne in awa hisa
   vepa mamsime
Haisa ne auka ne in awa hisa
   vepa mamsime

Ayaman ne seyewailo
   saniloata fayalikun
      weyekai
Kiane sea yolemta sea kuta wikoli
   nutakai
Sea yolemta sea vaka hiuwai ne
   yo yumatakai
Haisa ne auka ne in awa hisa
   vepa mamsime

What happened to me that my hands
   are over my antler crown?
What happened to me that my hands
   are over my antler crown?

What happened to me that my hands
   are over my antler crown?
What happened to me that my hands
   are over my antler crown?

What happened to me that my hands
   are over my antler crown?
What happened to me that my hands
   are over my antler crown?

Over there, I, in an opening
   in the flower-covered grove,
      as I am walking,
Just I, flower person's wooden bow
   has taken me.
Flower person's flower bamboo arrow
   has overpowered me in an enchanted way.
What happened to me that my hands
   are over my antler crown?

The deer, the deer, he is saying this as he is being carried. The hunters killed him, the pahkolam, *the ones who are the hunter persons.*

I also kill deer. I always place the hands on the top of the antlers when I carry one after killing it. The song says that, "what happened to me that my hands are over my antler crown?" Well, it is because his hands are placed there by the hunters, and he is being carried. He himself is saying that in that way and singing about himself.

He is killed, killed by a wooden bow.

Metaka weiyawa metaka weiyawa
   wana huyapo
      ne metaka weiyawa

Metaka weiyawa metaka weiyawa
   wana huyapo
      ne metaka weiyawa

Metaka weiyawa metaka weiyawa
   wana huyapo
      ne metaka weiyawa

Ayaman ne seyewailo
   huyata naisukuni
Kiane yevuku yolem ne
   yo yumatakai
Yo yevuku yolemem ne
   yo yumatakai
Metaka weiyewa
   wana huyapo
      ne mataka weiyawa

Killed and taken, killed and taken,
   there in the wilderness,
      I am killed and taken.

Killed and taken, killed and taken,
   there in the wilderness,
      I am killed and taken.

Killed and taken, killed and taken,
   there in the wilderness,
      I am killed and taken.

Over there, I, in the center
   of the flower-covered wilderness,
Just I, Yevuku Yoleme overpowered
   me in an enchanted way.
Enchanted Yevuku Yolemem overpowered
   me in an enchanted way.
Killed and taken,
   there in the wilderness,
      I am killed and taken.

Here he will enter the ramá *again, he will be carried into the* ramá. *Here he is talking about himself. "I am killed and taken. There in the wilderness, I am killed," it says. "The enchanted hunter people have gotten me," it says. He is talking about himself. "Dead, I am being taken," it says.*

Huyat ematekama
    sewailo yolemta seatakawa
Huyat ematekama
    sewailo yolemta seatakawa

Ai huyat ematekavo
    sewailo yolemta seatakawa
Huyat ematekama
    sewailo yolemta seatakawa

Ai huyat ematekavo
    sewailo yolemta seatakawa
Huyat ematekama
    sewailo yolemta seatakawa

Ayaman ne seyewailo
    yoyo yevuku yolemta seatevachiapo
        chikti yo huya
           aniwata nuka
Aet ematekama
    sewailo yolemta seatakawa

On branches, you lay
    flower-covered person's flower body.
On branches, you lay
    flower-covered person's flower body.

On branches, you lay
    flower-covered person's flower body.
On branches, you lay
    flower-covered person's flower body.

On branches, you lay
    flower-covered person's flower body.
On branches, you lay
    flower-covered person's flower body.

Over there, I, in Yevuku Yoleme's
    flower-covered, enchanted, enchanted flower patio,
        gather each plant
           from the enchanted wilderness world,
On them, you lay
    flower-covered person's flower body.

Here the singers are saying that to him. "On branches, you lay flower-covered person's flower body," it says. "In Yevuku Yoleme's flower patio, gather each plant from the wilderness world and lay him on them," it says. Lay the deer on them.

Any plant can be used. At the pahko, there is always cottonwood. On the ramá, there will be some cottonwood stuck there and out in the roadway. That can be used to place on him, on the deer.

This is where he will be butchered, where the pahkolam will butcher him. Once he is placed there on the branches, he will be covered with an old sack or blanket. I will say this song when they lay him on the branches. But then the tampaleo will sing differently, he will start to play a different one. While he is being placed on the branches, the tampaleo will start playing the spotted fly song. The deer singers do not have the spotted fly song, only the tampaleo. Then the pahkolam will play with that song, they will play with it. They will play round the deer, then they will pretend to defecate on him, on the dead deer. They will walk around him and pretend to defecate on him. Then they will say, "Let's butcher him right away." So they butcher him.

Nechem a seatua
  sewailo yolemta seatakawa
Nechem a seatua
  sewailo yolemta seatakawa

Ai nechem a seatua
  sewailo yolemta seatakawa
Nechem a seatua
  sewailo yolemta seatakawa

Ai nechem a seatua
  sewailo yolemta seatakawa
Nechem a seatua
  sewailo yolemta seatakawa

Ayaman ne seyewailo
  sea fayaliapo
    weyekai
  tolosailo
    weyekai
  vaiwawailo
    weyekai
Nechem a seatua
  sewailo yolemta seatakawa

Put a flower on me
  from flower-covered person's flower body.
Put a flower on me
  from flower-covered person's flower body.

Oh, put a flower on me
  from flower-covered person's flower body.
Put a flower on me
  from flower-covered person's flower body.

Oh, put a flower on me
  from flower-covered person's flower body.
Put a flower on me
  from flower-covered person's flower body.

Over there, I
  in the flower-covered flower opening.
    as I am standing,
  covered with dust,
    as I am standing,
  covered with mist,
    as I am standing,
Put a flower on me
  from flower-covered person's flower body.

Well, you see it is windy now, a dusty wind, a dusty wind. Tolosailo is when it is dusty and not too clear. That is the way it is too somewhere in Yevuku Yoleme's *flower patio out there.*

That tree, like those standing over there in the patio, yes, well, that tree is talking to him. This is what the tree is saying. In the patio, a tree will be standing. When the deer is laid there on the branches, the tree will ask for the tail, for the deer's tail. All the deer hunters cut off the tail and hang it on the tree. That is what the tree is asking for. The tree is asking for the tail. "Put a flower on me from flower-covered person's flower body," it says. The tree is saying that to the hunters, to the pahkolam. *It wants to tell the deer hunters to hang the tail on it. The tree will stand with the flower. The tree that is standing in the patio is the one that wants it as a flower, the deer's tail.*

In yo seatakawa
  tai vepa taiya
    hepela chawakame
In yo seatakawa
  tai vepa taiya
    hepela chawakame

In yo seatakawa
  tai vepa taiya
    hepela chawakame
In yo seatakawa
  tai vepa taiya
    hepela chawakame

In yo seatakawa
  tai vepa taiya
    hepela chawakame
In yo seatakawa
  tai vepa taiya
    hepela chawakame

Ayaman ne seyewailo
  yevuku yolemta seatevachiaposu
    inim ne naikim
      ne yotune
    inim ne naikim
      ne seatune
In yo seatakawa
  tai vepa taiya
    hepela chawakame

My enchanted flower body,
  fire, above the fire,
    side by side is hung.
My enchanted flower body,
  fire, above the fire,
    side by side is hung.

My enchanted flower body,
  fire, above the fire,
    side by side is hung.
My enchanted flower body,
  fire, above the fire,
    side by side is hung.

My enchanted flower body,
  fire, above the fire,
    side by side is hung.
My enchanted flower body,
  fire, above the fire,
    side by side is hung.

Over there, I, in Yevuku Yoleme's
  flower-covered, flower patio,
    here I am scattered,
      I become enchanted,
    here I am scattered,
      I become flower.
My enchanted flower body,
  fire, above the fire,
    side by side is hung.

The meat, as it is being roasted in that way, it speaks. There it will be skewered. "My enchanted flower body above the fire side by side is hung, skewered," it says. "Yevuku Yoleme's flower patio," it says. "Here I am scattered and become flower," it says. The deer's spirit stays in the wilderness. The deer says that about himself. He sings like that.

In yo seatakawa kalalipalipati
  machika wana yeu katekai
In yo seatakawa kalalipalipati
  machika wana yeu katekai

In yo seatakawa kalalipalipati
  machika wana yeu katekai
In yo seatakawa kalalipalipati
  machika wana yeu katekai

Ayaman ne seyewailo
  yevuku yolemta seatevachiaposu
    kiane kalalipalipati machika
      wana yeu katekai
      nim ne naikim
      ne yotune
In yo seatakawa kalalipalipati
  machika wana yeu katekai

My enchanted flower body is glistening,
  sitting out there.
My enchanted flower body is glistening,
  sitting out there.

My enchanted flower body is glistening,
  sitting out there.
My enchanted flower body is glistening,
  sitting out there.

Over there, I, in Yevuku Yoleme's
  flower-covered, flower patio,
    I am just glistening,
      sitting out there,
      here I am scattered,
      I become enchanted.
My enchanted flower body is glistening,
  sitting out there.

Guts, deer guts, it is the guts the song talks about here.

Ala senu kutataka	But one stick,
ka tui tuli	not good and beautiful,
machika weyekai	is standing,
Ala senu kutataka	But one stick,
ka tui tuli	not good and beautiful,
machika weyekai	is standing,

Ala senu kutataka	But one stick,
ka tui tuli	not good and beautiful,
machika weyekai	is standing,
Ala senu kutataka	But one stick,
ka tui tuli	not good and beautiful,
machika weyekai	is standing,

Ala senu kutataka	But one stick,
ka tui tuli	not good and beautiful,
machika weyekai	is standing,
Ala senu kutataka	But one stick,
ka tui tuli	not good and beautiful,
machika weyekai	is standing,

Ayaman ne seyewailo	Over there, I, in the center
huyata naisukunisu	of the flower-covered wilderness,
wana huyapo	there in the wilderness,
tui tuli machika weyekai	one, good and beautiful, is standing.
Ala senu kutataka	But one stick,
ka tui tuli	not good and beautiful,
machika weyekai	is standing.

With this song, it is finished. The pahkolam, *they themselves, will cut each other down. The one who is made into a post will be cut and will fall there. He will fall down, lie down backward, and straighten out. Forcefully, he will point his head toward the post in the ramá. Then, after pointing his head in a certain way, they will get an old sack or a blanket. They will wet it in some water and cover him up. In that way they tan the deer hide.*

After that is done they will be out there hitting the Baptized Ones with it, saying that they are still tanning it. That will be the last, nothing else will there be in the game. There it is ended. The run lasts to that point.

Yuku Bwikam: Rain Songs

Don Jesús talked with us about one other *yeuwame* that enacts the coming of rain. This game is accompanied by four rain songs. According to Don Jesús, the rain songs are sung during a *lutu pahko,* but only when the *maso me'ewa* songs are not sung. Others who have written about Yaqui ceremonies say that the rain songs may be sung along with the other games.[24] Juan Tampaleo told us that "either we do the *maso me'ewa* or we do the rain songs. We don't do both at the same *pahko.*" Don Jesús took a characteristically pragmatic approach in answering our question about this. "If they want to throw the water they can," he said, "but sometimes the *pahkolam* don't want to do it. During the winter they don't do it. It's not done all the time, just occasionally. When they want to throw it, we sing these songs."

Don Jesús sang his rain songs for us May 9, 1981, at Yoem Pueblo. The comments which follow our translations are those he made after singing each song.

Water in any form is rare in the Sonoran desert, and it is the rain that prompts the miracle of rebirth in this wilderness world.

TOSALI VAESEVOLIM

Tosali vaesevolimtea
  hepelamsum chasaka
Tosali vaesevolimtea
  hepelamsum chasaka

Tosali vaesevolimtea
  hepelamsum chasaka
Tosali vaesevolimtea
  hepelamsum chasaka

Tosali vaesevolimtea
  hepelamsum chasaka
Tosali vaesevolimtea
  hepelamsum chasaka

Tosali vaesevolimtea
  hepelamsum chasaka
Tosali vaesevolimtea
  hepelamsum chasaka

Ayaman ne seyewailo
  taa'ata yeulu weyevetana
    yeulu katekai
      sime huya aniwachi
        sea hepelamsum chasaka
Tosali vaesevolimtea
  hepelamsum chasaka

WHITE BUTTERFLIES

White butterflies, they say,
  in a row are flying.
White butterflies, they say,
  in a row are flying.

White butterflies, they say,
  in a row are flying.
White butterflies, they say,
  in a row are flying.

White butterflies, they say,
  in a row are flying.
White butterflies, they say,
  in a row are flying.

White butterflies, they say,
  in a row are flying.
White butterflies, they say,
  in a row are flying.

Over there, I, where the flower-covered
  sun comes out,
    they are emerging,
      all through the wilderness world,
        in a row they are flying.
White butterflies, they say,
  in a row are flying.

That is the butterflies. Any time, whenever it is going to rain, you will see them coming. When we sing this song, the pahkolam *will throw white corn kernels or dry leaves from a branch up into the air. "Here they come," they will say.*

CHUKULI NAMUTA

Ne ka yo toloko namutakaine
    kiane chukuli namuta hekau vetukun
        vichane wesime
Ne ka yo toloko namutakaine
    kiane chukuli namuta hekau vetukun
        vichane wesime

Ne ka yo toloko namutakaine
    kiane chukuli namuta hekau vetukun
        vichane wesime
Ne ka yo toloko namutakaine
    kiane chukuli namuta hekau vetukun
        vichane wesime

Ne ka yo toloko namutakaine
    kiane chukuli namuta hekau vetukun
        vichane wesime
Ne ka yo toloko namutakaine
    kiane chukuli namuta hekau vetukun
        vichane wesime

Ne ka yo toloko namutakaine
    kiane chukuli namuta hekau vetukun
        vichane wesime
Ne ka yo toloko namutakaine
    kiane chukuli namuta hekau vetukun
        vichane wesime

Ayaman ne seyewailo
    mekka bwiaponesu
        toloko bwiaponesu
            polopoloti komisu a yuyumao
Kiane chukuli namuta hekau vetukun
    vichane wesime

THE BLACK CLOUD

I am not the enchanted light blue cloud,
    I am just the black cloud blowing,
        under, I am moving.
I am not the enchanted light blue cloud,
    I am just the black cloud blowing,
        under, I am moving.

I am not the enchanted light blue cloud,
    I am just the black cloud blowing,
        under, I am moving.
I am not the enchanted light blue cloud,
    I am just the black cloud blowing,
        under, I am moving.

I am not the enchanted light blue cloud,
    I am just the black cloud blowing,
        under, I am moving.
I am not the enchanted light blue cloud,
    I am just the black cloud blowing,
        under, I am moving.

I am not the enchanted light blue cloud,
    I am just the black cloud blowing,
        under, I am moving.
I am not the enchanted light blue cloud,
    I am just the black cloud blowing,
        under, I am moving.

Over there, I, on the flower-covered
    distant earth, I am,
        on the light blue earth, I am,
            as, here and there, down it reaches.
I am just the black cloud blowing,
    under, I am moving.

It is going to rain, to rain. This song will be going toward the time when it will rain. The black cloud says that it is moving. "*I am moving under on the distant earth,*" *it says.* "*When the rain drops, here and there, down,*" *it says,* "*I am moving toward there.*"

All the time we sing, the pahkolam *stick out their tongues, like they are the lightning. And they hit the* tampaleo's *drum on the post of the* ramá *or the ground for the thunder.*

NE CHE VAULINA

Ne che vaulina
  yo yevuku yoleme
    machiwa yoleme
Ne che vaulina
  yo yevuku yoleme
    machiwa yoleme

Ne che vaulina
  yo yevuku yoleme
    machiwa yoleme
Ne che vaulina
  yo yevuku yoleme
    machiwa yoleme

Ne che vaulina
  yo yevuku yoleme
    machiwa yoleme
Ne che vaulina
  yo yevuku yoleme
    machiwa yoleme

Ne che vaulina
  yo yevuku yoleme
    machiwa yoleme
Ne che vaulina
  yo yevuku yoleme
    machiwa yoleme

Ayaman ne seyewailo
  naisukuni ika yoyovata
    nuka
Ne che ae vaulina
  yo yevuku yoleme
    machiwa yoleme

WASH MY FACE

Wash my face,
  enchanted Yevuku Yoleme
    dawn person.
Wash my face,
  enchanted Yevuku Yoleme
    dawn person.

Wash my face,
  enchanted Yevuku Yoleme
    dawn person.
Wash my face,
  enchanted Yevuku Yoleme
    dawn person.

Wash my face,
  enchanted Yevuku Yoleme
    dawn person.
Wash my face,
  enchanted Yevuku Yoleme
    dawn person.

Wash my face,
  enchanted Yevuku Yoleme
    dawn person.
Wash my face,
  enchanted Yevuku Yoleme
    dawn person.

Over there, I,
  in the flower-covered center,
    this enchanted, enchanted water, bring me.
Wash my face with it,
  enchanted Yevuku Yoleme
    dawn person.

With this song, the deer washes himself. He goes to the deer singers' water, the water in the water drum, and sticks his face in there, right in front of us. Well, not really, but it is as if he sticks his face in there, as if he washes his face.

YUVALI YUVALIKA

Yuvali yuvalika
  tolo bwiapo
    yeyewe
Yuvali yuvalika
  tolo bwiapo
    yeyewe

Yuvali yuvalika
  tolo bwiapo
    yeyewe
Yuvali yuvalika
  tolo bwiapo
    yeyewe

Yuvali yuvalika
  tolo bwiapo
    yeyewe
Yuvali yuvalika
  tolo bwiapo
    yeyewe

Yuvali yuvalika
  tolo bwiapo
    yeyewe
Yuvali yuvalika
  tolo bwiapo
    yeyewe

Ayaman ne seyewailo
  huyatanaisukuni
    kiane yo tevulia namulia
      vaiwa sililiti komisu yuyumao
Yuvali yuvalika
  tolo bwiapo
    yeyewe

BATHING, HE IS BATHING

Bathing, he is bathing,
  on the light blue earth,
    playing.
Bathing, he is bathing,
  on the light blue earth,
    playing.

Bathing, he is bathing,
  on the light blue earth,
    playing.
Bathing, he is bathing,
  on the light blue earth,
    playing.

Bathing, he is bathing,
  on the light blue earth,
    playing.
Bathing, he is bathing,
  on the light blue earth,
    playing.

Bathing, he is bathing,
  on the light blue earth,
    playing.
Bathing, he is bathing,
  on the light blue earth,
    playing.

Over there, I, in the center
  of the flower-covered wilderness,
    just I, as the enchanted rain cloud
      in a drizzling fog reaches down,
Bathing, he is bathing,
  on the light blue earth,
    playing.

Yuvali yuvalika
tolo bwiapo
yeyewe

Bathing, he is bathing,
on the light blue earth,
playing.

The deer is bathing. He will run outside to run about in the rain. That is where he will bathe. The pahkolam *will run after him. They will be knocking each other over. They will be running into each other. And then the* pahkolam *will get some water in the deer singers' gourds, and they will throw it on the people. The* pahkolam *will throw the water that we have sung with all night. They will take it from the water drum. They will sprinkle the people with that water. Then they will pour different water into the basin, and we will finish singing with that. Then we throw that water too, the water we finished with, on the ground like a cross. When we do that we are blessing the ground. The water will bless it.*

28. Summer rain clouds ...

EPILOGUE

✠ Larry always wants to know what it means. Sometimes I can say, because I know or because I have learned something from one of the elders. But sometimes I know and I can't explain. There are things you can't understand unless you are a *yoeme*. And sometimes no one can really understand. It is like the time my friend Don Jesús died.

Teka sevo'i is a horsefly. This kind of fly is considered a warning of somebody's death by Yaquis. *Teka sevo'i* is translated as "heaven fly." We believe that these flies are like messengers from heaven to earth. These flies usually visit somebody at home or when he is out in the wilderness. When the fly lands close by, it means that somebody known to the person will meet with death. My grandmother told me that it was very important to try to destroy the fly right away if you saw it, before it got away. She told me that it had visited her many times during her lifetime, and that people had died, if she didn't have a chance to kill the heaven fly.

I became aware of this fly's power when Don Jesús died. On Tuesday afternoon after Easter Sunday, I was drinking water outside my aunt's house in Potam.

As I was drinking I looked to the kitchen wall. There on the bamboo I saw a *teka sevo'i*. I looked at it, and right away I felt uneasy. I thought of my mother back in Eloy, Arizona. I worry about her because she is a diabetic. Usually these flies sit around for awhile in a place or just fly around one location. I wanted to kill it, but I couldn't find anything to do it with. Finally I took my straw hat off and tried. It flew away and didn't come back, so I thought that somebody back home was going to die.

That same evening Don Jesús became ill. We had talked with him in the morning. He was strong and happy. He talked about wanting to come up to Arizona with us again. He talked about the talking stick and sang about it. He told us about the time when the earth was becoming new again. When he looked a little tired, we left him and drove some of our friends from Potam down to Obregón to shop and over to Pueblo Yaqui to see the apparition of our Lady of Guadalupe everybody was talking about. We saw it in the glass of a school window there, and my aunt touched it with a flower. In the evening when we came back to Potam we stopped to check on

Don Jesús. We found him sitting on his cot with his son. He was mumbling and moaning. We got the ambulance for him from the clinic, but his son didn't want him to go. We went to the store and got him some juice and tried to talk with him about going to the clinic. Finally the ambulance came again and they took him in to the hospital at Obregón. We followed on the highway in the truck and took two of his friends to stay with him in the hospital. I wasn't thinking about the *teka sevo'i*, but I felt terrible. His son and his friends said that it was good we could be with Don Jesús that day because he loved to sing and to talk more than anything. Larry and I talked about it all during the night and early the next morning on our way back to Tucson. We had to come back to work.

Don Jesús died on the next Saturday at the hospital in Obregón. The Governor called from Potam to tell us. There was a dream too. The people tell me that Don Jesús' heart was over here in Arizona during his last hours and that is why I had the dream. Larry saw Don Jesús in a dream that night too, and he woke his wife up to tell her about it. My dream occurred as I was sleeping in my house Friday night, April 16, 1982. It started when I was near my house in Yoem Pueblo. I was walking toward the Jehovah Kingdom Hall across the road from my house.

As I was walking toward the Kingdom Hall, I saw my friend and *komai* Juana and her two daughters making tortillas out in the open near the Kingdom Hall. I said "Hi" to them and stayed to watch them make tortillas. As I stood there, to her amazement Juana discovered an image of Our Lady of Guadalupe on one of her tortillas. The image was in color. I saw it too. It was a little like the one we saw on the school window in Pueblo Yaqui but more clear. All of us there were astonished, and Juana quickly ran across the street to show some of the people in Yoem Pueblo.

People came running to see the image. The discovery spread quickly in the Pueblo. All the people who saw the image were very interested. All of them gathered around Juana. She held the tortilla proudly. The people who were there were talking much about why it appeared on the tortilla and were asking each other what it meant. I could never really hear exactly what the people were saying, but I think they were saying that the image was to be a warning from heaven.

While the people were viewing the image, big black and gray clouds started to gather in the sky. Immediately it started to rain in a thick mist, and water was already running in the street in front of my house. My house started to leak immediately. Some of the people ran for cover when the rain started, but I was already inside because when the clouds started forming I knew it was going to rain so I started for my house before the rain came down.

My brother was at my house. We stood near the window looking out at the strange rain. I had never seen that kind of rain before. This thick misty rain lasted about five minutes, but the water was running all over like a quick little desert wash. As we stood there the rain turned to fire. We got scared and we didn't know what to do. Immediately I thought about my truck which was parked under our brush ramada. I told my brother I was going to move the truck out of the ramada, but at the same time I remembered that we recently covered the roof with fresh bamboo reeds. I was thinking it wouldn't burn. Also I was afraid of the fire rain drops. The rain was mixed with fire and, as it hit the ground, smoke and embers were left smoldering. This fire rain lasted about two minutes.

After the rain let up I went over to my Uncle Tomás next door to ask if he saw the rain because he is almost deaf and blind. He opened the door when I knocked on it and told me to come in and sit down on a chair. I asked him if he saw the rain and he said he did. I asked him when it happened and why. He told me it happens once in many centuries to clean things up, and he mentioned the name. It sounded like *wichiki*. And he also started to sing a song that goes with that rain. He sang the song. It sounded like a deer song, and he sang the first stanza three times but he didn't sing the concluding stanza. As he sang, he became Don Jesús.

REFERENCES

29. Felipe Molina adjusts Angel Duarte's headdress.

ACKNOWLEDGMENTS

THOSE OF YOU who have read this far will know that this is a book we could not have written alone. We thank all who have helped us. Special thanks to the following:

Don Jesús Yoilo'i, who taught us more than anyone about the subject of this book, and the other Yaqui deer singers and consultants who worked with us: Adan, Aleho Alvarez, Guillermo Amarillas, Irma Acuña, Tani Maso Bwikame, Paula Castillo, Luis Cinfuego, Miguel Cinfuego, Timothy Cruz, Hopom, Miguel Matus Hu'upame'a, Guadalupe Molina, Mollie Rivera, Marcos Savivae, Luis Valenzuela, Sr., Luis Valenzuela, Jr., Luciano Velasquez, and Porfirio Yokiwa.

The families who gave us a place to be at home when we were in Yaqui country: Teresa and Vicente Balthazar, Potam; Antonia and Ignacio Amarillas, Potam; and Juana and Alfonso Flores, Guasimas; Fernaldo and Hipolito Flores, for the memorable boat ride across the bay to *Yasikwe*.

Danny Leon, for permission to photograph and print his mural; Mini Valenzuela Kaczkurkin, for writing *Yoeme*; and Anselmo Valencia, for his many public explanations of Yaqui culture.

Edward H. Spicer and Rosamond Spicer, for the work without which we could not have begun; Dorothy Fannin, for offering us more of her rich collection of photographs than we could use here; David Burckhalter, for helping us during the final stages; Richard Felger, for telling us what non-Yaqui scientists call the *tamkokochi*; Peter Warshall, for teaching us other names for the birds and animals mentioned in the songs; Roseann Gonzales, for help translating some passages from Pérez de Ribas; Peter Wild, for writing a wrong comment at the right time and for consistently helpful conversation; Barbara Babcock, for telling us we could do better; Leslie Marmon Silko, for maintaining the Idle Hour and for the use of that place while we worked on this book; and James S. Griffith, for advice throughout the project.

Barbara Babcock, James S. Griffith, Birgit Hans, Karl Kroeber, N. Scott Momaday, Jarold Ramsey, Carter Revard, Emory Sekaquaptewa, Leslie Marmon Silko, Rosamond

Spicer, Michelle Taigue, Barre Toelken, and Ofelia Zepeda, for reading the whole of the manuscript and for offering suggestions.

The Folk Arts Division of the National Endowment for the Arts, for two grants that supported some of the work represented in this book.

The National Endowment for the Humanities, for the Summer Stipend that helped Evers get the writing started.

Larry Evers remembers the early encouragement of Paul A. Olson, Les Whipp, Mark DuPree, John and Susette Turner, and John Mangan; and the continuing support of his parents, Lois and Lawrence Evers. He thanks his wife, Barbara Grygutis, and his children, Elly and Noah, for their support and love.

Felipe Molina remembers the many deer singers who have taught him. He thanks his mother, Paula Castillo; his grandmother, Anselma Angwis Tonopuamea; and his grandfather, Rosario Bacaneri Castillo, for teaching him the Yaqui language and for helping him to respect and continue Yaqui ways.

READING YAQUI WORDS:
AN ORTHOGRAPHY

THROUGHOUT THIS BOOK we use a system for writing Yaqui developed by Felipe S. Molina. Reading the Yaqui words transcribed with it is not difficult. For the most part the letters sound the same as they do in English, with only a few closer to Spanish.

Yaqui *vowels* sound like these vowels:

	English word	Yaqui word
a	f*a*ther	*a*chai (father)
e	b*e*t	*e*teho (to tell)
i	m*ee*t	v*i*cha (to see)
u	m*oo*n	k*u*chu (fish)
o	is pronounced like the Spanish p*o*co	*o*hvo (blood)

Yaqui uses *double vowels* which sound the same as those above but are held for a longer time:

aa	m*aa*so (whitetail deer)
ee	*ee*ye (red ant)
ii	m*ii*si (cat)
oo	k*oo*vo'e (turkey)
uu	ch*uu*'u (dog)

Yaqui also has *diphthongs:*

ai	l*i*ke	h*ai*vu (already)
ei	l*a*te	w*ei*ya (to take)
oi	c*oy*	m*oi*te (to plow)
ui	g*ooe*y	chuk*ui* (black)

The *glottal stop* (') indicates that the voice stops before the next syllable. In English it is the break your voice makes before the second "Oh" when you say "Oh Oh!"

chuu'u (dog)

The Yaqui *consonants* follow:

bw	no English equivalent, <u>b</u> as in <u>b</u>all with <u>w</u> as in <u>w</u>ent together as one sound	<u>bw</u>a'ame (food)
ch	<u>ch</u>urch	<u>ch</u>oki (star)
h	<u>h</u>ard	<u>h</u>o'o (back)
k	<u>k</u>ick	<u>k</u>ookam (necklace)
l	<u>l</u>ed	<u>l</u>ovolai (sphere)
m	<u>m</u>et	<u>m</u>acham (thigh)
n	<u>n</u>ice	<u>n</u>ooka (to talk)
p	<u>p</u>oem	<u>p</u>aaros (jackrabbit)
r	Spanish <u>r</u>ico	<u>r</u>eepam (earrings)
s	<u>s</u>ee	<u>s</u>ochik (bat)
t	Spanish <u>t</u>engo	va<u>t</u> (first)
v	<u>v</u>ote	<u>v</u>iicha (wasp)
w	<u>w</u>ent	<u>w</u>ata (willow tree)
y	<u>y</u>es	<u>y</u>ena (to smoke)

Yaqui forms the plural in most cases by adding an *m* to the end of the singular: *pahkola, pahkolam; aaki, aakim; yoeme, yoemem;* and so on.

YAQUI COMMUNITIES

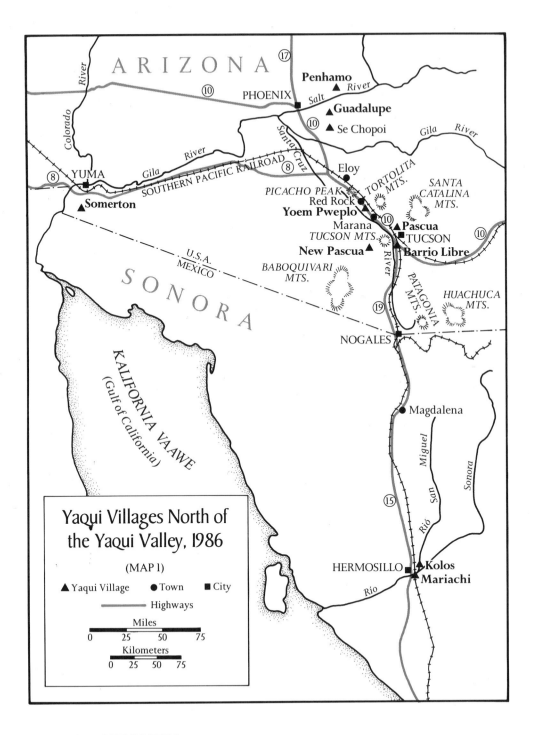

ARIZONA

⑰

Penhamo ▲ *River*

⑩ PHOENIX *Salt*

▲ **Guadalupe**

⑩ ▲ Se Chopoi

River *Colorado River* *Gila* *River* *Gila* *River*

SOUTHERN PACIFIC RAILROAD ⑧ *Santa Cruz*

Eloy

PICACHO PEAK *TORTOLITA MTS.* *SANTA CATALINA MTS.*

⑧ YUMA *Gila River* Red Rock **Yoem Pweplo**

▲ **Somerton** Marana ⑩ ■ **Pascua**

TUCSON MTS. ▲ TUCSON

New Pascua ▲ **Barrio Libre** ■

U.S.A. *MEXICO*

BABOQUIVARI MTS. *River* *PATAGONIA MTS.* *HUACHUCA MTS.*

SONORA ⑲

NOGALES ■

● Magdalena

KALIFORNIA VAAWE *(Gulf of California)*

Río San Miguel *Río Sonora*

⑮

Yaqui Villages North of the Yaqui Valley, 1986

(MAP 1)

▲ Yaqui Village   ● Town   ■ City

—— Highways

Miles
0   25   50   75

Kilometers
0   25   50   75

HERMOSILLO ■ ▲ **Kolos**
▲ **Mariachi**

Río

Hiak Pweplom:
Yaqui Villages (1984)

Most Yaquis trace their roots back to one of *Ume Wohnaiki Pweplom*, The Eight Pueblos, along the Río Yaqui which have been the centers of Yaqui culture since the seventeenth century. We first give the Yaqui name for the pueblo, with English translation in parentheses, then the name by which it is known to non-Yaquis:

Ko'oko'im (chile peppers)	Cocorit
Vahkom (lagoons)	Bacum
Torim (wood rats)	Torim
Vikam/Vika Pweplo (arrow points)	Vicam
Potam (ground moles)	Potam
Rahum (hardened ones)	Raum
Wivism (bronzed cowbirds)	Huirivis
Veenem (abandoned) (flat, sloping place)	Belem

Other named Yaqui settlements in the Río Yaqui area include:

Wasiman (name of tree, in Yaqui *aiya*)	Las Guasimas
Pitaya (organ pipe cactus, in Yaqui *aaki*)	Pitahaya

Oros (gold)	Oros
Vika Suichi (arrow point switch)	Vicam Switch
Tapiro	Tapiro
Lovom (wolves)	Lobos
Lencho (Lawrence, for Lorenzo Cardenas)	Lencho
Kompwertam (water gates)	Compuertas
Koasepe	Corasepe
Vatakomsikapo (where the water went down)	Bataconsica
Loma Wamuchil (plant name, in Yaqui *makochini*)	Loma de Guamuchil
Tahimaroa (thrown fire)	Tahimaroa
Kolonia Militar (military colony)	Colonia Militar

Two Yaqui communities in Hermosillo, Sonora, are:

Kolos	Colos
Mariachi	Mariachi

Communities in Arizona are referred to by Yaquis in one or more of the three languages they speak. We give the most common Yaqui usages, followed by those most common among the non-Yaqui community.

Pahkua/Pascua/Old Pascua	Pascua/Old Pascua/Pascua Viejo
Vemela Pahkua/New Pascua	Pascua Pueblo/New Pascua/Pascua Nueva
39/Treinta y nueve	Barrio Libre/39th Street
Kampo/Yoem Pweplo	Marana/Yaqui Camp/Yoem Pueblo
Se Chopoi (sand hill)	High Town
Penhamo/Camino de Vista/Eskatel	Camino de Vista/Scottsdale
Walupe/Warupe	Guadalupe
Somerten/Hollywood/Siva Kovi/Pinacate	Somerton

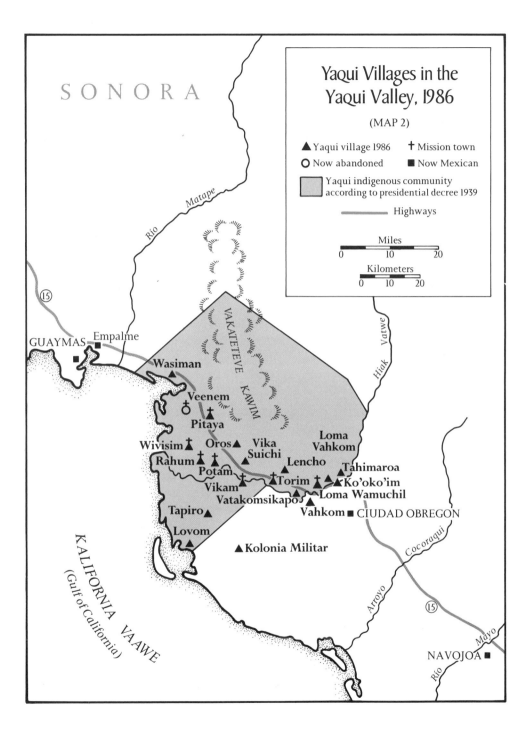

SONORA

Yaqui Villages in the Yaqui Valley, 1986

(MAP 2)

▲ Yaqui village 1986   ✝ Mission town
○ Now abandoned   ■ Now Mexican

Yaqui indigenous community
according to presidential decree 1939

Highways

Miles
0   10   20

Kilometers
0   10   20

Rio Matape

⑮

GUAYMAS Empalme

Wasiman

Veenem

Pitaya

VAKATETEVE KAWIM

Hiak Vatwe

Wivisim Oros Vika
Rahum   Suichi

Loma
Vahkom

Potam   Lencho   Tahimaroa
Vikam   Torim   Ko'oko'im
Vatakomsikapo   Loma Wamuchil

Tapiro   Vahkom ■ CIUDAD OBREGON

Lovom

KALIFORNIA VAAWE
(Gulf of California)

▲ Kolonia Militar

Cocoraqui

⑮

Arroyo

Rio Mayo

NAVOJOA ■

NOTES ON THE TEXT

Yopo Nooki: Enchanted Talk

1. The image of the Yaqui deer dancer in the contemporary culture of Sonora in particular and Mexico generally is discussed by Edward H. Spicer in "La Danza Yaqui Del Venado En La Cultural Mexicana," *América Indígena* 25, No. 1 (1965), pp. 117 – 39. Spicer contrasts the way in which the Ballet Folklórico de México transformed the Yaqui deer dance when they took it into their repertory with the way the deer dance and deer singing continue in Yaqui communities. He returns to the subject in *The Yaquis: A Cultural History* (Tucson: Univ. of Arizona Press, 1980), pp. 275 – 76. See also his "Context of the Yaqui Easter Ceremony," in Tamara Comstock, ed., *New Dimensions in Dance Research: Anthropology and Dance—the American Indian*, CORD Research Annual VI (New York: Committee on Research in Dance, 1974), pp. 309 – 46.

2. We will take up the question of how the *Yoemem* became known as Yaquis in the next section. We have chosen to use both names throughout, as do most Yaquis we know. *Yoemem* seems to be increasingly popular in those situations when the people want to call special attention to themselves as a tribal people. See, for example, the title of the first Yaqui-authored book to be published, Mini Valenzuela Kaczkurkin's *Yoeme: Lore of the Arizona Yaqui People* (Tucson: Sun Tracks, 1977) or the T-shirt design prepared for Pascua Pueblo which reads "Yoemem/Pascua Yaqui."

3. Ruth Finnegan talks about "an aesthetics of regularity" in her book *Oral Poetry* (Cambridge: Cambridge Univ. Press, 1977), p. 131.

4. Kenneth Rexroth's comment was made in reference to translations published by Frances Densmore in "American Indian Songs: The United States Bureau of Ethnology Collection," *Perspectives USA* 16 (1956), p. 200.

5. James Clifford's "On Ethnographic Authority," *Representations* 1, No. 2 (1983), pp. 118 – 46, gives a sophisticated description of the development of polyphonic exposition in anthropology. Arnold Krupat calls attention to polyphony as a defining feature of American Indian autobiography in *For Those Who Come After: A Study of Native American Autobiography* (Berkeley: Univ. of California Press, 1985). H. David Brumble's "Anthropologists, Novelists and Indian Sacred Material," *The Canadian Review of American Studies* 11, No. 1 (1980), pp. 31 – 48, and his subsequent exchange with Karl Kroeber, "Reasoning Together," *The Canadian Review of American Studies* 12, No. 2 (1981), pp. 253 – 70, raise questions of exploitation in literary relationships

between native and non-native peoples. Marcia Herndon traces the evolution of the "savage informant" into the "collaborator" in *Native American Music* (Norwood, PA: Norwood Editions, 1980); see especially her second chapter "History of the Euro-American Study of Native American Music," pp. 32 – 55. An exemplary collaboration is represented in Ben Black Bear, Sr., and R. D. Theisz, *Songs and Dances of the Lakota* (Rosebud, SD: Sinte Gleska College, 1976), a work which is complemented by both audio and video cassettes of Lakota songs being performed.

6. See Kenneth Hale, "A New Perspective on American Indian Linguistics," in *New Perspectives on the Pueblos,* Alfonso Ortiz, ed. (Albuquerque: Univ. of New Mexico Press, 1972), 87 – 88; as well as his "Afterword" to Ofelia Zepeda's *When It Rains* (Tucson: Univ. of Arizona Press, 1982).

7. *Seyewailo: the Flower World: Yaqui Deer Songs* is a 51-minute color videotape narrated by Felipe Molina and produced by Larry Evers in cooperation with KUAT-TV, University of Arizona, Tucson. It is part of a series of eight tapes distributed by Clearwater Publishing Company, 1995 Broadway, New York, NY 10023, as *Words and Place: Native Literature from the American Southwest. Seyewailo* is accompanied by a printed guide.

8. Peter Wild makes the comment about the first western verse in a collection of work by eight contemporary poets titled *New Poetry of the American West* (Durango, CO: Logbridge-Rhodes, Inc., 1982). See page 10 of the Introduction. Such a view proceeds directly from the pronouncements of Puritans like William Bradford that the continent they were colonizing was "unpeopled." For the extent to which that convenient assumption continues through American literary study, see Richard Drinnon, *Facing West: The Metaphysics of Indian-Hating and Empire Building* (New York: NAL, 1980). Mary Austin sounds an early call for a wider definition of American literature in her entry "Aboriginal" in *The Cambridge History of American Literature* (New York: Macmillan Co., 1917), William Peterfield Trent et al., eds., pp. 610 – 34; her biographer T. M. Pearce echoes it in "American Traditions and Our Histories of Literature," *American Literature* 14 (1942), pp. 277 – 84.

9. Harry Levin is quoted from page xiii of the "Preface" to *The Singer of Tales* by Albert B. Lord (Cambridge, MA: Harvard Univ. Press, 1960). William Bright goes a step further and urges that "we . . . make conscious efforts to recapture some of the virtues of illiteracy." See *American Indian Linguistics and Literature* (Berlin: Mouton, 1984), p. 157.

10. Edward H. Spicer's book *Cycles of Conquest: The Impact of Spain, Mexico, and the United States on the Indians of the Southwest, 1533 – 1960* (Tucson: Univ. of Arizona Press, 1962) asks, "What are the chief ways in which Indians have responded to Western civilization and what has happened to their cultures as a result of contact?" To answer those questions Spicer draws on his own extensive experience with native peoples in the Mexican Northwest and the American Southwest, as well as on the voluminous historical, ethnological, and linguistic studies available, to construct a synthesis which stands as the best single account of the ethnohistory of the region.

11. As a continuation of the work he initiated during the Deer Song Project, Felipe set up a series of community meetings at Yoem Pueblo which he called *Yo'owem Etehopo:* Where the Elders Talk. During each of these meetings he invited elders from one of the Yaqui communities

in southern Arizona to reflect on their past, discuss the present, and look to the future. Copies of the sound recordings that Felipe made of these meetings, which were conducted in Yaqui, are available through him to Yaqui speakers. Felipe also prepared a cassette with selections from the original tapes of these sessions which he duplicated and distributed in Arizona Yaqui communities.

12. A visa issued to Don Jesús April 4, 1952, listed his birth date as December 24, 1904. The marker on his grave gives his age as 70 when he died in 1982. Don Jesús told us of participating in the fighting against the Mexican soldiers when "Obregón was captured at Vikam Suichi." Probably this would have been the event in September 1926 which went into Mexican history as the "last Yaqui revolt." See Spicer, *The Yaquis*, p. 235, for a description of the episode. Because Don Jesús was teacher to Guadalupe Molina (b. 1892) and because Don Jesús's eldest son "looks 70," Felipe believes that Don Jesús was born much earlier, perhaps as early as 1890.

13. When Felipe and his grandfather met Don Jesús during the *pahko* at Potam, Don Jesús was taking part in a religious drama introduced to Yaquis by the Jesuits. The conquest of the Moors by the Christians, as it is presently enacted in the Río Yaqui area, consists of a series of ritual contests between villagers representing the two sides. The "Christian" side is marked by blue colors; the "Moors" by red. Each of the sides sets up a *ramá* on opposite sides of the plaza, and different deer singers, deer dancers, and *pahkolam* perform in them. There is keen competition for the Yaqui audiences, which walk back and forth across the plaza to watch and compare the two performances. At Potam, where Don Jesús took part as a Moor, the village *pahko* is celebrated on *Santísima Trinidad:* Holy Trinity Day. See Spicer, *The Yaquis*, pp. 70 – 71, 187 – 94, for a discussion of the drama.

14. See Spicer, *Pascua* (1940; rprt. Tucson: Univ. of Arizona Press, 1984), p. 196, and "Yaqui," in *Perspectives in American Indian Culture Change*, Edward H. Spicer, ed. (Chicago: Univ. of Chicago Press, 1961), p. 81. See a similar assessment by G. P. Kurath in "The Kinetic Ecology of Yaqui Dance Instrumentation," *Ethnomusicology* 10, No. 1 (1966), p. 40. Spicer saw things differently by the time he published *The Yaquis: A Cultural History* in 1980. That book ends with a moving description of the Yaquis as one of the "enduring peoples" of the world and looks to the continuance of deer dancing and deer singing as a major proof. See the last two paragraphs of the book.

15. Donald Bahr, Joseph Giff, and Manuel Havier in "Piman Songs on Hunting," *Ethnomusicology* 23, No. 2 (1979), p. 268. See Ruth Underhill's *Singing for Power* (1938; Berkeley: Univ. of California Press, 1976), pp. 53 – 62, for Papago deer song texts and literary reconstruction of their place in aboriginal Papago society. Karl W. Luckert, *The Navajo Hunter Tradition* (Tucson: Univ. of Arizona Press, 1975), p. 133, uses the term "prehuman flux" to refer to "man's primeval kinship with all creatures of the living world." He continues: "Examples of prehuman flux have survived from a hunter background in many mythologies of the world. I am now inclined to regard this stratum of human awareness as perhaps the most basic in the history of man's religious consciousness—at least as the oldest still discernible coherent world view."

16. The Yaqui language and its relation with other native languages is discussed by Wick R. Miller, "Uto-Aztecan Languages," in Alfonso Ortiz, volume editor, *Southwest*, Volume 10,

Handbook of North American Indians (Washington, DC: Smithsonian Institution, 1983), pp. 120 – 21. In the same volume, see Spicer's succinct description of the present situation of Yaquis, pp. 250 – 63. Carroll G. Barber explores Yaquis' use of Spanish, English, and their native language in "Trilingualism in an Arizona Yaqui Village," in Paul R. Turner, ed., *Bilingualism in the Southwest* (Tucson: Univ. of Arizona Press, 1973), pp. 295 – 318.

17. We quote Anselmo Valencia from "Trust Status for the Pascua Yaqui Indians of Arizona," Hearing before the United States Select Committee on Indian Affairs, September 27, 1977 (Washington, DC: Government Printing Office, 1977), p. 6.

18. Native oral traditions about the deer have an important place in much contemporary Indian writing. See Joseph L. Concha, *Lonely Deer* (Taos, NM: Red Willow Society, 1969); Harold Littlebird, *On Mountains' Breath* (Sante Fe, NM: Tooth of Time, 1982); and Leslie Marmon Silko, *Storyteller* (New York: Seaver Books, 1981) for three examples. Assessing the contemporary literary scene, Paula Gunn Allen looks to the deer and oral traditions for an emblem of the survival of all Indian people: "If, in all these centuries of death, we have continued to endure, we must celebrate that fact and the fact of our vitality in the face of what seemed, to many, inevitable extinction." See "Answering the Deer," *American Indian Culture and Research Journal* 6 (1982), p. 44.

19. Documentary historian Evelyn Hu-DeHart warns that the recollective character of Pérez de Ribas's memoirs suggests that they are "vague, general, or incomplete" in many parts. See *Missionaries, Miners, and Indians* (Tucson: Univ. of Arizona Press, 1981), p. 31. An English translation of portions of his narrative is *My Life Among The Savage Nations of New Spain* (Los Angeles: Ward Ritchie Press, 1968), trans. Tomás Antonio Robertson.

20. Miguel León-Portilla's *Pre-Columbia Literatures of Mexico* (Norman: Univ. of Oklahoma Press, 1969) provides samples of the riches Sahagún and other early translators were able to preserve. León-Portilla gives a more extended consideration of their early translation practices in "Translating the Amerindian Texts," *Latin American Indian Literatures* 7, No. 2 (1983), pp. 101 – 22. John Bierhorst gives a superb contemporary translation of Nahuatl songs transcribed under Sahagún's supervision in *Cantares Mexicanos: Songs of the Aztecs* (Stanford: Stanford Univ. Press, 1985).

21. Dr. Letherman is quoted by Washington Matthew's *Navaho Legends* (New York: Houghton, Mifflin and Company, 1897), p. 22. An accessible version of one of the chantways is *Four Masterworks of American Indian Literature* (1974; rprt. Tucson: Univ. of Arizona Press, 1984). For a demonstration of the beauty and complexity of Navajo "grunts," see Gary Witherspoon, *Language and Art in the Navajo Universe* (Ann Arbor: Univ. of Michigan Press, 1977). Paul Zolbrod's essay "From Performance to Print: Preface to a Native American Text," *The Georgia Review* 35, No. 3 (1981), pp. 456 – 509, describes his initiation into the complexities of translating Navajo narratives.

22. For Mexican attitudes toward the Yaqui verbal arts in the nineteenth and early twentieth centuries, see Spicer, *The Yaquis*, p. 275.

23. Evers reviews some of the early attempts to appreciate American Indian story and song as literature in "Cycles of Appreciation," in *Studies in American Indian Literature* (New York: Modern Language Association, 1983), Paula Gunn Allen, ed., pp. 23 – 32. Brinton is quoted

from the conclusion of *Aboriginal American Authors and Their Productions: Especially Those in the Native Languages. A Chapter in the History of Literature* (1883; rprt. Chicago: Checagou Reprints, 1970), pp. 59 – 60; quotes regarding the mission of the American Folk-Lore Society are from editorial statements in the first issue of the *Journal of American Folklore* 1, No. 1 (1888).

24. *Yuman and Yaqui Music* was published in 1932 as Bulletin 110 of the Bureau of American Ethnology. Charlotte J. Frisbie notes that Densmore "produced over 140 publications of American Indian music, about twenty of which were monographs" and confirms J. C. Hickerson's judgment that Densmore was "the most prolific collector and publisher of North American Indian music." See Hickerson's "Annotated Bibliography of North American Indian Music North of Mexico," an M.A. thesis submitted at Indiana University in 1961. Frisbie gives a valuable chronological survey of collections and studies of American Indian song in *Music and Dance Research of Southwestern United States Indians: Past Trends, Present Activities, and Suggestions for Future Research*, Detroit Studies in Music Bibliography, No. 36 (Detroit: Information Coordinators, Inc., 1977).

25. Frances Toor edited the "Yaqui Number" of *Mexican Folkways* in July 1937. Francisco Domínguez's contributions to the issue included "Costumbres Yaquis/Yaqui Customs," pp. 6 – 25, which ends with a report on a visit to the elementary school at Potam, and "Música Yaqui/Yaqui Music," pp. 32 – 44. Francisco Domínguez's "Música Yaqui Recognida en la Ciudad de México, Distrito Federal en 1931" and his "Informe Sobre la Investigación Folklórico-Musical Realizada en las Regiones de los Yaquis, Seris, y Mayos, Estado de Sonora, Abril y Mayo de 1933," are published in Baltasar Samper, ed., *Investigación Folklórica en México* (Mexico City: Instituto Nacional de Bellas Artes, 1962).

26. The Satanic "deer song" is on page 333 of *A Treasury of Mexican Folkways* (New York: Crown, 1947).

27. See *My Life Among the Savage Nations of New Spain*, p. 128.

28. J. Frank Dobie, *Apache Gold and Yaqui Silver* (1939; rprt. Albuquerque: Univ. of New Mexico Press, 1976), pp. 152 – 160.

29. See, for example, Dobie's story from borderlands folklore about the vaquero who "roped a *nagual* " in *Tongues of the Monte* (1935; rprt. Austin: Univ. of Texas Press, 1975), pp. 45 – 55.

30. See "Just What's All This Fuss About White Shamanism Anyway?" in Bo Schöler, ed., *Coyote Was Here* (Aarhus, Denmark: Univ. of Aarhus, 1984), p. 21.

31. See *Castaneda's Journey: The Power and the Allegory* (Santa Barbara, CA: Capra Press, 1976) and *The Don Juan Papers: Further Castaneda Controversies* (Santa Barbara, CA: Ross-Erickson Publishers, 1980).

32. Zane Grey's version of the wild Yaqui village hidden deep in the mountains is "Yaqui," a short story that was collected with another Yaqui story "Escape" in *Yaqui and Other Great Indian Stories* (1920; rprt. New York: Belmont Tower Books, 1976). We refer readers interested in fictional treatments of Yaqui life to two novels which have been well received among Yaqui readers: Curry Holden's *Hill of the Rooster* (New York: Henry Holt and Company, 1956) and Virginia Sorensen's *The Proper Gods* (New York: Harcourt, Brace, and Co., 1951). See also the short stories about Yaquis written by the Chicano writer Miguel Mendez in, for example, *Tata Casehua y Otros Cuentos* (Berkeley, CA: Editorial Justa, 1980).

33. Spicer did publish a few deer song texts. A paraphrase of one appears in *Pascua: A Yaqui Village in Arizona* (1940; rprt. Tucson: Univ. of Arizona Press, 1984), p. 242. Of that song text, Spicer wrote to us October 2, 1980, that "[the singer] always insisted that he couldn't remember the words correctly unless he were singing at a fiesta with other singers. The result was that we merely talked *about* Deer Songs." In the same letter Spicer commented on the man who contributed the deer song published in Kurath and Spicer, *A Brief Introduction to Yaqui*, Univ. of Arizona Bulletin, No. 15 (1947), p. 43: "Jorge claimed at first to be a Deer Singer, but it turned out he wasn't."

Muriel Thayer Painter's *With Good Heart: Yaqui Beliefs and Ceremonies in Pascua Village* (Tucson: Univ. of Arizona Press, 1986) represents a life-long study, begun in 1939 at the urging of Bronislaw Malinowski and continued, with advice from Edward H. Spicer, until Mrs. Painter's death in 1975. The book contains many statements by Yaquis concerning the deer songs and beliefs associated with them. Mrs. Painter's collection of some twenty deer song texts, most fragments, was not published in *With Good Heart* but is available in the archives of the Arizona State Museum.

A number of sound recordings of Yaqui deer songs have been released. Working with Professor Spicer, John Green recorded several kinds of Yaqui music at Pascua village on Holy Saturday 1941. Included among the music he released on the record album *Yaqui Indian Music*, General G-18 (1941), is one deer song sung by Juan Silvas. In May of 1946 Henrietta Yurchenco recorded deer songs from Filomeno Flores and L. Tapia at Vicam, Sonora. One of these songs was released on *Indian Music of Mexico*, Ethnic Folkways Library, FE 4413 (1952). The "free translation" given in the liner notes seems to bear little relation to the words of the song. Musicologist Laura Boulton included three Yaqui deer songs she recorded in Tlaxcala on *Indian Music of Mexico*, Folkways FW 8851. More recently, Raymond Boley of Canyon Records in Phoenix, Arizona, has released two albums of Yaqui music. The deer songs on the first, *Yaqui: Music of the Pascola and Deer Dance*, Canyon C-6099 (1973), were recorded from Guadalupe Flores, Luis Aldamas, and Luis A. Valenzuela on May 27, 1972, during the Tiniran Fiesta in Potam, Sonora. The second, *Yaqui Ritual and Festive Music*, Canyon C-6140 (1976), includes deer songs recorded from Marcos Zaviva Cochemea, Luis Jiocamea Cupis, and Conrado Madrid Molina at Old Pascua village, Easter 1975. Finally, as we have mentioned above, the two of us produced a videotape *Seyewailo: The Flower World: Yaqui Deer Songs*, working with Anselmo Valencia and Fern Cupis, and in cooperation with KUAT-TV. The videotape includes six deer songs sung, October 20, 1976, by Loretto Salvatierra, Juan Buli, and Leonardo Buitimea.

34. Felipe's review of song texts and translations in Carleton S. Wilder, *The Yaqui Deer Dance*, BBAE 186 (Washington, DC: Government Printing Office, 1963), revealed few mistranslations of any note. In Wilder's Song Twelve, for example, "cho?i" [*choi*] should be translated as "palo verde" rather than "cholla."

35. Kenneth Lincoln gives an account of the history, evolution, and promise which the flowering of the native American verbal arts holds for all of American letters in *Native American Renaissance* (Berkeley: Univ. of California Press, 1983). Michael Castro's *Interpreting the Indian: Twentieth-Century Poets and the Native American* (Albuquerque: Univ. of New Mexico Press, 1983) looks at the subject from the point of view of its effect on modern and contem-

porary American poets. Dennis Tedlock's *The Spoken Word and the Work of Interpretation* (Philadelphia: Univ. of Pennsylvania Press, 1983) and Dell Hymes's *"In Vain I Tried to Tell You": Essays in Native American Ethnopoetics* (Philadelphia: Univ. of Pennsylvania Press, 1981) represent the collected essays of the two linguistic anthropologists most responsible for the surge of interest in native American verbal arts in anthropology.

The term "ethnopoetics" has served as a place name for the intersection in native America where many with diverse interests have gathered to work. An early use of the word was in the subtitle of the journal edited by Tedlock and Jerome Rothenberg throughout the 1970s. "As the first magazine of the world's tribal poetries," the two wrote in a statement of intention in the first issue (autumn 1970), "*Alcheringa* will not be a scholarly 'journal of ethnopoetics' so much as a place where tribal poetry can appear in English translation & act (in the oldest & newest of poetic traditions) to change men's minds & lives." The third issue (winter 1971) featured a photo of a Yaqui deer dancer on the cover but no deer songs. Jerome Rothenberg and Diane Rothenberg have more recently edited a *Symposium of the Whole: a Range of Discourse Toward an Ethnopoetics* (Berkeley: Univ. of California Press, 1983) which enlarges "ethnopoetics" considerably to include "an exploration of creativity over the fullest human range, pursued with a regard for particularized practice as much as unified theory and further 'defined,' as in this book, in actual discourse."

SAIL, Studies in American Indian Literatures, a newsletter edited by Karl Kroeber at Columbia University, has served as a regular forum for those in literary studies interested in native American verbal arts. Paula Gunn Allen, ed., *Studies in American Indian Literature* (New York: Modern Language Association, 1983) offers some critical perspectives and course outlines, while Karl Kroeber, ed., *Traditional American Indian Literatures: Texts and Interpretations* (Lincoln: Univ. of Nebraska Press, 1981) is a collection made from close readings of individual native American narratives. A good introductory bibliography has been published by A. LaVonne Brown Ruoff and Karl Kroeber as *American Indian Literatures in the United States: A Basic Bibliography for Teachers* (New York: Association for Study of American Indian Literatures, 1983). Andrew O. Wiget's study for the Twayne U.S. Authors Series *Native American Literature* and a companion volume *Critical Essays on Native American Literature,* both published by G. K. Hall in 1985, are valuable introductions to an area he feels is "maturing as a genuinely interdisciplinary enterprise."

36. See "Poem, Dream, and the Consuming of Culture," *The Georgia Review* 32 (1978), p. 272.

37. See *Yuman and Yaqui Music,* p. 157.

38. We quote Dell Hymes, "Some North Pacific Coast Poems: A Problem in Anthropological Philology," from *"In Vain I Tried to Tell You,"* p. 37, who believes that "with most Amerindian poetry, the most one can expect in a living tradition of translation is philological recognition of the original, not bilingual control." As he notes, even such "philological recognition of the original" is rarely present in so-called efforts at "re-translation." Like Rexroth, Jerome Rothenberg relines and rewords some of Densmore's paraphrases of deer song texts into poems in *Shaking the Pumpkin: Traditional Poetry of the Indian North Americas* (New York: Doubleday, 1972), pp. 444 – 45. Brian Swann makes one more pass in *Song of the Sky: Versions of Native American Songs and Poems* (Ashuelot, NH: Four Zoas Night House Ltd., 1985), where, on p. 40 under the title

"Yaqui Deer Dance," he arranged the Densmore paraphrases in a circle on the page to form a concrete poem, one in which "shape creates tension and movement." Jeffrey F. Huntsman gives a balanced evaluation in "Traditional Native American Literature: the Translation Dilemma," in *Smoothing the Ground*, pp. 87 – 97.

39. See "The Words of Indian Songs as Unwritten Literature," *Journal of American Folklore* 63 (1950), p. 458.

40. Tahirussawichi is quoted from Fletcher, *The Hako: a Pawnee Ceremony*, 22nd Annual Report of the Bureau of American Ethnology, Part 2 (Washington, DC: Government Printing Office, 1904), p. 126. James R. Murie, a native speaker of Pawnee, served as Fletcher's collaborator.

41. See *Traditional Poetry of the Yaqui Indians*, p. 55.

42. That verbal art will not "hold still for analysis" and appreciation is an inevitable frustration for all of us who would translate ephemeral live performances into static printed texts. See Elizabeth C. Fine, *The Folklore Text: From Performance to Print* (Bloomington: Indiana Univ. Press, 1984), for a full discussion of various models for print representation of performances of verbal art.

43. See Leticia T. Varela-Ruiz, *Die Musik im Leben der Yaqui* (Regensburg: Gustav Bosse Verlag, 1982), for notation and musical analysis of two deer songs.

44. See Leanne Hinton, "Vocables in Havasupai Song," in Charlotte J. Frisbie, ed., *Southwestern Indian Ritual Drama* (Albuquerque: Univ. of New Mexico Press, 1980), pp. 275 – 305, and her Havasupai song translations in *Spirit Mountain: An Anthology of Yuman Story and Song*. Donald Bahr urges use of the song language, before "translation" to ordinary language, as a "template" for creation of an English language translation in "A Format and Method for Translating Songs," *Journal of American Folklore* 96 (1983), pp. 170 – 82.

45. An elaborate attempt to find English language sound equivalents for the Navajo sounds in Frank Mitchell's horse songs is reported in Jerome Rothenberg's "Total Translation: An Experiment in the Presentation of American Indian Poetry," in Abraham Chapman, ed., *Literature of the American Indians* (New York: New American Library, 1975), pp. 292 – 307. See also the system proposed by Bahr in "A Format and a Method for Translating Songs."

46. Simon J. Ortiz, "Song/Poetry and Language—Expression and Perception: A Statement on Poetics and Language," *Sun Tracks* 3 (1977), p. 9.

Yeu A Weepo: Where It Comes Out

1. We print translations in lines when we are able to work from sound recordings of the original Yaqui statement. Line breaks represent pauses in the original Yaqui statement. We print translations in a prose paragraph format when Felipe is translating from memory without a sound recording and, of course, when we are quoting translations done in that format by others.

2. We asked another deer singer about this connection between the talking stick and deer singing. With his brother Luis as his deer dancer, Miguel Cinfuego is an active deer singer in the

Río Yaqui area today, where his strong voice and wide knowledge have gained him a large audience. The two brothers have become so identified with their singing and dancing that they are known not by their given names now but as Luis and Miki Maaso. Whether it was intended or not we don't know, but Miki is well aware of the Walt Disney character his deer singing name calls to mind, and, when we were with him during the Holy Trinity *pahko* at Potam in June of 1983, his friends joked with him about it for the benefit of us English speakers.

Miki's response to our questions about the talking stick was more serious. Like Don Jesús, he sang a deer song, the one we use as an epigram for this chapter. When we asked him to explain, Miki Maaso talked about the song this way:

The tree that talked like that,
The people in the beginning, the people heard it too.
They themselves asked about it.
They understood each other.
And it is still that way today,
It is still that way.
Because here where we walk around,
     it is here too,
The one that is singing,
The enchanted fawn stick,
That is the only one that talks like that now.
Not just any stick talks like that.
Yes, where the flower person walks about,
     you can see him dancing,
It will be shown to you.
In the beginning it was much better.
Now it is here, too, but it is a little
     difficult.
But it is still going on,
The wilderness world listens to itself even now.

In the understanding of both Miki Maaso and Don Jesús, then, deer songs continue the kind of language which was spoken by the talking stick. It is to that language that "the flower person walks about," that the deer dancer dances.
3. Mini Valenzuela Kaczkurkin's *Yoeme: Lore of the Arizona Yaqui People* (Tucson: Sun Tracks, 1977) contains contemporary Yaqui accounts of the *Surem* and the talking tree recorded at Pascua Pueblo; see pp. 6 – 9. Ruth Warner Giddings's *Yaqui Myths and Legends* (Tucson: Univ. of Arizona Press, 1959) gives a version from Lucas Chavez, pp. 25 – 27. Chavez identifies the interpreter as Yomumuli. Giddings's thesis "Folk Literature of the Yaqui Indians" (Univ. of Arizona, 1945) contains a version from Ambrosio Castro which identifies the woman as *Yueta*; cf. pp. 36 – 37. Savala's literary version of the story, "The Singing Tree," was first published in the *Arizona Quarterly* 1, No. 1 (1945) and is reprinted with commentary in his *Autobiography of*

a *Yaqui Poet* (Tucson: Univ. of Arizona Press, 1980), pp. 39 – 43. Savala's editor, Kathleen M. Sands, analyzes several previously published versions of the story in "The Singing Tree: Dynamics of a Yaqui Myth," *American Quarterly* 35 (1983), pp. 355 – 75. She suggests that "the Singing Tree is a symbol of the poetic process itself." Edward H. Spicer gives a version of the story in *The Yaquis: A Cultural History,* p. 172. He writes, "The myth of the Talking Tree provides sanction for the conception of the dual universe and therefore appears to have developed in the post-Jesuit period." Jarold Ramsey's essay on "Retroactive Prophecy in Western Indian Narrative" describes some analogous stories: "'Retroactive' because, without denying the possibility of authentic prophecy (by which most Indian groups set great store), I think that these texts poignantly suggest that during the Contact era, Western Indians tried to assert the traditional continuity of their disrupted disordered lives by retroactively fixing upon or inventing prophecies, set in past times, of present calamities." See *Reading the Fire: Essay in the Traditional Indian Literatures of the Far West* (Lincoln: Univ. of Nebraska Press, 1983), pp. 152 – 65.

4. Edward H. Spicer, "Highlights of Yaqui History," *The Indian Historian* 7, No. 2 (1974), pp. 4 – 5. Evelyn Hu-DeHart notes that "from the beginning, Yaquis demonstrated a practical flexibility and tended to seize the initiative in establishing their relationship with alien groups interested in them." See *Missionaries, Miners and Indians: Spanish Contact with the Yaqui Nation of Northwestern New Spain 1533 – 1820* (Tucson: Univ. of Arizona Press, 1981), p. 20.

5. See Spicer's analysis in *The Yaquis: A Cultural History,* p. 96.

6. Ruth Warner Giddings's thesis "Folk Literature of the Yaqui Indians" and her "Yaqui Oral Folk Literature, Supplement to Chapter I of Folk Literature of the Yaqui Indians," which is a manuscript of material collected in conjunction with work on her Master's Thesis for the files of the Arizona State Museum, are a rich source for Yaqui narratives of all kinds. Ambrosio Castro's story about the Resurrection is printed in "Folk Literature of the Yaqui Indians," p. 50, where it is titled "Gate of Glory." Another version from Ambrosio Castro which is titled "Gate of Heaven" differs hardly at all. It is a part of Spicer's papers, "Yaqui Tales and Myths. Notes, Correspondence; Pascua and Potam (1940 – 42)," Arizona State Museum Archive File A-0670. Oral narratives with Biblical themes and references have been called "The Bible of the Folk" by Francis L. Utley, *California Folklore Quarterly* 4 (1945), pp. 1 – 17. Many recorders of American Indian verbal art have, like Nellie Barnes, restricted themselves to include "only forms preceding the influence of white men; at least forms showing no obvious influence of white men or of Christian teaching." See *American Indian Verse: Characteristics of Style,* Bulletin of the University of Kansas 22 (Lawrence: Univ. of Kansas, 1921), p. 1. Jarold Ramsey and others have more recently pointed out that Indian versions of Biblical stories present "a cultural and literary convergence that can tell us some interesting things about the importance of mythology to the Indians and about how it felt . . . to encounter the Gospel as astonishing, but not necessarily good, news." See "The Bible in Indian Mythology," *Reading the Fire,* p. 168.

7. Savala makes this comparison as part of an analysis of the deer dance he prepared for Muriel T. Painter. (See pp. 188 – 89.) Spicer's notes indicate that Frank Acuña of Pascua said "the deer songs are like prayers." He is quoted in Carleton Stafford Wilder, *The Yaqui Deer Dance: A Study in Cultural Change,* Bureau of American Ethnology Bulletin 186 (Washington, DC: Smithsonian Institution, 1963), p. 204. Spicer writes of deer songs in *Potam* (Menasha, WI:

American Anthropological Association, 1954), p. 130, that "it is not necessary to regard them as true, says the head maestro, in order to appreciate them as beautiful. He himself takes great delight in them, but speaks of them as something quite apart from what he calls 'Yaqui religion.'" Writing in *Pascua* (1940; rprt. Tucson: Univ. of Arizona Press, 1984), p. 198, however, Spicer notes another opinion: "It is because they are connected with the wild animals that the *pascolas* and deer-dancer dance in the *ramada* and not in the church. But, nevertheless, says a '*temasti*,' they are part of 'our religion,' too."

8. Spicer gives a synonymy in "Yaqui," *Southwest*, Volume 10, *Handbook of North American Indians* (Washington, DC: Smithsonian Institution, 1983), p. 262. He notes that A. L. Kroeber argued that *kaita* was inappropriate because of its meaning as early as 1911, but that his argument has gone largely unheeded. Both Spicer's sketch of Yaqui language and the chapter on "Uto-Aztecan Languages" by Wick R. Miller in the same volume use "Cahita."

9. *Triunfos de Nuestra Santa Fé entre Gentes las mas Bárbaras y Fieras del Nuevo Orbe*, volume 2 (1645; rprt. Mexico City: Editorial Layac, 1944), p. 65.

10. The "*aakim*" story is retold from Giddings, "Yaqui Oral Folk Literature, Supplement," p. 15.

11. Spicer, *The Yaquis*, p. 65. *Pocho'oku* is another Yaqui word which means desert, wilderness, or *monte*. The javalina is known to Yaquis both as *pocho'oku kowi* and *hua kowi* (desert pig). Felipe's sense is that *pocho'oku* is restricted to regular conversational use and does not extend to the spiritual dimensions of *huya*. Hayden White follows concepts of wildness from Greek classics and the Old Testament into contemporary usage in "The Forms of Wildness: Archaeology of an Idea," in *The Wild Man Within: An Image in Western Thought from the Renaissance to Romanticism* (Pittsburg: Univ. of Pittsburgh Press, 1972), pp. 3 – 53. Roderick Nash's *Wilderness and the American Mind* (third edition; New Haven: Yale Univ. Press, 1982) gives a superb account of the evolution of Euro-American definitions of wilderness but almost totally ignores native American views. Richard K. Nelson, *Make Prayers to the Raven: A Koyukon View of the Northern Forest* (Chicago: Univ. of Chicago Press, 1983), pp. 245 – 47, writes that he prefers "wildlands" to "wilderness" because "for the Western mind, it is wilderness because it is essentially unaltered and lacks visible signs of human activity, and it must therefore be unutilized. But in fact the Koyukon homeland is not a wilderness, nor has it been for millenia."

12. *Yoeme*, a collection of contemporary Yaqui statements collected and edited by Mini Valenzuela Kaczkurken, a Yaqui, gives a broad sampling of the range of experiences and narratives associated with the various *aniam*.

13. Ralph L. Beals, *The Aboriginal Culture of the Cahita Indians* (Berkeley: Univ. of California Press, 1943) describes the Yaquis' "religion of the woods."

14. See Beals, *The Aboriginal Culture*, p. 15, for a description of stalking and listening to the language of the deer. The encounter with *malichi* is described in Beals, *The Contemporary Culture of the Cahita Indians*, Bureau of American Ethnology Bulletin 142 (Washington, DC: Smithsonian Institution, 1945), pp. 12 – 13.

15. Amos Taub writes that the Yaquis he worked with first translated *yevuku yoeme* as "play-much creature" and later changed to "trainer or tamer-person," with the explanation that this was the title given by the deer, and by all animals in their natural state, to human (Yaqui)

hunters. See "Traditional Poetry of the Yaqui Indians," pp. 59 – 60. Taub refers to "elaborating discussions . . . in Mrs. M. T. Painter's field notes for her study of Yaqui ceremonials."

Professor Ake Hultkrantz explores the larger relationship implicit in the Taub/Painter translation in "The Owner of the Animals in the Religion of the North American Indians," in *Belief and Worship in Native North America* (Syracuse: Syracuse Univ. Press, 1981), pp. 135 – 46.

16. We have taken this story from Giddings, "Folk Literature of the Yaqui Indians," pp. 68 – 69. We have edited the part of the story we use here lightly and Felipe changed Yaqui spellings slightly. Note that we do not give the whole story. It continues in a second movement to tell of *Yevuku Yoeme's* marriage to a beautiful young girl named *Seahamut* who was sent by God to be his faithful companion. With the blessing of *Yevuku Yoeme's* mother, they set up house, and "Well, they were very happily married until they both died of old age."

17. *The Contemporary Culture,* p. 190.

18. Giddings, "Folk Literature of the Yaqui Indians," pp. 32 – 34. Again we have edited the narrative lightly, and Felipe has changed spellings of Yaqui words and translated the Yaqui names. One of Giddings's notes to the story cautions that "this is a loose translation of the Yaqui words of the song as they are remembered by [Ambrosio Castro] who is not a deer-singer."

19. See *The Autobiography of a Yaqui Poet,* p. 188.

20. Spicer discusses *seyewailo* in *The Yaquis,* p. 104: "Yaquis feel they cannot surely render [*seyewailo*] in English. The phrase is clearly archaic, and while in the song context it is felt to have real significance, it has no connections with Yaqui life outside the Deer Dance itself. Hence it is not readily translatable. It is here given three meanings in English each of which may be offered by the same Yaqui translator when pressed for explanation. Thus Seye Wailo 'means' (1) Home of All the Animals, (2) Home of the Deer, and (3) In the Midst of the Flowers. It is treated by Yaquis as a definite place name and has associations with the east." See Wilder, p. 177: "It is apparently a mythical place and is used in connection with animals as supernaturals."

21. The use of flowers as a metaphor is common among nearly all of the Yaquis' linguistic and cultural relatives, as, for example, among the Náhuatl speakers of the Aztec empire. The extensive manuscripts gathered in the late sixteenth century by Fray Bernardino de Sahagún and his team of well-trained native scholars at the Imperial College of Santa Cruz de Tlatelolco are rich with poetic dialogues on the nature of this basic metaphor. Professor Miguel León-Portilla gives a good sampling in *Pre-Columbian Literatures of Mexico* (Norman: Univ. of Oklahoma Press, 1969). See also Andrew O. Wiget, "Aztec Lyrics: Poetry in a World of Continually Perishing Flowers," *Latin American Indian Literatures* 4, No. 1 (1980), pp. 1 – 11, and Willard Gingerich, "La Comprensión del Mundo a Través de la Poética Náhuatl," *La Semana de Bellas Artes* 70 (1979), pp. 2 – 7.

22. *Seatakaa* is discussed at some length in Mary Elizabeth Shulter's "Disease and Curing in a Yaqui Community," in *Ethnic Medicine in the Southwest,* Edward H. Spicer, ed. (Tucson: Univ. of Arizona Press, 1977); see especially pp. 186 – 93.

23. See Giddings, "Folk Literature of the Yaqui Indians," p. 156.

24. Henry Munn's commentary on the Mazatec word *nai*[3] (the [3] indicates tone level with [4] the lowest) which is used extensively by Maria Sabrina in her chants reminds us of Yaqui *yo:*

"It has the connotation of age and therefore of what is worthy of respect. Sra. Gonzalez remembers once overhearing a woman say to another: 'Your mother's grandmother is a hundred and forty.' 'Poor grandmother,' the other replied, 'she is getting nai^3.' In other words, ancient. Asked whether nai^3 means old, the medicine woman, Irene Pineda, answered: 'Yes, it is what comes from the root.' It has the sense of what is primordial." See *Maria Sabina: Her Life and Chants* (Santa Barbara, CA: Ross-Erickson Inc., 1981), pp. 210–11.

25. See *Autobiography of a Yaqui Poet*, p. 39. Elsewhere Savala contrasts *seatakaa*, which he calls a "divine gift," with *yo ania*, which he calls "devil nature."

26. As an example, we give here an account of José Kukut from Don Jesús. It is very similar to an account of an encounter in the *yo ania* published by Refugio Savala in his *Autobiography of a Yaqui Poet*. Savala identifies Kukut as a "sniper" who was "still living when Porfirio Diaz was invading the Yaqui country to annihilate the tribe."

Some are able to kill after entering into the enchanted homes.
José Kukut was such a person.
He could destroy a whole batallion by himself.
He lives there where they call it Pilem.
Well, like that in the beginning Yaquis did not have guns.
They just had bows.
Later some had guns here and there.
Something happened to José Kukut over there.
Perhaps he fooled himself, I don't know,
But he got his ability in the mountains as a husband,
He was given a wife there.
Her name is Lola Kuuku'it.
Perhaps she is still alive,
Or perhaps she is dead already, I don't know.
But he met her over there in the mountains
    and she was given to him.
He was given ammunition over there.
She was the one bullet he was given.
Then somewhere in the wilderness he would meet up with fifty
    Mexican soldiers or more.
He could fell them with that woman, with his single bullet.

But he got angry once they say.
Elder Yaquis talk of it like this.
Something was not done for him and that's why he got angry.
He told them he would never help them again, they say.
"I'm never going to help you again.
Now I will go," he said.
Now he's over there at Pilem they call it.

Near Ortiz, he lives there.
Whoever wants to see him, they look for him at high noon,
Twelve o'clock, they talk to him in the mountains.
Then he will come out, they say.
He is heard over there.
Those who know of him say that he is over there.
Around twelve o'clock he is seen sitting outside on
*   some big rocks, they say.*
"Come inside, sir," they say he will say.
Then it will open for them, they say.
In there it looks much like here, they say.
There are other people there, too, they say.
After visiting there, you will go out again.
"Why don't you come and visit us often?" they say that man says.
José Kukut,
He lives there at Pilem.
He is just one.
There are many homes in the mountains,
Many enchanted homes.

Compare *Autobiography of a Yaqui Poet*, pp. 22 – 25. It is clear that the link between the *yo ania* and the Devil was made by the first missionaries to enter Yaqui country in 1617. Some stories about the *yo ania* in *Yoeme* include "*Sikil Kawi*," p. 13, which tells about a special cave within walking distance of Torim; "*Yo-Joara*," p. 14, in which Anselmo Valencia tells that it is possible to enter the Enchanted House by meditation and concentration alone; and "*Bakot* Pascola," p. 15, a story about a *pahkola* who received the ability to shrink himself smaller and smaller as he danced after a visit to the *yo ania*. Comparable accounts appear in Beals, *Contemporary Culture*, p. 127.

27. In 1931 Frances Toor visited each of the eight Yaqui villages. During her trip a Yaqui man described to her one of the games the *pahkolam* had performed at a recent *pahko*. The *pahkolam* are clowns, among other things, and in their clowning they do not hesitate to mock all aspects of Yaqui life. In the game he described they parody an encounter in the *yo ania*, the very source of their own power. The parody turns the whole idea of "enchantment" on its head, making an encounter with the enchanted world into a game of tag. See Frances Toor, "Apuntes Sobre Costumbres Yaquis," *Mexican Folkways* (1937), pp. 62 – 63.

28. Giddings, "Folk Literature of the Yaqui Indians," p. 156, is the only one we know to report composition: "new deer-songs and coyote-songs are reportedly composed by Yaquis in Sonora, occasionally, even by children." She may have had in mind events such as the one Domínguez reports in "A Visit to the Rural School at Potam," *Mexican Folkways* (1937), p. 25: "We also took some pictures of the children, who dance admirably the Deer and Pascolas dances accompanied by other companions with instruments improvised of all sorts of utensils that they have at hand. The perfection with which these children dance is surprising. Also the youngsters

accompany the dance with very simple pentatonic songs to which they have adapted original words such as these:

Maazo, Maazo,
Deer, Deer,
Scratch your spine,
Take out a white eye,
Seguata manaibe.

Felipe translates the last line as "want to set down the flower."

That traditional Yaqui singers do not compose songs is in marked contrast with current practice among such Uto-Aztecan speakers as the Papagos and Hopis. Papagos continue to dream new songs. See, for example, the song "Kiho Do'ak: Quijotoa Mountain" which was recorded and translated by Alice Listo in *The South Corner of Time* (Tucson: Univ. of Arizona Press, 1980), p. 127. Alice Listo writes that the "song was dreamed up by my grandfather for my uncle who was overseas during World War II at the time. He handed it down to each one of us, his granddaughters." Hopis continue to compose hundreds of new songs for *katsina* performances and other events. See George List, "The Hopi as Composer and Poet," in *Proceedings of the Centennial Workshop on Ethnomusicology*, Peter Crossley-Holland, ed. (Vancouver, B.C.: Univ. of British Columbia, 1970), pp. 43 – 53, and Emory Sekaquaptewa's "A Clown Story," in *The South Corner of Time*, pp. 18 – 20. Barbara Tedlock, "Songs of the Zuni Kachina Society: Composition, Rehearsal, and Performance," in *Southwestern Indian Ritual Drama*, pp. 7 – 35, reports a continuing tradition of composition at Zuni Pueblo.

29. See Densmore, *Yuman and Yaqui Music*, Bureau of American Ethnology Bulletin 110 (Washington, DC: Smithsonian Institution, 1932), p. 23.

Senu Tukaria Bwikam: One Night of Songs

1. See *Folk Literature of the Yaqui Indians*, p. 136.

2. Spicer defines the *pahko* as a "joint religious ceremony carried out by church and household or by church and other organized group." See *The Yaquis*, pp. 89 – 95, for his discussion of the event. See also Griffith and Molina, *Old Men of the Fiesta: An Introduction to the Pascola Arts* (Phoenix: The Heard Museum, 1980).

3. *The Yaqui Deer Dance*, p. 198.

4. Public lecture on deer songs, October 17, 1978.

5. Some observers find the movements of the deer dancer literal, virtually the movements of an actual deer. Others see an artful dance of free and complete interpretation. Mexican folklorist Francisco Domínguez writes: "It is a dance of free interpretation, in which the dancer is subject only to the rhythm . . . and develops his movements with extraordinary plastic and dynamic power." See *Mexican Folkways* (1937), p. 22. Arthur Tress, "Deer Dances I Have Seen: A First Hand View of Two Ancient Tributes to the Deer," *Dance Magazine* 42 (1968), pp. 58 – 61, 84 – 85, compares a Yaqui deer dance which he saw "at the Shrine of the Virgin of Guadalupe a few miles outside Mexico City" with a Japanese deer dance. Of the Yaqui deer dancer he

writes: "The dancer is practically naked and moves with direct brutal force. His mime is directed to the immediate sensual response. It is powerfully physical and dramatic—not subtle in any esoteric or symbolic way." By contrast he finds that in the Japanese dance "civilizing courtliness and mystical religion super-imposed itself over violent animism, making the movements become 'less realistic and more stylized.' " Spicer finds the deer dance "naturalistic only in a small degree, selecting two or three characteristic deer movements and employing these more symbolically than imitatively." See his discussion in *The Yaquis*, p. 105. Contrasting the Yaqui village style with the Ballet Folklórico de México version of the dance, Spicer finds that the Folklórico performers "have made it highly naturalistic, broadly expressive, and wasteful of space and movement." In contrast, the Yaqui village versions tend to be characterized by intensity and classical restraint. See his extensive comparison of the two in *New Dimensions in Dance Research* (New York: Committee on Research in Dance, 1974), pp. 339 – 42.

6. *Folk Literature of The Yaqui Indians*, p. 141.

7. Deer singers talk about their instruments in other ways. Like almost every other Yaqui ceremonial object, the instruments are known as *sewam*, flowers. We have also heard them called *sewa kuta*, flower stick; *yo kuta*, enchanted stick; *maso kuta*, deer stick; and *yo mali kuta*, enchanted fawn stick; in addition to *noka kuta*, talking stick, as we have earlier discussed. Late one night as he joked around during a break between songs, we heard one deer singer note the phallic possibilities and refer to his *kutahu'i*, promiscuous stick.

8. See *The Yaqui Deer Dance*, p. 168. The speed with which the lead singer sings is another quality that comes up in Yaqui evaluations of the performance. Mayo deer singers use a faster tempo. One Yaqui lead singer is repeatedly criticized for singing "too fast, like a Mayo."

9. See *Traditional Poetry of the Yaqui Indians*, p. 20. See also Spicer, *Pascua*, pp. 241 – 42, and Giddings, *Folk Literature*, p. 135.

10. Wilder's estimate that the "total number of deer songs is from 30 – 70" is, we believe, much too low. Felipe estimates that Don Jesús knew upward of three hundred.

11. We do not find agreement as to what these tunings are called. Refugio Savala writes that his father was "a harpist of outstanding merit by gift." He tells of a man who came to his father "to learn the three frequencies of Yaqui music. They are *campanilla* [evening], *partillo* or *una vahti* [midnight], and *vakothia weye* [dawn]." See *Autobiography of a Yaqui Poet*, p. 23.

12. Wilder, *The Yaqui Deer Dance*, p. 196, describes a sequence of those songs "necessary to any deer dance," including "introductory songs" and "procession songs." But two pages later he writes that there is no "sequential and meaningful interrelation of the songs." Asked about the sequence of deer songs during the Conference on Research in Dance (1972), Spicer responded: "There is a sequence at the beginning and a sequence at the ending of the night of deer dancing, but, in between, there is free selection . . . . Mrs. Painter has mentioned that at midnight the subject matter of the Deer Songs shifts to purely wild things . . . . They use songs only about wild creatures who live in the *monte*." See p. 345. Taub reports that deer singer Leonardo Alvarez described a sequence of opening songs, songs about flowers during the early part of the night, songs about various animals after midnight, songs about birds with the approach of dawn, followed by three final early morning songs: (1) blossom-woodpecker, (2) thundersong, and (3) pick up rasper. See p. 37. Densmore asserted that "each portion of the night [had] its

proper songs" (see p. 155); however, she gives no clue as to what the singer she worked with thought the sequence was. However, of Yuman songs she wrote of a well-developed narrative sense of the sequence of the songs. See *Yuman and Yaqui Music*, pp. 130 – 50.

The following chart summarizes the kinds of deer songs Don Jesús described in relation to the sequence of the *pahko*. We illustrate with the sequence of songs sung by Felipe and translated in this chapter:

Don Jesús Yoilo'i: Kinds of Deer Songs	Felipe S. Molina: A Sequence of Deer Songs

nate bwikam: beginning songs:
  1. *kanariom*
  2. *kanariom saila*
  3. *maso yeu weye:*
    the deer comes out
	1. *Sewailo Malichi:* Flower-covered Fawn
	2. *Elapo Yeu Wene:* Let the One Go Out
	3. *Wana Yeu Weyema:* There He Comes Out

kaminaroa bwikam: road or procession songs. Also called *yaiwame bwikam:* arriving songs.	4. *Seata Valumai:* Wash the Flower
hubwa kupteo bwikam: early evening songs. These are all *alavansas*.	5. *Sewau Hotekate:* Already We Sit Down to the Flower 6. *Maiso Yoleme:* Deer Person 7. *Awa Hisa Moelam:* Old Antler Crown 8. *Sewa Huya:* Flower Wilderness 9. *Semalulukut:* Hummingbird 10. *Empo Ka Yo Kausi Wolekame:* You Who Do Not Have Enchanted Legs 11. *Sewailo Wesime:* Flower-covered, Going
nasuktukaria bwikam: middle of the night songs. These are all *alavansas*.	12. *Sewa Huya Aniwa:* Flower Wilderness World 13. *Sewa Yotume:* Growing Flower 14. *Sewailo Sevoli:* Flower-covered Fly 15. *Tolo Pakuni:* To the Light Blue Outside
matchuo vicha bwikam: toward the morning songs. Usually *wiikit bwikam*, bird songs; and *yeu bwikam*, play songs.	16. *Tuka Yolemem:* Night People 17. *Sikili Suva'i:* Red Quail 18. *Kau Satema:* Mountain Buzzard 19. *Chukuli Poutela:* Black Cowbird
alva bwikam: dawn songs or morning service songs	20. *Malisu Ka Seatene:* The Fawn Will Not Make Flowers
limohnaim: donated ones	21. *Tosali Wiikit:* White Bird 22. *Ili Maso:* Little Deer 23. *Sewa Huli:* Flower Badger

ansu bwikam: finishing song	24. *Hilukiam Tovoktiane:* Pick Up Raspers
kaminaroa bwikam: procession songs. Also called *sakawame bwikam:* leaving songs	25. *Sea Yoleme Huya Sika:* Flower Person Is Going to the Wilderness

13. There is a tradition of performance of deer songs and the deer dance outside Yaqui communities for audiences of non-Yaquis. Yaqui deer singers and a deer dancer have long been a central attraction when the Mexican village of Magdalena in northern Sonora celebrates the feast of St. Francis Xavier on October 4. In a special issue of the *Kiva* 16 (1950) devoted to the fiesta of St. Francis Xavier in Magdalena, Sonora, Henry F. Dobyns writes: "Papagos are deeply impressed by the deer and pascola dances continually put on in Magdalena by Sonora Yaquis and Mayos. They are generous in supporting the dancers financially, though many smile at such pagan antics. They take pictures with their box cameras." Dobyns attended the fiesta in 1949 and 1950. See "Papago Pilgrims on the Town," p. 29.

Within the United States, Yaqui deer singers have performed at such intertribal gatherings as the Navajo Tribal Fair in Window Rock, Arizona. Performances for the purpose of entertaining and instructing non-Indian audiences date at least to the 1920s, when Yaqui performers demonstrated the deer dance for Mexican, American, and European artists and writers in Mexico City and Tlaxcala. A description of the deer dance as performed at Tlaxcala, with many photographs and drawings of regalia, is G. Montell's "Yaqui Dances," *Ethnos* 3 (1938), pp. 145–65. With the encouragement of federal funding for "cultural education" during the 1970s and early 1980s, performances of this sort have flourished in Arizona. On a number of occasions deer singers and a deer dancer performed for the benefit of conferences of non-Yaqui academics with specialties ranging from anthropology and music education to dance and performance studies. For example, October 17, 1978, Yaqui deer singers and a deer dancer performed on stage in an auditorium of the University of Arizona as a part of a series of programs on dance titled "Dance Probe." The program was sponsored by Arizona State Humanities Council and, in addition to the singing and dancing, featured analysis and discussion by both Edward H. Spicer and Anselmo Valencia, who served as the lead deer singer. A sound recording of the evening is at the Southwest Folklore Center, University of Arizona. Likewise, Felipe and other deer singers have regularly given performances in elementary and junior high schools throughout the Tucson and Phoenix areas as a part of various federally sponsored Indian education programs. All of these performances are attempts to evoke performances at a *pahko* within Yaqui communities. Felipe feels that such presentations "are only a small portion of the Yaqui all-night ceremonial, and the result is something not too real. The feeling I get at these events is usually not something good. Many times people who are viewing don't understand the meaning of the dance, so they don't really appreciate the performances. There is no true spiritual meaning in the performance like there is at a Yaqui household or ceremonial plaza. There is a different, good feeling when a deer dancer dances in his *kolensia* in a Yaqui community."

14. See Alan Dundes, "Texture, Text and Context," *Southern Folklore Quarterly* 28 (1964), pp. 251–65, and "Metafolklore and Oral Literary Criticism," *The Monist* 50 (1966), pp. 505–16.

Maso Me'ewa: Killing the Deer

1. The statement is used as part of his narration on the videotape *Seyewailo: The Flower World: Yaqui Deer Songs*.

2. See Barbara Abel, "Peaceful Death Comes to Victor on the Wings of Owl," *Tucson Citizen*, January 16, 1985, and Cindy Hubert, "Gift Deer Dancer Captures Late Youth's Power, Belief," *Arizona Daily Star*, July 12, 1985.

3. Donald Bahr translates a set of eighteen songs dreamed by a Pima named Hummingbird around 1900 and sung for Bahr by Blaine Pablo at Sacaton Flats, Arizona, in 1981–82. In those songs the singer gives voice to a persona that he explicitly identifies as Jesus Christ speaking before his descent "to bad earth," during his crucifixion on the "shining tree/That is my cross," and as he ascends to a heaven that seems especially Piman, one where "Rainhouse many stretch/ And I just then arrive." See "Piman Heaven Songs," unpublished essay, 1985. We know of no such Yaqui songs in which Jesus Christ is represented as speaking directly.

4. See *The Yaquis*, pp. 96–113, for a discussion of Yaqui drama.

5. See Painter, *A Yaqui Easter*.

6. See James S. Griffith and Felipe S. Molina's *Old Men of the Fiesta: an Introduction to the Pascola Arts* (Phoenix: The Heard Museum, 1980) for a concentrated and readable discussion of Yaqui and Mayo *pahkolam*. Spicer (*The Yaquis*, p. 10) discusses the way in which *pahkolam* "[build] up a fictional world through the employment of devices of words and actions which are traditional but which are always spiced and supplemented by the individual imaginations of the different Pascolas." We quote his comment on the ability of the *pahkolam* to twist incidents into odd forms from "Yaqui," in *Perspectives in American Indian Culture Change* (Chicago: Univ. of Chicago Press, 1961), p. 63. Ruth Giddings, *Folk Literature*, pp. 150–51, discusses the *pahkolam's* repertory of stories.

7. See *Pascua* (1940), p. 196; Montell, "Yaqui Dances," *Ethnos* 3 (1938), p. 154; Ralph L. Beals, *The Contemporary Culture of the Cahita Indians*, BBAE 142 (Washington, DC: Smithsonian Institution, 1945), pp. 130–31. J. Frank Dobie writes: "The deer dance of the Yaqui Indians pantomimes two coyotes and two buzzards trailing down a deer together." See *The Voice of the Coyote* (1949; rprt. Lincoln: Univ. of Nebraska Press, 1961), p. 80.

8. Quoted from Wilder, *The Yaqui Deer Dance*, pp. 206–7.

9. Spicer, "La Danza Yaqui del Venado en La Cultura Mexicana," *América Indígena* 25 (1965), p. 129: "La cacería del venado es una parte del absurdo mundo de los pascolas, no del ritual de la danza del venado."

10. We have been told that in addition to the song sets we give here there is a set of songs about the lizard and one about the tortoise which may be used as a part of *maso me'ewa*.

11. "Piman Song on Hunting," p. 245. Bahr amplifies this thesis in "Piman Heaven Songs," as he calls attention to the lengthy "song myths" collected by A. L. Kroeber from the Mohaves. Bahr estimates that the thirteen "song myths" included some 2,400 songs.

12. See *The Yaquis*, p. 5.

13. See *Rainhouse and Ocean: Speeches for the Papago Year* (Flagstaff: Museum of North Arizona Press, 1979), p. 81.

14. See Wilder, p. 197.

15. See *The Experience of Song* (New Haven: Yale Univ. Press, 1981), p. 24.

16. See Albert B. Lord, *The Singer of Tales*, p. 115.

17. See Finnegan, *Oral Poetry*, p. 69.

18. See "The Clown's Way," *Teachings From The American Earth* (New York: Liveright, 1975), p. 109. The chapter titled "Sacred Fools and Clowns" in Peggy V. Beck and A. L. Waters, *The Sacred: Ways of Knowledge, Sources of Life* (Tsaile, AZ: Navajo Community College Press, 1977), gives a broad and well-illustrated account of native American clowning.

19. *South Corner of Time*, pp. 14–17.

20. "Arrange Me into Disorder: Fragments and Reflections on Ritual Clowning," in John MacAloon, ed., *Rite, Drama, Festival, Spectacle: Rehearsals Toward a Theory of Cultural Performance* (Philadelphia: ISHI Press, 1984), p. 120.

21. Of the long sets of Mohave songs he called "song myths," Kroeber writes, "a myth might be characterized as a web loaded with a heavy embroidery of songs which carry an emotional stimulus of their own, and at the same time endow the plot with a peculiar decorative quality and charge it with a feeling tone which renders of secondary importance the sort of consistency of character, motivation, and action which we expect of a narrative." See "Seven Mojave Myths," *University of California Anthropological Records* 11, no. 1 (1948), p. 1. Quoted in Bahr, "Pima Heaven Songs."

22. *A Rhetoric of Motives* (1950; rprt. Berkeley: Univ. of California Press, 1969), p. 39.

23. Frances Toor, "Apuntes sobre costumbres Yaquis," *Mexican Folkways*, p. 55, writes: "The deer's tail is never lacking in any house, for they believe that it brings success, and they call it 'la flor sequa' or the flower of the dark twig. They say that an old man can change the course of a river with the deer's tail, and they also attribute to it curative powers." Working in a Tucson Yaqui community in 1958–59, Mary Elizabeth Shutler writes that the Yaquis she talked with said "that the deer's tail brought success in hunting but not in curing." See "Disease and Curing in a Yaqui Community," p. 188. See also Underhill et al., *Rainhouse and Ocean*, pp. 78–80, for description of the curative powers of the deer's tail in Papago verbal art and ritual.

24. See Giddings, *Folk Literature of the Yaqui Indians* (1945), pp. 132–33 and the Savala quote above, for example. Spicer writes: "at the first show of light, it is said, the deer dancer went to the gourd drum and began scattering water at persons in the crowd. If it fell on a woman, it would help her to have children." See *Pascua*, p. 196.

NOTES ON
THE PHOTOGRAPHS

1. Credit: David Burckhalter

2. Don Jesús Yoilo'i. Photo taken with permission April 13, 1983.

Credit: Larry Evers

3. Deer dancer Luis Cinfuego, from Rahum, Sonora, is so identified with the deer dance that he is known as Luis Maaso.

He wears a headdress that he made from the head of a whitetail deer. The scarf he has tied to the antlers is pink and sequined and decorated with flowers to represent the flower world. The white cloth, *vuam*, and a small flat stick fixed to it help to hold the headdress in place. The necklace consists of several strands of glass beads and abalone shells that Luis has carved into the form of the Yaqui cross. These are said to help protect him from evil thoughts, *erim*. He also wears a beadwork necklace that he acquired in the United States.

Photograph taken with permission November 20, 1976, 8008 South Mission Road, Tucson, Arizona, during the videotaping of *Seyewailo: The Flower World: Yaqui Deer Songs*.

Credit: Scott Blake

4. Tenhawe, Open Mouth, is a name from the days of our ancestors the Surem. A huge serpent came out of the mountains near *Takalaim*, the forked mountain near the place they now call San Carlos. The serpent ate animals and the people. It was as large as a small village when it lay curled up. The serpent caused such great concern that the *Wohnaiki Pueblom*, the Eight Pueblos, met to discuss the problem.

North of Benem Pueblo lived a magician named *Wo'ochime'a*, Grasshopper Kill. The governors of the Eight Pueblos agreed to go hire *Wo'ochime'a* to kill the serpent with his talent. Their own weapons could do nothing to the serpent. When the governors met with *Wo'ochime'a*, they told him what they wanted. He told them he was just a poor man. But later, he agreed to help them.

Wo'ochime'a asked for green branches from all the trees around his place: mesquite, paloverde, all of them. He told them how to squeeze the juice from these branches into a *soto'i*, a big pot, over a fire. After the juice boiled and cooled, he told the people to smear the green mixture all over his muscular body. In this way they made the small man green all over.

Then he was ready. He ordered the people to go out east and west and to move the serpent south to him. *Wo'ochime'a* climbed into a large mesquite tree with his *tepwam*, his ax. It too was covered with the green mixture.

Then when the serpent was close enough, *Wo'ochime'a* jumped from the tree and sliced the serpent in the middle. The serpent's head fell off. It moved and shook for a long time. *Wo'ochime'a* kicked the rest of the serpent away. The body he sent to the northeast, the tail to the northwest. The serpent's head is now *Tenhawe*, Open Mouth, near the highway to Las Guasimas. The body is the mountain we call *Wo'ochime'a* after the Sure magician. The tail landed on the last land before the ocean. We call it *Yasikwe*.

Alfonso Flores told this narrative to us February 21, 1981, at his home in Las Guasimas.
Credit: David Burckhalter

5. Juan Tampaleo's drum, photographed with permission November 20, 1976, 8008 South Mission Road, Tucson, Arizona, during the videotaping of *Seyewailo: The Flower World: Yaqui Deer Songs.*
Credit: Scott Blake

6. Taking a break from deer singing during the 1984 Arts Festival celebration at Old Pascua are (from left) Timothy Cruz, water drummer; Felipe Molina, lead deer singer; and Benjamin Lucero, deer singer.
Photo taken with permission May 15, 1984, Old Pascua.
Credit: Dorothy Fannin

7. Reyno Romero's *tenevoim* are made from the cocoons of the giant silk moth. The cocoons are difficult to find, and in recent years Yaquis have had to go into the Mayo River area in search of them.
Photograph taken with permission November 20, 1976, 8008 South Mission Road, Tucson, Arizona, during the videotaping of *Seyewailo: The Flower World: Yaqui Deer Songs.*
Credit: Scott Blake

8. Totoitakusepo, Where the Rooster Crows, is one of the sacred peaks in the Vacateteve Mountains that rise north and east of the Yaqui Pueblos in Sonora. Another sacred peak, Samawaka, named for the saawas, an edible root, is visible on the left edge of the photograph. These mountains served as a refuge for the Yaquis who fought to protect their homeland during the Mexican Revolution. A fictionalized version of events that took place in the Vacateteve Mountains around that time may be found in Curry Holden's *Hill of the Rooster.*
Credit: David Burckhalter

9. Luis Maaso's gourd rattles are called *ayam* in Yaqui.
Photograph taken with permission November 20, 1976, 8008 South Mission Road, Tucson, Arizona, during the videotaping of *Seyewailo: The Flower World: Yaqui Deer Songs.*
Credit: Scott Blake

10 – 13. Photographs taken with the permission of the muralist Danny Leon, September 1, 1982, Old Pascua.
Credit: Larry Evers

14. Practicing at Yoem Pueblo, (from left) Joaquin "Bumper" Garcia dances to the deer singing of Benjamin Lucero, Felipe Garcia, and Timothy Cruz. The boys practice at the home

of their teacher Felipe S. Molina. Other children from Yoem Pueblo give them an audience: John Gabriel, Tammy Alvarez, Emma Garcia, Ray Romero (the baby), and Rachel Miranda.

The bundles of bamboo at the left are cut along irrigation ditches in the farming area west of the village. They are used for a variety of purposes. Bamboo canes cover the roof of the *ramá* at the left: they were used like lath to support adobe plaster on some of the walls of Felipe's house; they were used to construct the traditional fence, *vaka kora*, behind the children; and they are split and woven to make mats, *hipetam*, such as the one on which the boys sit. A holy cross, *santa kus*, of paper flowers and willow branches protects the entrance of the house on the left. The gas meter on the right was installed in 1971 when water and natural gas first came to the village.

Photograph taken with permission August 4, 1982, Yoem Pueblo.

Credit: Larry Evers

15. Joaquin "Bumper" Garcia dances the words of the song without the *masokova*, deer head, on this afternoon; at some other practice sessions he and the other boys use it. He uses gourd rattles, *ayam*. Benjamin and Felipe use raspers, *hirukiam*, on gourd resonators. Timothy plays the water drum, *va kuvahe*. Gourds for the instruments are often grown in the village.

Photograph taken with permission August 4, 1982, Yoem Pueblo.

Credit: Larry Evers

16. At the center of the *kolensia*, Luis Maaso dances to a deer song sung by lead deer singer Loretto Salvatierra (white shirt) and Juan Buli (on Salvatierra's left). The water drummer, Leonardo Bultimea, is to Salvatierra's right, behind the deer dancer. Juan Amarillas, the *tampaleo*, seated on the cushion, rests during the deer singers' performance. Damacio Romero, the *moro*, looks on from his seat in the right corner. All musicians customarily wear broad-brimmed hats when they perform in formal situations.

The photograph shows the *maaso's* regalia, *attea*: the deer headdress, *masokova*; the abalone shell necklace, *hoporosim*; the beaded necklace, *kokam*; the deer-hoof belt rattles, *rihhutiam*; the shawl-kilt, *hiniam*; the cocoon leg rattles, *tenevoim*.

The dancer begins and ends facing the deer singers. As the dancer performs, his movements are usually restricted to the area immediately in front of the deer singers and within the *ramá*. This area is often called the *kolensia*.

Photograph taken with permission, November 20, 1976, 8008 South Mission Road, Tucson, Arizona, during videotaping of *Seyewailo: The Flower World: Yaqui Deer Songs*.

Credit: James S. Griffith

17. Angel Duarte anticipates his first performance as *saila maso* during the Guadalupe Day *pahko* at Yoem Pueblo.

Photograph taken with permission December 12, 1981, Yoem Pueblo.

Credit: Dorothy Fannin

18. *Pakola* Francisco Alame'a dances late in the night during the Guadalupe Day *pahko* at Yoem Pueblo. The deer dancer, David from Hermosillo, Sonora, holds a characteristic pose.

Photograph taken with permission December 12, 1981, Yoem Pueblo.

Credit: Dorothy Fannin

19. The *pahkome*, those who sponsor the *pahko*, serve a traditional meal to the deer singers and others who will perform with them during the *pahko* held at Yoem Pueblo to celebrate the purchase of the land upon which the village was built.

Photograph taken with permission May 16, 1980, Yoem Pueblo.

Credit: Dorothy Fannin

20. Leonardo Bultimea's water drum, photographed with permission November 20, 1976, 8008 South Mission Road, Tucson, Arizona, during the videotaping of *Seyewailo: The Flower World: Yaqui Deer Songs*.

Credit: Scott Blake

21. Loretto Salvatierra's instruments: the notched rasper, *hirukiam*; the smooth rubber or baby rasper, *hirukia aso'olam*; and the half-gourd resonator, the *bweha*. Salvatierra carved these raspers from brazilwood, *huchahkom*. "When I can go to the mountains, I use *huchahkom*," Don Jesús told us, "if I don't want to go to the mountains, I use *hu'upa keka'a* [a variety of mesquite]."

Photograph taken with permission November 20, 1976, 8008 South Mission Road, Tucson, Arizona, during the videotaping of *Seyewailo: The Flower World: Yaqui Deer Songs*.

Credit: Scott Blake

22. To celebrate the blessing of the village grounds that they purchased from the Cortaro Water Users Association in May 1980, residents of Yoem Pueblo held a *pahko*. This *ramá* was constructed for that occasion.

Railroad ties and mesquite posts serve as uprights. Bamboo and willow branches, freshly cut from the nearby Santa Cruz river bosque, cover the roof and sidewalls. The Arizona State flag (left), the United States flag, and the Yaqui flag (right) are raised for all village *pahkom*. The area on the left side of the *ramá* without walls is used as a kitchen to prepare and serve the traditional meals. The part of the *ramá* with enclosed sidewalls is divided into two areas: the *kolensia*, on the right side of the *ramá*, where the deer singers, deer dancer, the *pahkolam*, and their musicians perform; and the *santo heka*, the holy shade, between the kitchen and the *kolensia*, where the altar is set up. Speakers on the roof enable the large audience that will gather to hear the ceremonial music. In the right foreground of the photograph is the *tevat kus*, the patio cross, that marks the edge of the *santo tevat*, the holy space, that extends east from the open side of the *pahko rama*. The *matachinim* dance before the altar between the *tevat kus* and the open side of the *ramá*.

Photograph taken with permission May 16, 1980, Yoem Pueblo.

Credit: Dorothy Fannin

23. Yoem Pueblo residents and visitors crowd around the open side of the *pahko ramá* to watch the deer dance and to hear the deer songs during the *pahko* held to bless the village ground at Yoem Pueblo.

Photograph taken with permission May 16, 1980, Yoem Pueblo.

Credit: Dorothy Fannin

24. After months of practice, Angel Duarte dances deer for the first time during a village *pahko*. Deer singers, Felipe S. Molina, Felipe Garcia, and Victor Lucero sing for him. *Pahkola* Francisco Alame'a looks on. David, from the Yaqui community in Hermosillo, Sonora,

served as the principal deer dancer on this occasion. He relaxes (upper right) while Angel tries out his newly learned talent. That night the *pahkolam* joked to David that he had had a baby, "a little fawn."

Photograph taken with permission December 12, 1981, Yoem Pueblo.

Credit: Dorothy Fannin

25. The altar is ready for the vespers service during the Our Lady of Guadalupe *pahko* at Yoem Pueblo. Holy pictures and statues belong to various village residents. Many families place their *animam*, books of departed souls, on the altar during the *pahko*. One may be seen on the right side of the altar.

Photograph taken with permission December 12, 1981, Yoem Pueblo.

Credit: Dorothy Fannin

26. Summer rain clouds gather over Yoem Pueblo and the *Mochik Kawim*, Tortolita Mountains, in the Santa Cruz River valley north of Tucson.

Credit: Dennis Carr

27. Playing with the deer, *pahkolam* Jose Alvarez, Reyno Romero, and Felipe Galaviz act out a *yeuwame*, a play, in which they take on the roles of coyotes who chase and capture a deer. In this sequence, which is recorded in the videotape *Seyewailo*, they chase the deer out of the *ramá*, round and round a saguaro cactus, and then back to the *ramá* again where they fight over the deer head, making growling sounds and entertaining the audience with their scuffling.

Photograph taken with permission November 20, 1976, 8008 South Mission Road, during videotaping of *Seyewailo: The Flower World: Yaqui Deer Songs.*

Credit: Scott Blake

28. See note on photograph 26.

29. Felipe Molina adjusts Angel Duarte's headdress. See notes to photographs 17 and 24 above.

Photograph taken with permission December 12, 1981, Yoem Pueblo.

Credit: Dorothy Fannin

WORKS CONSULTED

Abel, Barbara. "Peaceful Death Comes to Victor on Wings of Owl." *Tucson Citizen*. January 16, 1985.

Alexander, Hartley Burr. "Indian Songs and English Verse." *American Speech* 1 (1926): 571–75.

Allen, Paula Gunn. "Answering the Deer." *American Indian Culture and Research Journal* 6 (1982): 35–45.

————, ed. *Studies in American Indian Literature*. New York: Modern Language Association, 1983.

Altman, G. J. "The Yaqui Easter Play of Guadalupe, Arizona." *The Master Key* 20 (1946): 181–89; 21 (1947): 19–23, 67–72.

Astov, Margot. *The Winged Serpent*. New York: The John Day Co., 1946.

Austin, Mary. "Aboriginal." In *The Cambridge History of American Literature*, pp. 610–34. William Peterfield Trent et al., eds. New York: Macmillan Co., 1917.

Babcock, Barbara. "Arrange Me into Disorder: Fragments and Reflections on Ritual Clowning." In *Rite, Drama, Festival, Spectacle: Rehearsals Toward a Theory of Cultural Performance*, pp. 102–28. John MacAloon, ed. Philadelphia: ISHI, 1984.

Bahr, Donald. "A Format and Method for Translating Songs." *Journal of American Folklore* 96 (1983): 170–82.

————. "Pima Heaven Songs." Unpublished essay, 1985. 31 pp.

Bahr, Donald, Joseph Giff, and Manuel Havier. "Piman Songs on Hunting." *Ethnomusicology* 23 (1979): 247–96.

Bahr, Donald M., and Richard Haefer. "Song in Piman Curing." *Ethnomusicology* 22 (1978): 89–122.

Barber, Carroll. "Trilingualism in an Arizona Yaqui Village." In *Bilingualism in the Southwest*, pp. 295–318. Paul R. Turner, ed. Tucson: Univ. of Arizona Press, 1973.

Barker, George C. "The Yaqui Easter Ceremony at Hermosillo." *Western Folklore* 16 (1957): 256–62.

————. "Some Aspects of Penitential Processions in Spain and the American Southwest." *Journal of American Folklore* 70 (1957): 137–42.

————. "Some Functions of Catholic Processions in Pueblo and Yaqui Culture Change." *American Anthropologist* 60 (1958): 449–55.

Barnes, Nellie. *American Indian Verse: Characteristics of Style*. Bulletin of the University of Kansas 22.18. Lawrence: Univ. of Kansas, 1921.

Beals, Ralph L. *The Aboriginal Culture of the Cahita Indians*. Ibero-Americana 19. Berkeley: Univ. of California Press, 1943.

—————. *The Contemporary Culture of The Cahita Indians*. Bureau of American Ethnology Bulletin 142. Washington, DC: Government Printing Office, 1945.

Beck, Peggy V., and Anna L. Walters. *The Sacred: Ways of Knowledge, Sources of Life*. Tsaile, AZ: Navajo Community College Press, 1977.

Bierhorst, John, ed. *Four Masterworks of American Indian Literature*. 1974. Reprint. Tucson: Univ. of Arizona Press, 1984.

—————. *Cantares Mexicanos: Songs of the Aztecs*. Stanford: Stanford Univ. Press, 1985.

Bingham, Sam and Janet, eds. *Between Sacred Mountains: Navajo Stories and Lessons from the Land*. Tucson: Sun Tracks and Univ. of Arizona Press, 1984.

Black Bear, Ben, Sr., and R. D. Theisz. *Songs and Dances of the Lakota*. Rosebud, SD: Sinte Gleska College, 1976.

Bogan, Phoebe M. *Yaqui Indian Dances of Tucson, Arizona: An Account of the Ceremonial Dances of the Yaqui Indians at Pascua*. Tucson: The Archeological Society, 1925.

Booth, Mark W. *The Experience of Songs*. New Haven: Yale Univ. Press, 1981.

Bowra, C. M. *Primitive Song*. New York: World, 1962.

Bright, William. *American Indian Linguistics and Literature*. Berlin: Mouton, 1984.

Brinton, Daniel. *Aboriginal American Authors*. 1883. Reprint. Chicago: Checagou Reprints, 1970.

Brown, Emily. *The Passion at Pascua*. Tucson: Tucson Chamber of Commerce, 1941.

Burke, Kenneth. *A Rhetoric of Motives*. Berkeley: Univ. of California Press, 1969.

Castaneda, Carlos. *The Teaching of Don Juan: A Yaqui Way of Knowledge*. Berkeley: Univ. of California Press, 1968.

Castro, Michael. *Interpreting The Indian: Twentieth Century Poets and The Native American*. Albuquerque: Univ. of New Mexico Press, 1983.

Chapman, Abraham, ed. *Literature of the American Indians: Views and Interpretations*. New York: New American Library, 1975.

Clements, William M., and Frances M. Malpezzi, eds. *Native American Folklore, 1879–1979: An Annotated Bibliography*. Athens: Swallow Press, 1984.

Clifford, James. "On Ethnographic Authority." *Representations* 1 (1983): 118–46.

Concha, Joseph L. *Lonely Deer*. Taos, NM: Red Willow Society, 1969.

Cook de Leonard, Carmen. "Máscaras de Sonora." *Yan* 1 (1953): 9.

Cronyn, George W. *The Path on the Rainbow: An Anthology of Songs and Chants from the Indians of North America*. New York: Boni and Liveright, 1918.

Crumrine, Lynn S. *The Phonology of Arizona Yaqui*. Anthropological Papers 5. Tucson: Univ. of Arizona Press, 1961.

Crumrine, N. Ross. *The Mayo Indians of Sonora: A People Who Refuse to Die*. Tucson: Univ. of Arizona Press, 1977.

Curtis, Natalie. *The Indians' Book.* 2nd ed. 1923. Reprint. New York: Dover, 1968.

Day, A. Grove. *The Sky Clears: Poetry of The American Indians.* 1951. Reprint. Lincoln: Univ. of Nebraska Press, 1964.

De Mille, Richard. *Castaneda's Journey: The Power and the Allegory.* Santa Barbara, CA: Capra Press, 1976.

——————. *The Don Juan Papers: Further Castaneda Controversies.* Santa Barbara, CA: Ross-Erikson, 1980.

Densmore, Frances. "The Words of Indian Songs as Unwritten Literature." *Journal of American Folklore* 63 (1950): 450–58.

——————. *Yuman and Yaqui Music.* Bureau of American Ethnology Bulletin 110. Washington, DC: Government Printing Office, 1932.

Dobie, J. Frank. *Apache Gold and Yaqui Silver.* 1939. Reprint. Albuquerque: Univ. of New Mexico Press, 1976.

——————. *Tongues of The Monte.* 1935. Reprint. Austin: Univ. of Texas Press, 1975.

——————. *The Voice of the Coyote.* 1949. Reprint. Lincoln: Univ. of Nebraska Press, 1961.

Dobyns, Henry F. "Papago Pilgrims on the Town." *The Kiva* 16 (1950) 27–32.

Domínguez, Francisco. "Costumbres Yaquis/Yaqui Customs." *Mexican Folkways* (1937): 6–25.

——————. "Informe sobre la Investigación Folklórico-Musical Realizada en las Regiones de los Yaquis, Seris y Mayos, Estado de Sonora, Abril y Mayo de 1933." In *Investigación Folklórica en México,* vol. I, pp. 113–226. Baltasar Samper, ed. Mexico City: Instituto Nacional de Bellas Artes, 1962.

——————. "Música Yaqui: Recogida en la Ciudad de México, Distrito Federal, in 1931." In *Investigación Folklórica en México,* vol. I, pp. 65–83. Baltasar Samper, ed. Mexico City: Instituto Nacional de Bellas Artes, 1962.

——————. "Música Yaqui: Yaqui Music." *Mexican Folkways* (1937): 32–44.

Dundes, Alan. "Metafolklore and Oral Literary Criticism." *The Monist* 50 (1966): 505–16.

——————. "Texture, Text, and Context." *Southern Folklore Quarterly* 28 (1964): 251–65.

Edmondson, G. C. *Chapayeca.* Garden City, NY: Doubleday, 1971.

Estrada, Álvaro. *Maria Sabina: Her Life and Chants.* Santa Barbara, CA: Ross-Erikson, 1981.

Evers, Larry. "On the Power of Yaqui Deer Songs." *Telescope* 2 (1981): 99–109.

——————, prod. *Seyewailo: The Flower World: Yaqui Deer Songs.* Tucson: KUAT-TV, 1978. Distributor: Clearwater Publishing Company, 1995 Broadway, New York, NY.

——————, ed. *The South Corner of Time: Hopi, Navajo, Papago, and Yaqui Tribal Literature.* 1980. Tucson: Univ. of Arizona Press, 1981.

Fabila, Alfonso. *Las Tribus Yaquis de Sonora y su Anhelada Autodeterminación.* México: Departamento de Asuntos Indígenas, 1940.

Felger, Richard Stephen, and Mary Beck Moser. *People of the Desert and Sea: Ethnobotany of the Seri Indians.* Tucson: Univ. of Arizona Press, 1985.

Fine, Elizabeth C. *The Folklore Text: From Performance to Print.* Bloomington: Indiana Univ. Press, 1984.

Finnegan, Ruth. *Oral Poetry*. New York: Cambridge Univ. Press, 1977.

Fletcher, Alice C. *The Hako: A Pawnee Ceremony*. 22nd Annual Report of the Bureau of American Ethnology, Part 2. Washington, DC: Government Printing Office, 1904.

————. *Indian Story and Song from North America*. Boston: Small, Maynard and Co., 1900.

Frisbie, Charlotte J. *Music and Dance Research of Southwestern United States Indians*. Detroit Studies in Music Bibliography 36. Detroit: Information Coordinators, 1977.

————, ed. *Southwestern Indian Ritual Drama*. Albuquerque: Univ. of New Mexico Press, 1980.

Giddings, Ruth Warner. "Folk Literature of the Yaqui Indians." M.A. Thesis. Univ. of Arizona, 1945.

————. *Yaqui Myths and Legends*, Harry Behn, ed. Tucson: Univ of Arizona Press, 1959.

————. "Yaqui Oral Folk Literature." Supplement to Chapter 2 of "Folk Literature of the Yaqui Indians." Unpublished typescript. Arizona State Museum.

Gill, Sam D. *Native American Religions: An Introduction*. Belmont, CA: Wadsworth, 1982.

Gingerich, Willard. "La Comprensión del Mundo a Través de La Poética Náhuatl." *La Semana de Bellas Artes* 70 (1979): 2 – 7.

Grey, Zane. *Yaqui and Other Great Indian Stories*. Loren Grey, ed. 1920. Reprint. New York: Belmont Tower Books, 1976.

Griffith, James S., and Felipe S. Molina. *Old Men of the Fiesta: An Introduction to the Pascola Arts*. Prepared in Coordination with an Exhibition by the Heard Museum, April 12 – August 15, 1980. Phoenix: The Heard Museum, 1980.

Herndon, Marcia. *Native American Music*. Norwood, PA: Norwood Editions, 1980.

Hickerson, J. C. "Annotated Bibliography of North American Indian Music North of Mexico." M.A. Thesis. Indiana Univ., 1961.

Hinton, Leanne. *Havasupai Songs: A Linguistic Perspective*. Ars Linguistica: Commentationes Analyticae et Criticaele. Tubingen: Gunter Narr Verlag, 1984.

Hinton, Leanne, and Lucille Watahomigie, eds. *Spirit Mountain: An Anthology of Yuman Story and Song*. Tucson: Sun Tracks and Univ. of Arizona Press, 1984.

Holden, Curry. *Hill of the Rooster*. New York: Henry Holt and Company, 1956.

Hubert, Cindy. "Gift Deer Dancer Captures Late Youth's Power, Belief." *Arizona Daily Star*. July 12, 1985.

Hu-DeHart, Evelyn. *Missionaries, Miners, and Indians: Spanish Contact with the Yaqui Nation of Northwestern New Spain, 1533 – 1820*. Tucson: Univ. of Arizona Press, 1981.

————. *Yaqui Resistence and Survival: The Struggle for Land and Autonomy, 1821 – 1910*. Madison: Univ. of Wisconsin Press, 1984.

Hultkrantz, Ake. *Belief and Worship in Native North America*. Edited, with an Introduction, by Christopher Vecsey. Syracuse: Syracuse Univ. Press, 1981.

Hymes, Dell. *'In Vain I Tried To Tell You': Essays in Native American Ethnopoetics*. Philadelphia: Univ. of Pennsylvania Press, 1981.

Indian Music of Mexico. Ethnic Folkways Library, FE4413, 1952.

Jahner, Elaine. "Indian Literature and Critical Responsibility." *Studies in American Indian Literatures* 1 (1977): 3 – 10.
Johnson, Broderick H., ed. *Stories of Traditional Navajo Life and Culture.* By Twenty-two Navajo Men and Women. Tsaile, AZ: Navajo Community College Press, 1977.
Johnson, Jean B. *El Idioma Yaqui.* Instituto Nacional de Anthropologiae Historia, Departamento de Investigaciones Anthropológicas 10. Mexico. 1962.

Kaczkurkin, Mini Valenzuela. *Yoeme: Lore of the Arizona Yaqui People.* Tucson: Sun Tracks, 1977.
Kelley, Jane Holden. *Yaqui Women: Contemporary Life Histories.* Lincoln: Univ. of Nebraska Press, 1978.
Kroeber, A. L. "Seven Mojave Myths." *University of California Anthropological Records* 11, no. 1 (1948), 1 – 70.
Kroeber, Karl. "Poem, Dream, and the Consuming of Culture." *The Georgia Review* 32 (1978): 266 – 80.
————, ed. *Traditional American Indian Literatures: Texts and Interpretations.* Lincoln: Univ. of Nebraska Press, 1981.
Kroeber, Karl, and H. David Brumble, III. "Reasoning Together." *The Canadian Review of American Studies* 12 (1981): 253 – 70.
Krupat, Arnold. *For Those Who Come After: A Study of Native American Autobiography.* Berkeley: Univ. of California Press, 1985.
Kurath, G. P. "The Kinetic Ecology of Yaqui Dance Instrumentation." *Ethnomusicology* 10 (1966): 28 – 42.
————. "The Sena'asom Rattle of the Yaqui Indian Pascolas." *Ethnomusicology* 4 (1960): 60 – 63.
Kurath, William, and Edward H. Spicer. *A Brief Introduction to Yaqui, a Native Language of Sonora.* Univ. of Arizona Social Science Bulletin 15. Tucson: Univ. of Arizona, 1947.

Laycock, George. *The Deer Hunters Bible.* New York: Doubleday, 1971.
León-Portilla, Miguel. *Pre-Columbian Literatures of Mexico.* Grace Lobanov and the Author, trans. Univ. of Oklahoma Press, 1969.
————. "Translating the Amerindian Texts." *Latin American Indian Literatures* 7 (1983): 101 – 22.
Lincoln, Kenneth. *Native American Renaissance.* Berkeley: Univ. of California Press, 1983.
Lindenfeld, Jacqueline. *Yaqui Syntax.* Berkeley: Univ. of California Press, 1973.
List, George. "The Hopi as Composer and Poet." In *Proceedings of Centennial Workshop in Ethnomusicology,* pp. 43 – 53. June 19 – 23, 1967. P. Crossley Holland, ed. Vancouver: Univ. of British Columbia, 1970.
Litvinoff, V. "Yaqui Easter." *Drama Review* 17 (1973): 52 – 63.
Littlebird, Harold. *On Mountains' Breath.* Santa Fe, NM: Tooth of Time Books, 1982.

Lord, Albert B. *The Singer of Tales.* Cambridge: Harvard Univ. Press, 1960.
Luckert, Karl W. *The Navajo Hunter Tradition.* Tucson: Univ. of Arizona Press, 1975.

Matthews, Washington. *Navaho Legends.* New York: Houghton, Mifflin and Co., 1897.
Mendez, Miguel. *Tata Casehua y Otros Cuentos.* Berkeley: Editorial Justa Publications, Inc., 1980.
Miller, Wick R. "Uto-Aztecan Languages." *Southwest.* Handbook of North American Indians. Vol. 10. pp. 113 – 24. Washington, DC: Smithsonian Institution, 1983.
Moises, Rosalio, Jane Holden Kelley, and William Curry Holden. *The Tall Candle: The Personal Chronicle of a Yaqui Indian.* Lincoln: Univ. of Nebraska Press, 1971.
Momaday, N. Scott. "A First American Views His Land." *National Geographic* 150 (1976): 13 – 18.
——————. "The Man Made of Words." In *Indian Voices: The First Convocation of American Indian Scholars,* pp. 44 – 84. San Francisco: Indian Historian Press, 1970.
Montell, G. "Yaqui Dances." *Ethnos* 3 (1938): 145 – 66.

Nash, Roderick. *Wilderness and the American Mind.* 3rd ed. New Haven: Yale Univ. Press, 1982.
Nelson, Richard K. *Make Prayers to the Raven: A Koyukon View of the Northern Forest.* Chicago: Univ. of Chicago Press, 1983.

Ortiz, Alfonso, volume ed. *Southwest.* Handbook of North American Indians. Vol. 10. Washington, DC: Smithsonian Institution, 1983.
——————, ed. *New Perspectives on the Pueblos.* Albuquerque: Univ. of New Mexico Press, 1972.
Ortiz, Simon J. "Song/Poetry and Language: Expression and Perception." *Sun Tracks* 3 (1977): 9 – 12.

Painter, Muriel Thayer, Refugio Savala, and Ignacio Alvarez. *A Yaqui Easter Sermon.* Social Science Bulletin 26. Tucson: Univ. of Arizona, 1955.
Painter, Muriel Thayer. *A Yaqui Easter.* 1950. Reprint. Tucson: Univ. of Arizona Press, 1983.
——————. *With Good Heart: Yaqui Beliefs and Ceremonies in Pascua Village.* Tucson: Univ. of Arizona Press, 1986.
Pearce, Thomas M. "American Traditions and Our Histories of Literature." *American Literature* 14 (1942): 277 – 84.
Pérez de Ribas, Andrés. *Triunfos de Nuestra Santa Fé entre Gentes Las Mas Bárbaras y Fieras del Nuevo Orbe.* 3 vols. 1645. Mexico City: Editorial Layac, 1944.
——————. *My Life Among the Savage Nations of New Spain.* Tomas Antonio Robertson, trans. Los Angeles: Ward Ritchie, 1968.

Radin, Paul. "The Literature of Primitive Peoples." *Diogenes* 12 (1955): 1 – 28.
Ramsey, Jarold. *Reading the Fire: Essays in the Traditional Indian Literatures of the Far West.* Lincoln: Univ. of Nebraska Press, 1983.
Rexroth, Kenneth. "American Indian Songs: U.S. Bureau of Ethnology Collection." *Perspectives USA* 16 (1956): 197 – 201.

—————. *Assays*. New York: New Directions, 1961.

Rothenberg, Jerome. *Shaking The Pumpkin*. New York: Doubleday, 1972.

Rothenberg, Jerome, and Diane Rothenberg, eds. *Symposium of The Whole: A Range of Discourse Toward an Ethnopoetics*. Berkeley: Univ. of California Press, 1983.

Rothenberg, Jerome, and Dennis Tedlock. "Statement of Intention." *Alcheringa* 1 (1970): 1.

Rue, Leonard Lee, III. *The Deer of North America*. New York: Crown Publishers, 1978.

Ruoff, A. LaVonne Brown, and Karl Kroeber. *American Indian Literatures in the United States: A Basic Bibliography for Teachers*. New York: Association for Study of American Indian Literature, 1983.

Samper, Baltasar, ed. *Investigación Folklórica En México*. Volume I: Materiales. Mexico City: Instituto Nacional de Bellas Artes, 1962.

Sands, Kathleen M. "The Singing Tree: Dynamics of a Yaqui Myth." *American Quarterly* 35 (1983): 355–75.

Savala, Refugio. *The Autobiography of a Yaqui Poet*. Kathleen M. Sands, ed. Tucson: Univ. of Arizona Press, 1980.

—————. "Two Yaqui Legends." *Arizona Quarterly* 1 (1945): 20–24.

Schöler, Bo, ed. *Coyote Was Here: Essays on Contemporary Native American Literary and Political Mobilization*. Dolphin 9. Aarhus, Denmark: Univ. of Aarhus, 1984.

Shutler, Mary Elizabeth. "Disease and Curing in a Yaqui Community." In *Ethnic Medicine in the Southwest*, pp. 169–237. Edward H. Spicer, ed. Tucson: Univ. of Arizona Press, 1977.

Silko, Leslie Marmon. *Storyteller*. New York: Seaver Books, 1981.

Sorensen, Virginia. *The Proper Gods*. New York: Harcourt, Brace, and Co., 1951.

Spicer, Edward H. "Context of the Yaqui Easter Ceremony." In *New Dimensions in Dance Research: Anthropology and Dance—The American Indian*, pp. 309–46. Tamara Comstock, ed. New York: Committee on Research in Dance, 1974.

—————. *Cycles of Conquest: The Impact of Spain, Mexico, and the United States on the Indians of the Southwest, 1533–1960*. Tucson: Univ. of Arizona Press, 1962.

—————. "Highlights of Yaqui History." *The Indian Historian* 7 (1974): 1–14.

—————. "La Danza Yaqui del Venado en la Cultura Mexicana." *América Indígena* 25 (1965): 119–39.

—————. Letter to the authors. October 2, 1980. Archives of Southwest Folklore Center, University of Arizona, Tucson.

—————. *Pascua: A Village in Arizona*. 1940. Reprint. Tucson: Univ. of Arizona Press, 1984.

—————. *Potam: A Yaqui Village in Sonora*. Menasha, WI: American Anthropological Association, 1954.

—————. "Yaqui." In *Perspectives in American Indian Culture Change*. Chicago: Univ. of Chicago Press, 1961.

—————. "Yaqui." In *Southwest*, Handbook of North American Indians, vol. 10, pp. 250–63. Washington, DC: Smithsonian Institution, 1983.

—————. *The Yaquis: A Cultural History*. Tucson: Univ. of Arizona Press, 1980.

—. "Yaqui Tales and Myths. Notes, Correspondence, Pascua and Potam. 1940 – 42." File A-0670. Arizona State Museum, Tucson.

Spinden, Herbert Joseph. "American Indian Poetry." *Natural History* 19 (1919): 301 – 8.

—. *Songs of the Tewa.* 1933. Reprint. Santa Fe: Sunstone Press, 1976.

Swann, Brian, ed. *Smoothing The Ground: Essays on Native American Oral Literature.* Berkeley: Univ. of California Press, 1983.

—. *Song of the Sky: Versions of Native American Songs and Poems.* Ashuelot, NH: Four Zoas Night House, 1985.

Taub, Amos. "The Traditional Poetry of the Yaqui Indians." M.A. Thesis. Univ. of Arizona, 1950.

Tedlock, Barbara. "The Clown's Way." In *Teachings from the American Earth: Indian Religion and Philosophy,* pp. 105 – 18. Dennis Tedlock and Barbara Tedlock, eds. New York: Liveright, 1975.

Tedlock, Dennis. *Finding the Center: Narrative Poetry of the Zuni Indians.* 1972. Rev. ed. Lincoln: Univ. of Nebraska Press, 1978.

—. *The Spoken Word and the Work of Interpretation.* Philadelphia: Univ. of Pennsylvania Press, 1983.

Toelken, Barre. *The Dynamics of Folklore.* Boston: Houghton Mifflin Company, 1979.

Toor, Frances. "Apuntes Sobre Costumbres Yaqui/Notes on Yaqui Customs." *Mexican Folkways* (1937): 52 – 63.

—. "Los Fiesteros de la Fiesta de San Juan en el Pueblo de Vicam/The Yaqui Festival-Makers." *Mexican Folkways* (1937): 26 – 31.

—, ed. *A Treasury of Mexican Folkways.* New York: Crown, 1947.

Tress, Arthur. "Deer Dances I Have Seen: A First Hand View of Two Ancient Tributes to the Deer." *Dance Magazine* 42 (1968): 58 – 61, 84 – 85.

Underhill, Ruth. *Singing For Power,* 1938. Berkeley: Univ. of California Press, 1976.

Underhill, Ruth, Donald Bahr, Baptisto Lopez, José Pancho, and David Lopez. *Rainhouse and Ocean: Speeches for the Papago Year.* Flagstaff: Museum of Northern Arizona Press, 1979.

United States. Senate Select Committee on Indian Affairs. "Trust Status for the Pascua Yaqui Indians of Arizona." Ninety-Fifth Congress, First Session on S.1633. Sept. 27, 1977.

Utley, Francis L. "The Bible of the Folk." *California Folklore Quarterly* 4 (1945): 1 – 17.

Valencia, Anselmo. Performance of Deer Songs and Lecture. "Dance Probe," Univ. of Arizona. Tucson, October 17, 1978.

Varela-Ruiz, Leticia T., *Die Musik im Leben der Yaqui.* Regensburg: Gustav Bosse Verlag, 1982.

Walton E. L., and T. T. Waterman. "American Indian Poetry." *American Anthropologist* 27 (1925): 25 – 52.

Welsh, Andrew. *Roots of the Lyric: Primitive Poetry and Modern Poetics.* Princeton: Princeton Univ. Press, 1978.

White, Hayden. "The Forms of Wildness: Archaeology of an Idea." In *The Wild Man Within: An Image in Western Thought from the Renaissance to Romanticism,* pp. 3 – 38. Edward Dudley and Maximillian E. Novak, eds. Pittsburg: Univ. of Pittsburg Press, 1972.

Wiget, Andrew O. "Aztec Lyrics: Poetry in a World of Continually Perishing Flowers." *Latin American Indian Literatures* 4 (1980): 1 – 11.

————, ed. *Critical Essays on Native American Literature.* Boston: G. K. Hall, 1985.

————. *Native American Literature.* Boston: Twayne Publishers, 1985.

Wild, Peter, and Frank Graziano, eds. *New Poetry of the American West.* Durango, CO: Logbridge-Rhodes, 1982.

Wilder, Carleton Stafford. *The Yaqui Deer Dance: A Study in Cultural Change.* Bureau of American Ethnology Bulletin 186. Washington, DC: Government Printing Office, 1963.

Witherspoon, Gary. *Language and Art in the Navajo Universe.* Ann Arbor: Univ. of Michigan Press, 1977.

Yaqui Indian Music. General, G-18, 1941.

Yaqui: Music of the Pascola and Deer Dance. Canyon Records, C-6099, 1973.

Yaqui Ritual and Festive Music. Canyon Records, C-6140, 1976.

Yazzie, Ethelou, ed. *Navajo History.* Tsaile, AZ: Navajo Community College Press, 1971.

Zepeda, Ofelia, ed. *When It Rains: Papago and Pima Poetry.* Tucson: Sun Tracks and Univ. of Arizona Press, 1982.

Zolbrod, Paul. "From Performance to Print: Preface to a Native American Text." *The Georgia Review* 35 (1981), 465 – 509.

INDEX

Aapaleo (harp player), 83, 140
Abel, Barbara, 217
Acuña, Frank, 24
Akitavampokatekapo (where the organ pipe cactus is in the water), 41
Alavansa (hymn; song; deer songs sung during the pahko between the opening and the closing processions), 36, 84
Alcalá, Jerónimo de, 20
Allen, Paula Gunn, 202, 205
Aniam (worlds, in the sense of realm or domain), 45. See also Yo Ania; Sea Ania
Ariwares, Juan, 22, 26
Asum Kawi (Grandmothers' Mountain), 38
Austin, Mary, 200
Aztec, 19, 39

Babcock, Barbara, 150
Badger, 121
Bahr, Donald, 29, 139, 140
Baptized Ones. See Vato'im
Bats, 109
Beals, Ralph, 47, 50, 64, 134
Bierhorst, John, 202
Black Bear, Ben, 200
Booth, Mark, 143
Bradford, William, 200
Bright, William, 200
Brinton, Daniel, 21
Brumble, H. David, 199
Burke, Kenneth, 154
Butterflies, 175
Bwikam (songs), 84. See also Deer songs

Canyon Records, 67
Cárdenas, Lázaro, 19
Carter, President, 19
Castaneda, Carlos, 23
Castillo, Rosario, 15, 62, 67
Castro, Ambrosio, 37, 43, 49
Castro, Michael, 204
Catholicism, 39–40, 130
Chapayekam ("those with long noses," masked ceremonial dancers), 24, 55, 60, 130
Chavez, Lucas, 74
Chupiarim (completed ones), 62
Cinfuego, Luis (Luis Maaso), 6
Cinfuego, Miguel (Miki Maaso), 5, 13, 33, 89, 108, 112, 206–7
Ciudad Obregón, 7, 38
Clark, Captain William, 11
Clifford, James, 199
Clowns, 150. See also Pahkola
Collaborative authorship, 8–9, 10–11, 199–200
Colonia Militar, 38
Concha, Joseph L., 202
Cowbird, 112
Coyote Society, 79, 97
Coyote, 147, 149
Cruz, Timothy, 87
Cupis, Fern, 10

De Mille, Richard, 23–24
Deer dance, and hunting, 18, 47–48, 50, 134–35; origin, 50–51; performance, 18, 213–14, 216
Deer dancer, 6, 55, 59–61, 64, 73, 129; image in borderlands society, 7; relation to songs, 73–74